TRIATHLON 2.0

DATA-DRIVEN PERFORMANCE TRAINING

Jim Vance

Human Kinetics

Library of Congress Cataloging-in-Publication Data

Names: Vance, Jim, 1976-
Title: Triathlon 2.0 : data-driven performance training / Jim Vance.
Description: Champaign, IL : Human Kinetics, [2016] | Includes
   bibliographical references and index.
Identifiers: LCCN 2015042251| ISBN 9781450460026 (print)
Subjects: LCSH: Triathlon--Training.
Classification: LCC GV1060.73 .V36 2016 | DDC 796.42/57--dc23 LC record available at http://lccn.loc.
gov/2015042251

ISBN: 978-1-4504-6002-6 (print)

This publication is written and published to provide accurate and authoritative information relevant to the subject matter presented. It is published and sold with the understanding that the author and publisher are not engaged in rendering legal, medical, or other professional services by reason of their authorship or publication of this work. If medical or other expert assistance is required, the services of a competent professional person should be sought.

The web addresses cited in this text were current as of September 2015, unless otherwise noted.

Acquisitions Editor: Tom Heine; **Developmental Editor:** Kevin Matz; **Managing Editor:** Nicole O'Dell; **Copyeditor:** Mark Bast; **Indexer:** Bobbi Swanson; **Permissions Manager:** Martha Gullo; **Graphic Designer:** Denise Lowry; **Cover Designer:** Keith Blomberg; **Photograph (cover):** Arne Dedert/picture-alliance/dpa/AP Images; **Photo Production Manager:** Jason Allen; **Art Manager:** Kelly Hendren; **Associate Art Manager:** Alan L. Wilborn; **Illustrations:** © Human Kinetics, unless otherwise noted; **Printer:** Versa Press

Human Kinetics books are available at special discounts for bulk purchase. Special editions or book excerpts can also be created to specification. For details, contact the Special Sales Manager at Human Kinetics.

Printed in the United States of America   10 9 8 7 6 5 4 3 2 1

The paper in this book is certified under a sustainable forestry program.

Human Kinetics
Website: www.HumanKinetics.com

United States: Human Kinetics, P.O. Box 5076, Champaign, IL 61825-5076
800-747-4457
e-mail: info@hkusa.com

Canada: Human Kinetics, 475 Devonshire Road Unit 100, Windsor, ON N8Y 2L5
800-465-7301 (in Canada only)
e-mail: info@hkcanada.com

Europe: Human Kinetics, 107 Bradford Road, Stanningley, Leeds LS28 6AT, United Kingdom
+44 (0) 113 255 5665
e-mail: hk@hkeurope.com

Australia: Human Kinetics, 57A Price Avenue, Lower Mitcham, South Australia 5062
08 8372 0999
e-mail: info@hkaustralia.com

New Zealand: Human Kinetics, P.O. Box 80, Mitcham Shopping Centre, South Australia 5062
0800 222 062
e-mail: info@hknewzealand.com

E6013

TRIATHLON 2.0

DATA-DRIVEN PERFORMANCE TRAINING

CONTENTS

FOREWORD

Only three things can be measured in endurance training: frequency of workouts, duration of the workout, and intensity of the workout. Frequency is simple. All that's required is a calendar. Measuring duration is also easy. Any clock will do. Intensity is the hard one to measure. I've been trying to do that accurately for about 50 years. This book reveals the current state of the art of intensity measurement in sport.

When I started training as a collegiate runner in the 1960s the most advanced technology available for measuring intensity was a stopwatch. And we didn't wear it on the wrist; it was handheld. I've still got my silver Hanhart shockproof watch, scratched crystal and all, from when I was a high school track coach in the 1970s. By the early 1980s, when I was a triathlete, the heart rate monitor came along. I recall thinking there could be nothing more advanced than this; it was the ultimate measure of intensity. It took a couple of years to figure out zone-based training by sport. Once we had it, we were off to the races! That was the late 1980s.

In the early 1990s I heard about something called a power meter. I had no idea at first what it was all about, but somehow it measured intensity on the bike. Of course, there was no Internet, let alone search engines, so I had to wait for magazine articles on it. That seldom happened. But slowly I began to gather information. In 1995 I started writing a book called *The Cyclist's Training Bible* and decided I should include something about power meters. So I wrote to SRM, the German company that was the only power meter manufacturer in the world. The owner, Uli Schoberer, was kind enough to loan me one for three months so I could become familiar with it. It's been 20 years since I first tried training with power meters, and the learning continues. What an amazing tool! And the list of high-tech tools for measuring intensity goes on and on. Just when I think we've reached the pinnacle, something new comes along. The problem it creates for us as athletes and coaches is deciding what is best for us and then learning how to use it.

I've known Jim for many years and consider him one of the best triathlon coaches in the United States. I was his coach in the latter part of his career as a professional triathlete. When he retired and decided to become a coach, I was pleased because I knew he would be one of the best. That's certainly proven to be right. His greatest strength as a coach has always been his understanding of producing the best possible race performances from the athletes with whom he worked. And that is based on understanding how to measure what's important. He is one of the sport's leaders in this regard.

By reading *Triathlon 2.0: Data-Driven Performance Training*, you will become much more capable of determining your priorities and how you can measure and analyze them. Your improved performance will reflect your newfound knowledge.

Joe Friel, cofounder, TrainingPeaks

ACKNOWLEDGMENTS

This book wouldn't have come to fruition if not for the support of some amazing and wonderful people in my life. Thank you to my parents, Rhonda and Bob, for all their work in raising me, and the appreciation they helped me learn for all they taught me and did for me. Thanks to my wife, Orlanda, for her love and support through all the years. Thanks to my young sons, Alistair and Alden, who motivate me every time I look at them and see their beautiful smiles. Thanks to Adam Zucco, who has been a great friend and colleague in the coaching business. Thanks to Joe Friel, Greg Welch, Bob Seebohar, and Peter Reid for teaching me a lot through their coaching during my racing career. And thanks again to Joe, who has mentored me from athlete to coach to writer. Finally, thanks to Lydia Kaulapai, who introduced me to writing and showed me what a great tool it can be in life.

INTRODUCTION

BENEFITS OF TECHNOLOGY IN TRAINING

In all my days of racing as an elite triathlete, there was never a single piece of equipment I could use that would allow me to train poorly, or dumb, and make up for it on race day. There was no magical wheel set, aerodynamic frameset or helmet, pair of race shoes, or innovative wetsuit that changed the fact that how well I trained on a daily basis made all the difference on race day.

Look in most transition areas and you'll find the latest and greatest of these items, but probably few items devoted to executing daily training better. Most of the athletes who come into these races are undertrained or overtrained, and no bike or other piece of equipment will change that fact to any significant degree.

A small segment of athletes in the race are poised to do well. They have figured out how to balance training stress, recovery, life and job demands, and family commitments. They were able to see the signals that their training was going well and were able to keep it that way. They are likely the athletes you train with and are beating in the sessions but somehow lose to each race. Or they are the athletes who never seem to have a bad race. Or they're the athletes who always seem to peak perfectly at the biggest races. To many, these athletes are either very lucky or they know some magical formula we're all dying to know.

Many athletes scour articles and blogs, reading all they can, trying to process all the information out there, convinced it will make clear how to train. What tends to happen though is the exact opposite. Athletes read and try to put into practice everything they read about the latest interval set, or strength equipment, or long ride with big gear climbs, and so on. With so much information bombarding athletes, they get more confused and never stick to one plan, trying to do every plan out there, much of it not addressing their own needs, just what is popular.

Athletes get power meters, heart rate monitors, and GPS systems and look at screen after screen of data from their training, trying to figure out what it all means and where the secret information within it shows what to do next.

There is an infinite amount of information available on training for a triathlon, but in the end it is all about filtering that information so it makes sense for the individual athlete. This is the purpose of this book. We can't all be Ironman world champions, so training like one isn't going to work for the majority of athletes. Athletes simply need to understand their own goals and then decipher the information from their training that matches their goals, according to the time of year and amount of time until race day.

Athletes who have purchased generic training plans or taken a free one out of a recent magazine inevitably find some challenge with it, because it can't account for their whole race schedule, their past training history, their strengths and weaknesses, and what training groups and resources are available in their area.

A frustration I've had with most training plans, and many traditional coaches, is the belief that there is a set number of weeks to devote to a specific type of training. For example, many coaches say that athletes need 12 weeks of aerobic base-building work and then 12 weeks of race-specific work to be ready to perform well. That might work for some, but what if they really need 16 to 20 weeks of aerobic base work? What if their basic aerobic fitness is lacking so much that it should be almost all they focus on for many months? Otherwise, the athlete is coming to the start line with not enough aerobic fitness to make any race-specific work worthwhile. If an athlete hasn't shown he or she can last at an aerobic intensity for 12 hours, how is he or she going to break 12 hours in an Ironman? These things can't be rushed, and setting some arbitrary number because of historical norms doesn't help the individual athlete meet his or her specific needs.

What if the athlete has been doing multiple long-course races each year, for many years? Do you think that athlete needs to still do 12 weeks of aerobic base-building work? No, of course not. The athlete's aerobic fitness isn't lacking; it's the ability to hold a higher intensity during the race that needs to be addressed. This athlete would waste 12 weeks of opportunities to address his or her weakness and miss the potential for a huge breakthrough!

THE POWER OF DATA

I run into many athletes who think power meters and other technological tools are a waste of money. It's ironic that usually these athletes own some sort of smartphone, use complex software at their day jobs, or use computers in just about every aspect of their daily lives, and yet there is a disconnect that prevents them from realizing that technology could be as much of a benefit to their training as it is for their daily life.

If you're still wondering if using technology is best for you, let me ask you a few questions. What if I told you there was a way to determine exactly when you had enough aerobic fitness, so you could maximize training time by focusing more time on weaknesses, instead of aerobic work?

What if you could see your exact weaknesses and get direct, measurable feedback on how well your training is addressing them?

What if you could see exactly how many intervals you should do in a workout to get just the right amount of training stress, so you can recover quicker and pack in a better week of training?

What if you found the perfect tapering strategy and wanted to replicate it perfectly for each major race? What if you could actually see into the future to where your fitness will be down the road and how well your taper will be executed?

What if I told you that once you hit a certain performance marker in your training, the chances of achieving your goal or exceeding it just increased dramatically?

What if I told you we could look back at your training from the past season or longer and see where you made training mistakes or errors in judgment for your training load, what training load got you sick or injured, or where you plateaued, all in a matter of minutes?

What if you could be shown your training tendencies so you could come up with a new and better stimulus to get the fitness and performance jump you're looking for?

Believe it or not, all this can be done, and it really isn't that hard. You just have to know what data to collect, the elements of the data to look at, and when to look at them, according to your goals and timeline to race day.

What data should you collect? Depending on how many variables of your training you want to control, you should consider a power meter for your bike, a speed-distance device for your running (GPS or accelerometer-based watch), a heart rate monitor that will work for both devices, and something that can measure your swim pace and distance. If you have and regularly use all of these, you will be able to do all the things I've mentioned.

If you've been training old-school style, without any of these tools, this book will show you how to begin training by the numbers and open up a whole new world of training performance and efficiency. With so much data collection it appears difficult to isolate what is important, but that is exactly what you will learn to do in this book, making training with these tools simple and rewarding.

Everyone knows there's more than one way to train, and that's the fun of training in general, to find your own way. It's why I enjoy coaching athletes so much, helping them find the way that works for them. What way best helps athletes to reach their potential, given the resources available, strengths and weaknesses, and race goals, can be calculated and measured, giving you the freedom and power to create your best way of training.

GOING BY FEEL

I once had a very famous and successful triathlete tell me he liked "to go by feel" in his training and therefore didn't want to use data. It is perfectly fine to go by feel; no one is saying athletes should be robots and simply follow a set program of numbers. At the highest levels of the sport, athletes must use their feel and sense of their bodies to get that extra percentage point of improvement and performance. But collection and analysis of the data are what helps an athlete better understand and improve his or her sense of feel. In the end, the data are simply numbers, representing what has been done in training and helping us project what still needs to be done. The real art of coaching and training comes from the decisions made from what the data tell us. Those decisions become easier with a clearer picture, as we begin to know more and more about the athlete.

DATA AND THE MIND

In all my days of racing, the differences between my best races and my worst races usually only came down to one thing, and it wasn't health, injury, or equipment. It was what I was thinking on that start line. When I was timid and unsure of myself, I raced poorly. When I knew I was ready, I was eager to prove myself against the best. It wasn't really my training as much as my confidence in how the training had prepared me. When you've been tracking and seeing the improvement in your training, it is hard not to be confident in the preparation, which keeps you motivated to train and step to the start line ready to race.

ABOUT THIS BOOK

Part I, Triathlon Training Technology, will introduce you to the key training devices for cycling, running, and swimming. These chapters will help you make intelligent choices if you decide to purchase a new training device. Before using these devices in your training, you will need to assess your current fitness level and then set some training goals. That's where Part II, Planning Your Training, comes in.

Every training and racing decision you make, including equipment, nutrition, volume, and intensity, along with timing, depends on your goals. Determining the training to meet your goals in different times of the year, is where individuality is most important. The training decisions you make should support those goals and your needs as an athlete. In Part II we dive into better assessing your needs as an athlete, using the data from these tools, and then planning on how to meet those needs through the season, according to the goals you have set.

In Part III, High-Tech Periodization, we go step by step through the season, understanding how to prioritize training needs and analyzing how effective the current training decisions are, according to the goals you have set and the timeline available until race day. This allows you to make sure you are on a consistent improvement track and preparing to meet your goals.

In Part IV, Race Analysis for Winning Results, we use the data from prerace, during the race, and postrace, as well as from the entire season, to better examine athlete tendencies (both positive and negative), what types of race strategies and training the athlete responds best to, and how effective the overall training decisions for the season were. We can also use this to better plan paces and even nutrition strategies.

As an added benefit, many of the figures provided throughout this book are screenshots from actual races or training sessions with the coach's notes and comments left exactly as they were in real time, giving you an inside look at the coach/athlete relationship.

This book is a guide on this journey to help you find your best way of training, so you can be on the start line confident and ready to maximize your fitness and training. Let's get started.

PART I

TRIATHLON
TRAINING
TECHNOLOGY

1
CYCLING TECHNOLOGY

What gets measured gets improved.

Robin Sharma, best-selling author

If you watch cycling, are a fan of cycling, or train with some devoted cyclists or triathletes, the topic of power and watts is likely to come up. It sounds great to talk big numbers about watts, but what do they really mean? And are they really that important? How do watts and a power meter really tell an athlete anything more than heart rate monitors do?

Heart rate (**HR**) is probably the second most overrated metric in training, second only to volume (more on that later). No one ever won a race based on the heart rate achieved. HR is measured by beats per minute, or bpm. How high your HR can reach doesn't mean a thing, but you'll sometimes hear athletes brag about the bpm they reached in a workout or race.

In truth, if you have an out-of-shape, overweight individual go for a jog, that person's HR will likely be higher than that of someone who is fit. So does that mean the overweight individual's performance is better or the person is fitter? Of course not. My wife can reach heart rates over 200 bpm in a run workout, while I can go as hard as possible and never break 185 bpm. Does this mean she is faster than me? No, of course not.

I realize that for a lot of you, this sounds earth-shattering. Why wouldn't you pay attention to HR in a workout or race? How am I supposed to judge how I'm doing? What if my HR gets too high? What if it doesn't get high enough? The answer is, it doesn't matter. HR is variable from athlete to athlete, and even day to day within the same athlete, sometimes due to training and sometimes due to things that have nothing to do with training, such as temperature, stress, or diet.

Many times HR will only tell you something you already know, that you're going hard or easy. But you don't need a HR monitor to tell you that; you can feel it. HR plays an important role in determining a few important metrics we will discuss and use in this book, but HR by itself doesn't really mean much.

You've probably noticed that when you start an interval, HR lags behind because it takes a while to catch up. If you're doing very short intervals, say 15 seconds or less, there isn't enough time for HR to catch up to truly represent the intensity of the effort. It's just an input metric, communicating how your body is responding to the stress you're giving it in the moment—and sometimes doing it too late. You can't do much with that.

Output metrics, on the other hand, such as the pace you run at, mean something. If I told you I did a run at 150 bpm, you wouldn't really know what that means. Was it a fast run? A slow run? But if I told you I did a 5K run in 15 minutes, now you understand how fast that is. Output is what we care about, and every major metric in this book is based on output. Output is the entire point of performance and competition, and if you're reading this book, that is likely what you care most about.

I want to be clear about HR though: you should collect HR during just about all training sessions. Sometimes you should actually pay attention to it during the session, but those sessions will be outlined later on. Otherwise HR should be given no attention during a session. It is important to collect it for later analysis, but otherwise don't let it dictate the workout, and *never* let it dictate your racing.

POWER (WATTS)

If you're reading this book, it's likely because you have purchased, or are considering purchasing, a power meter and want to know how to use it to maximize your training. Two of the biggest things you're probably wondering are, *What is power exactly?* and *How does the power meter actually calculate it?*

Remember that HR is an input metric. Power is an output metric, one of the most important output metrics there is for training. You might be asking, "Isn't speed of the bike most important on race day?" Yes, it is on race day, but speed can vary so much based on wind, hills, altitude, road surface, weight, aerodynamics, stop signs and lights, and even whether there is a pack of riders around you. Speed is not something you can use to judge the quality of daily training, even if training on the race course each day, because these variables can change daily, positively and negatively. This is why power data is so important; it stays the same, despite the conditions and those variables.

Power is a work rate, measured in watts. Work is the basis here, and it is important to understand the actual work being done is the movement of your body and bike. The fitter you are, the higher the work rate you can perform and the longer you can hold it.

When you apply a force to the bike through the pedals and crank arms, the bike moves you. If you apply a force and don't move, no work has actually been done, just like pushing on a brick wall. The wall doesn't move, so you have done no work. The one exception of no movement on a bike is in the case of a stationary trainer, where the wheel actually does move, but you as a rider stay put.

In other words, the force you apply to the pedals times the distance you go equals work. We can express this with the following equation where work is W, force is F, and distance is D:

$$W = F \times D$$

We know that power is a work rate, so the equation for work simply needs to be divided by time to be a rate. This gives us

$$P = W / T$$

or

$$P = (F \times D) / T$$

If you think back to all the story problems you did in elementary school, you know that distance is equal to rate of speed, or velocity, times the time you travel at that speed, or

$$D = V \times T$$

Now comes the algebra you have always wondered if you would ever actually use in your lifetime outside of school. We will substitute this equation for D into the work equation:

$$P = (F \times D) / T$$

becomes

$$P = [F \times (V \times T)] / T$$

Now we have time on the top and bottom of the fraction, which allows them to cancel each other out. This leaves us with

$$P = [F \times (V)]$$

And this leaves us with our basic equation to define power, which is force times velocity:

$$P = F \times V$$

In basic terms, this means power is equal to the force you apply times the speed at which you apply it. When riding your bike, this means how hard you press on the pedals and how fast you turn the pedals.

Power meters measure or estimate the force we apply and then, based on the brand and model used, simply multiply the revolutions of the pedals or crank arm to get the work rate. The more fit the athlete, the higher the producible work rate or the longer or more efficiently the athlete can produce a certain work rate (watts). We will discuss the efficiency aspect more later.

Some power meters measure from the crank arm or bottom bracket, while others measure at the pedal or the hub. Some older models actually measured the tension on the chain to determine force. Another brand uses reactive forces (Newton's third law), measuring force applied in a direction, to estimate what amount of that force is being applied to the bike and in what direction.

The more precise the power meter is at measuring the work rate of the athlete, and the more user-friendly or mobile it is, generally the more expensive it is.

So now that you know what power is, there are a few key terms to know and understand, to help you maximize learning from the data.

CADENCE (RPM)

In the previous equation, V represented how fast you turn the pedals or crank arms when applying the force. This speed of revolutions is called cadence, and it is measured in terms of revolutions per minute, or **rpm.**

KILOJOULES (KJ)

Kilojoules are the measurement of actual work accomplished in a ride. One watt is equal to one joule of work done in one second. The unit for this metric is called the kilojoule, or KJ. Your long, intensive rides, such as those in an Ironman, will likely have the biggest KJs of your season.

AVERAGE POWER (AP)

Average power, or **AP**, is just the average watts generated for a given amount of time. This is a basic measurement but very important, and we will refer back to it many times.

NORMALIZED POWER (NP)

Normalized power, or **NP**, can be confusing to some athletes, because it isn't quite average power but many times can be similar or even the exact same value. Let me explain.

When you ride your bike and look at your power meter, you get values that jump around and even surge. Coast for a while, and you'll get zero watts. You can imagine that if you did a steady ride on a flat course, you'd get an average power that probably wouldn't vary much from what you saw on the power meter while you were riding. But if you did a group ride and threw in a lot of attacks, then sat in the pack for a while coasting, then attacked more and pushed hard to stay on a wheel in front of you, suddenly you've had a workout that was pretty challenging, that might actually have a lower average power than the easier steady ride, simply from the time spent drafting and coasting.

Compare a ride where the athlete might ride steady for 150 watts average power on a flat course with a ride where the athlete does hill repeats, spending equal time going uphill at 300 watts and downhill coasting at zero watts. It's the same average watts for the two rides, but they are much different in terms of the stress on the body to do that 150 watt average. This is where NP is a great metric. Normalized power takes all these surges into consideration, plugs the data from the workout into a complex algorithm, and calculates a power value that is more representative of the stress incurred during the ride.

FUNCTIONAL THRESHOLD POWER (FTP)

The best power output an athlete can sustain for 1 hour is called his or her functional threshold power, or **FTP**. For clarity, when referring to FTP on the bike, we use **bFTP**. If you take anything away from this chapter, the concept of FTP is paramount.

You've likely heard about threshold heart rate, which is expressed as a heart rate for the maximal sustainable effort of what an athlete could do for about an hour. However, if you're using power, we can actually express this maximal sustained effort as watts instead, which we can track and see if it improves throughout the season. Your threshold heart rate likely won't change at all over the course of the season, but the watts you can produce for an hour can and should change positively. This helps put the focus on what is most important—the output!

The time used for bFTP is still approximately 1 hour, and this is probably the most important metric for an athlete training with technology. In fact, Andrew Coggan wrote, "Power at lactate threshold (**LT**) is the most important physiological determinant of endurance cycling performance, since it integrates $\dot{V}O_2max$, the percentage of $\dot{V}O_2max$ that can be sustained for a given duration, and cycling efficiency" (Coggan 2008).

This metric must have your attention. It should be monitored regularly for changes as your fitness changes, both positively and negatively, because many of the other metrics we use are calculated based on this value. It also is the basis point for where your fitness and performance are.

If you go for a 2-hour ride and tell me it was 200 watt AP, then I can only compare how that was for me as an athlete, based on my threshold watts (bFTP). If my bFTP is 180 watts, then 200 watts is above my threshold power and impossible for me to accomplish for 2 hours. However, if my threshold is 350 watts, then this would be considered an active recovery ride.

Luckily, software programs now can recognize when this value has likely changed, but also knowing the appropriate intensities for given time values can help signal when your bFTP has changed. A basic example of this is when an athlete has a ride that lasts more than 1 hour and the NP or AP are higher than the athlete's specified bFTP. We know that by definition of bFTP, this is impossible, since bFTP is the best sustained output for 1 hour. So it is likely that the athlete's bFTP is higher than we have estimated or that the data are inaccurate.

Bits of inaccurate data, such as an unexplained surge or spike, are not that uncommon, and thankfully we can cut out those bits easily within many analysis software programs.

Of course, the best way to calculate this value initially is with a performance test of close to an hour. For example, a 40K time trial (**TT**) on the bike, or 1-hour all-out ride or race, will give a close indication. However, this is a very hard effort and requires a lot of mental motivation. In chapter 4, Assessing Triathlon Fitness, we discuss all the ways you can estimate bFTP.

POWER ZONES (Z)

Just like we have HR zones, there are also power zones. We base these zones, just like we do with HR zones, on threshold. In this case, we use bFTP. For the purposes of this book, we follow power levels developed by Dr. Andrew Coggan, commonly referred to as Coggan power zones (see table 1.1). His zones are the predominant ones used by most cyclists and triathletes.

TABLE 1.1   Power-Based Training Levels (Coggan Power Zones)

Level	Name	Average power (Relative to bFTP)	Average HR (Relative to LT HR)	Perceived exertion	Description
1	Active recovery	<55%	<68%	<2	Easy spinning or light pedal pressure, i.e., very low-level exercise, too low in and of itself to induce significant physiological adaptations. Minimal sensation of leg effort or fatigue. Requires no concentration to maintain pace, and continuous conversation possible. Typically used for active recovery after strenuous training days (or races), between interval efforts, or for socializing.
2	Endurance	56–75%	69–83%	2–3	All-day pace, or classic long slow distance (LSD) training. Sensation of leg effort or fatigue generally low but may rise periodically to higher levels (e.g., when climbing). Concentration generally required to maintain effort only at highest end of range or during longer training sessions. Breathing is more regular than at level 1, but continuous conversation still possible. Frequent (daily) training sessions of moderate duration (e.g., 2 hrs.) at level 2 possible (provided dietary carbohydrate intake is adequate), but complete recovery from very long workouts may take more than 24 hrs.

Level	Name	Average power (Relative to bFTP)	Average HR (Relative to LT HR)	Perceived exertion	Description
3	Tempo	76–90%	84–94%	3–4	Typical intensity of fartlek workout, spirited group ride, or briskly moving paceline. More frequent or greater sensation of leg effort or fatigue than at level 2. Requires concentration to maintain alone, especially at upper end of range, to prevent effort from falling back to level 2. Breathing deeper and more rhythmic than level 2, such that any conversation must be somewhat halting, but not as difficult as at level 4. Recovery from level 3 training sessions more difficult than after level 2 workouts, but consecutive days of level 3 training still possible if duration is not excessive and dietary carbohydrate intake is adequate.
4	Lactate threshold	91–105%	95–105% (may not be achieved during initial phases of effort)	4–5	Just below to just above TT effort, taking into account duration, current fitness, environmental conditions, etc. Essentially continuous sensation of moderate or even greater leg effort or fatigue. Continuous conversation difficult at best due to depth or frequency of breathing. Effort sufficiently high that sustained exercise at this level is mentally very taxing, therefore typically performed in training as multiple repeats, modules, or blocks of 10–30 min. Consecutive days of training at level 4 possible, but such workouts generally only performed when sufficiently rested or recovered from prior training so as to be able to maintain intensity.
5	$\dot{V}O_2max$	106–120%	>106%	6–7	Typical intensity of longer (3–8 min.) intervals intended to increase $\dot{V}O_2max$. Strong to severe sensations of leg effort or fatigue, such that completion of more than 30–40 min. total training time is difficult at best. Conversation not possible due to often ragged breathing. Should generally be attempted only when adequately recovered from prior training; consecutive days of level 5 work not necessarily desirable even if possible. Note: At this level, the average heart rate may not be high due to slowness of heart rate response or ceiling imposed by maximum heart rate.

(continued)

TABLE 1.1 *(continued)*

Level	Name	Average power (Relative to bFTP)	Average HR (Relative to LT HR)	Perceived exertion	Description
6	Anaerobic capacity	>121%	N/A	>7	Short (30 sec. to 3 min.), high-intensity intervals designed to increase anaerobic capacity. Heart rate generally not useful as guide to intensity due to non-steady-state nature of effort. Severe sensation of leg effort or fatigue, and conversation impossible. Consecutive days of extended level 6 training usually not attempted.
7	Neuro-muscular power	N/A	N/A	*(Maximal)	Very short, very high-intensity efforts (e.g., jumps, standing starts, short sprints) that generally place greater stress on musculoskeletal rather than metabolic systems. Power useful as guide but only in reference to prior similar efforts, not TT pace.

Adapted, by permission, from H. Allen and A. Coggan, 2010, *Training and racing with a power meter*, 2nd ed. (Boulder, CO: Velo-Press), 48. "Description" column reprinted, by permission, from A.R. Coggan, 2008, Power training zones for cycling. [Online.] Available: http://home.trainingpeaks.com/articles/cycling/power-training-levels,-by-andrew-coggan.aspx [August 25, 2015].

The power zones can be calculated automatically in your analysis and training software, if you have the bFTP value for the athlete, but for your knowledge and for comparison with HR, table 1.1, written by Dr. Coggan (2008), explains it well.

You will notice the HR and power zone percentages don't correlate exactly with each other (evidence of the inaccuracies of training with HR alone). And when doing shorter intervals, HR plays no role in determining the quality of the training—it lags too far behind.

READING A POWER FILE

The power graph is usually expressed with watts on the *y*-axis and time on the bottom of the graph (*x*-axis), but it can also be expressed as distance traveled (*x*-axis), if the file includes speed data, like in figure 1.1*b*. When you add in more data, such as elevation, speed, and cadence, the graph can get busy, so it is advised that as you are first learning, you keep the graph simple with fewer metrics displayed at one time (see figure 1.1*a*), or you end up with an image like in figure 1.1*c*.

You might be asking why there are such big spikes in the graphs. It seems so jagged, like the movements are varied, but when you watch them in person they seem smooth. This is because so much of the pedal stroke is not used to pedal and produce force. We can't produce force on a pedal when coming up in the pedal stroke, and because the pedals are in opposition to each other, only one is pro-

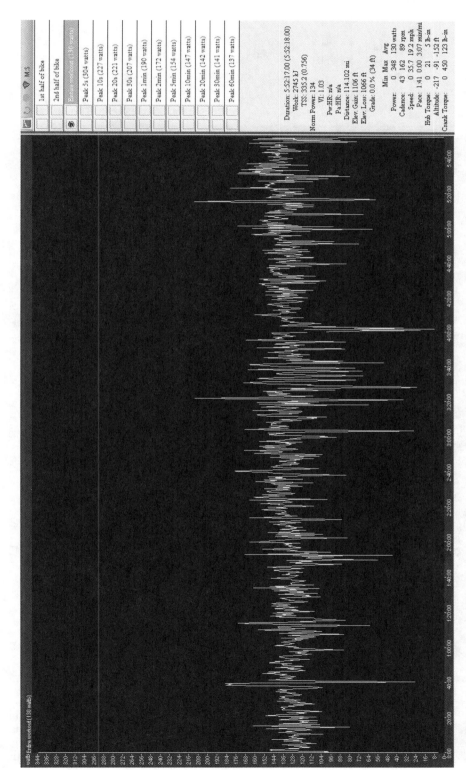

FIGURE 1.1A Power data from an Ironman, expressed as time on the x-axis, horizontal.

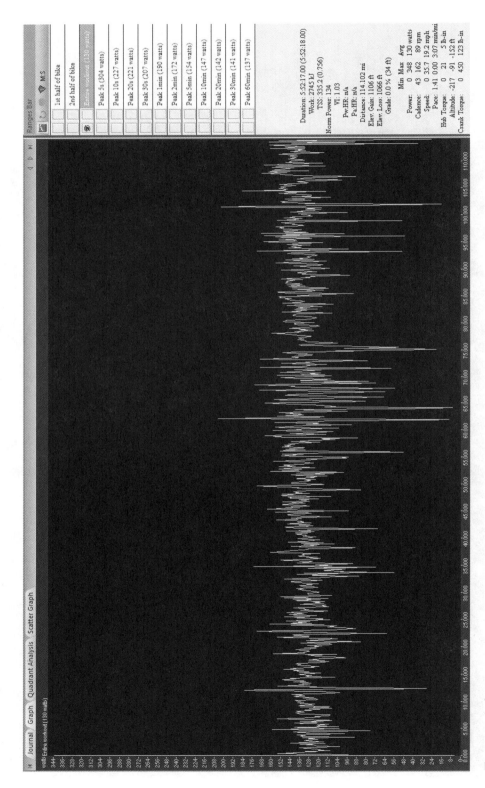

FIGURE 1.1B Speed data from an Ironman. Distance is on the x-axis, horizontal.

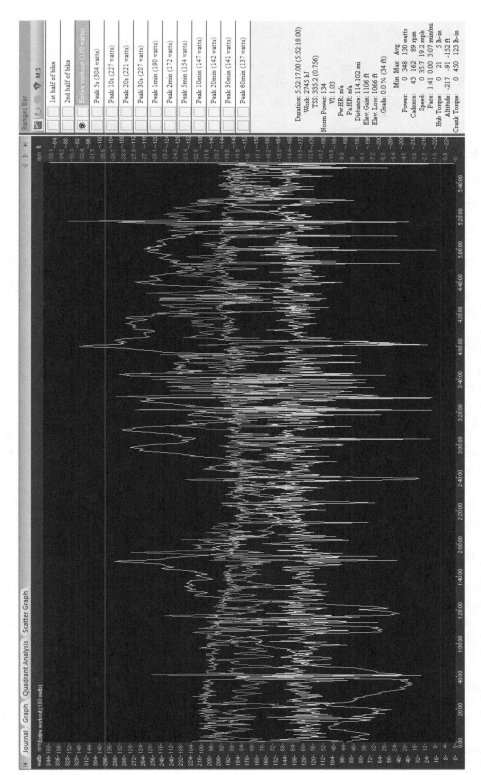

FIGURE 1.1C Typical power file from an Ironman event, with power displayed.

ducing a downward force, while the other is producing nothing. Also, the most force is produced during the downward part of the pedal stroke, so there are even fluctuations while pedaling, which are hard to see with the naked eye.

Some of these metrics and lines are simple and self-explanatory, such as speed, altitude, and HR. Other metrics and numbers you see listed in the graphs may not be familiar to you. Here are a few of the important ones shown and what they represent.

INTENSITY FACTOR (IF)

The intensity factor of a ride is just the quotient of NP / bFTP.

Since NP is the value that represents what the athlete basically rode at, then comparing that value with the bFTP value for the athlete shows us how intense that session was for the athlete.

If an athlete does an hour effort at his or her threshold output, the IF value is 1.00. This value can never be seen for efforts greater than 1 hour, because again, by definition the athlete's FTP is the maximal sustained effort for 1 hour. If a session is an hour or longer and has an IF of more than 1.00, that is a clear sign the athlete's FTP has improved and needs to be modified.

PEAK POWER (P)

The best average power an athlete can produce for a given amount of time is his or her peak power. The term was called *critical power* (**CP**) for many years, and you might still find it called that, but in this book we call it peak power, or simply **P**.

Peak power is expressed with a number after it that represents the time period it is referring to, usually in minutes. (In the images of the power file in figure 1.1, the word *peak* is written, followed by the time range, but you will see it a lot as just the letter P.) If we are to discuss an athlete's best power output for 1 minute, we would express this as his or her P1. If we wanted to refer to the best output for 30 seconds, we would express this as P.5. When we begin tracking times less than 30 seconds, such as best 5- or 12-second outputs, we would express it as P5s or P12s.

In the power file image (see figure 1.1c), the peak power outputs for those time intervals within that single file can be highlighted and easily found, to help isolate when and where they happened during the session.

An important power metric for a half Ironman athlete would be P120, or the athlete's best 2-hour power output, because this is a race-specific value. An Ironman athlete would want to look more at P180, or even P240 (although you won't find that value commonly written or discussed). A more common peak power value tracked is 30 minutes, since athletes tend to have a lot of 30-minute samples to track.

VARIABILITY INDEX (VI)

Some rides have a lot of variance in the output of watts, while others are very steady and consistent. This variance can be expressed by the variability index, or **VI**, and shows the difference between the NP and the AP of a ride. Bigger differences in NP and AP mean the ride was quite varied in its output intensities.

Efficiency Factor (EF)

Remember how I said that HR played an important role with other metrics? Here is a perfect metric for explaining the importance. It isn't that HR is useless, it's just that it needs an output metric to give it context. If I told you a number, such as 10, you would probably respond with "10 what? 10 pounds? 10 days? 10 seconds?" Because 10 doesn't mean anything by itself, it needs something to base itself on. When we take the NP and divide it by average HR, we get watts per beat, or what we call efficiency factor, **EF**. As the athlete's aerobic fitness improves, if we track the aerobic intensity workouts, we should see an increase in this value, either because the NP goes up for a given HR, or if NP stays the same, the HR to maintain that effort goes down. All are signs of fitness improvements.

Decoupling (Pw:HR)

Much as with EF, there is another way to measure aerobic economy of an athlete on the bike and the run. In long-course triathlon, aerobic endurance is critical. The relationship of power output to HR, and how much HR drifts or rises over time at a constant aerobic output intensity, tells us how aerobically fit or economical the athlete is. If an athlete is maintaining an effort at or near his or her aerobic threshold (AeT), then this effort should show a HR that is relatively stable, not climbing during this effort to higher rates. The reverse should also be true, that for a given HR, the athlete's output of power or pace doesn't decrease dramatically.

When we look at this relationship over time, such as 4 hours on the bike at zone 2 watts for an Ironman athlete, or 2.5 to 3 hours for a half Ironman athlete, then we can get some measurement of the athlete's aerobic bike fitness, expressed as a percentage of variance between the two, labeled as Pw:HR.

If an athlete doesn't keep a low value of drifting, or what we call *decoupling*, then we know the athlete needs to continue working on aerobic fitness. (This is expressed as a percentage of how the athlete deviated.) If the athlete can't show basic aerobic fitness for those time periods on the bike, how can we expect that athlete has the aerobic fitness to do well in a race? We can't.

In figure 1.2, we have an athlete who has done 2.5 hours steady at zone 2 endurance watts, according to Coggan's power zones. This athlete is training for a half Ironman race, and you'll notice when we highlight the trend of the two lines, there is a drift of 3.95 percent between the two lines. If the lines were perfectly parallel, the percentage would be zero, and these lines would be considered coupled. Since they are breaking apart slightly, they are decoupling, in this case by 3.95 percent.

In figure 1.3, we have an athlete who is clearly lacking aerobic fitness on the bike because Pw:HR decouples by more than 21 percent, over just a short 74-minute period.

In the next chapter, we'll take a look at running technology and how to better understand it for training analysis.

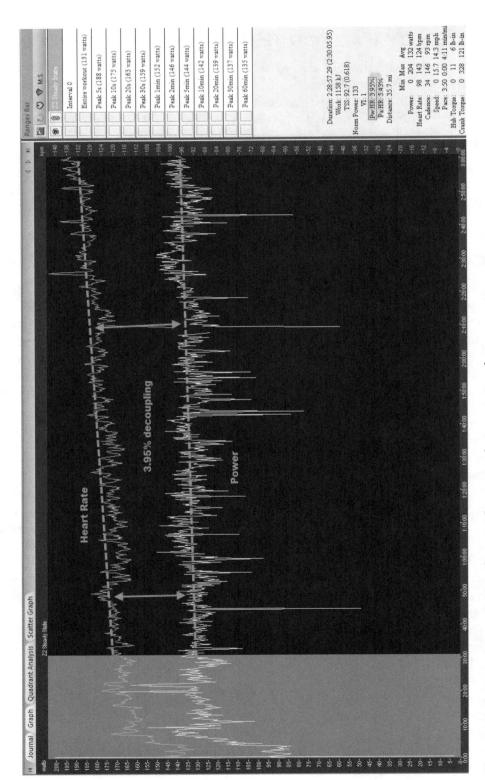

FIGURE 1.2 An athlete who has done 2.5 hours steady at zone 2 endurance watts.

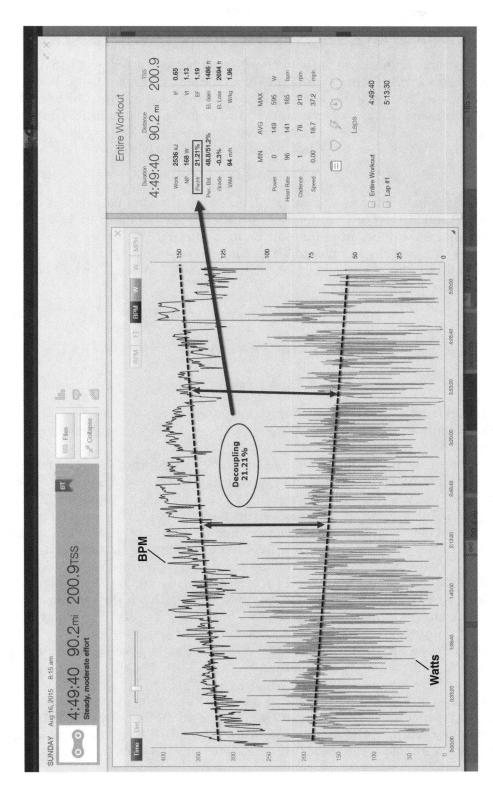

FIGURE 1.3 An athlete who is clearly lacking aerobic fitness on the bike.

TRAINING STRESS SCORE FOR BIKE (bTSS)

Imagine if every workout you did could have a number associated with it, a number that represents the performance and the toll of the stress it took on your body. The good news is we have this already! The better news is that it is just the beginning because this metric helps us better understand training, fatigue, fitness, tapering, and more. TSS (training stress score) is calculated in a software program usually, but for those looking to know what it means, here is the basic formula:

$$[(IF\^2) \times 100] \times (hours\ of\ workout) = TSS$$

You can see how intensity factor, IF, plays into this, and of course IF is dependent on NP and bFTP. If bFTP is not accurate, then IF and TSS are off. Again, more evidence that it is important to monitor for an accurate FTP.

To give you a baseline number to better understand TSS, let's say an athlete did a 1-hour all-out effort. This would be the athlete's FTP, so the IF would be 1.00. Plug 1.00 into the equation.

$$[(1.00\^2) \times 100] \times 1\ hour\ workout = TSS$$

$$[1 \times 100] \times 1 = TSS$$

$$100 = TSS$$

So a 1-hour, all-out, threshold effort would be equal to a TSS of 100. This is the same for swimming, biking, and running, where a 1-hour all-out effort in each sport is 100 TSS, specific to that sport.

When referring to TSS on the bike, we use bTSS; for running, TSS is referred to as **rTSS**. When we discuss training stress score as a whole, such as when we want to see the combination of both rTSS and bTSS, and possibly sTSS (swim TSS), we use just TSS. This will be an important distinction and value discussed later.

You're probably wondering why there would be a distinction between the disciplines of running and biking for TSS. Wouldn't training stress simply be training stress? In general, we can look at training stress as a whole, but 1 rTSS does not equal 1 bTSS. Still confused? Consider how your body would respond or feel after a run for 1 hour at rFTP, compared to an hour at bFTP. Given the weight-bearing aspect of running compared to cycling, the physical stress on the body is much higher for running.

When we combine the rTSS and bTSS values, we get a good sense of the total stress on the athlete. This is an important concept in this book, and we will dive more into this in chapter 6, Training Analysis Software.

There's also a new TSS metric, one not based on outputs like pace and power but the input metric of HR, called **hrTSS**. It uses an athlete's threshold HR and zones, and the workout HR data, to determine how much time was spent in each HR zone and estimate a TSS score for the athlete. This has been found to be fairly effective and accurate with estimating TSS from steady-state aerobic activities but obviously can't do as well with very stochastic sessions. Luckily, in training for long-course triathlon, the stochastic sessions are limited.

The hrTSS metric is not as accurate as power or running-based TSS scores but would probably be an effective alternative for athletes who might travel a lot and not be able to bring their bike with them, still looking to get in a ride perhaps on a stationary bike or even a rental or borrowed bike. It could also be effective in times when an athlete has a technology failure with power or pace data not able to be collected.

SUMMARY

Power is an output metric that signifies the work rate of an athlete. The most important output metric is an athlete's functional threshold, or the best output an athlete can do for 1 hour. On a bike, this is expressed as bFTP, the best watts an athlete can hold for the hour. Many of the other metrics used in training and racing analysis are based on the bFTP, so it is important for this value to be monitored for accuracy. Output metrics like these help give input metrics like HR a context that helps us better understand what is happening with the athlete and his or her fitness, as well as the athlete's needs.

2 RUNNING TECHNOLOGY

Train smarter, not harder.

Allan F. Mogensen

As popular as power meters are in the cycling world, GPS (global positioning system) units are even more popular in the running world. Just about every serious heart rate monitor brand on the market offers a GPS or some type of speed-distance device with it. And just about every GPS unit on the market now offers a heart rate monitor with it as well. If it doesn't use GPS satellites, it likely uses an accelerometer to measure speed and distance, usually a foot pod placed in the shoe that measures the accelerations and decelerations of the foot, to determine stride length and stride rate. In running, stride rate is the revolutions per minute (rpm) based on how many times the foot strikes the ground in a single minute. Running rpm are also referred to as cadence.

This chapter covers popular and useful technology used to train during runs, along with some useful terminology that will help you interpret and understand the data the technology provides.

GLOBAL POSITIONING SYSTEM (GPS)

Most athletes understand GPS units a lot more than power meters and power data because the information they provide is easier to conceptualize, for example, how fast one is running. If you produce more watts on the bike, you're not necessarily going faster (such as when going uphill), but if you push the pace on a run, you are definitely going faster. If you produce less watts on the bike, you're not necessarily going slower either (such as when coasting downhill or with a strong tailwind). If you run easier, you are almost always running slower than if you run hard.

A GPS device uses a network of 24 satellites that have been placed into orbit by the U.S. Department of Defense. GPS works in any weather, anywhere in the world, 24 hours a day without subscription or fee (Garmin 2015). These GPS satellites circle the earth transmitting information back to earth where GPS devices use triangulation to calculate the user's exact location.

The GPS receivers are very accurate due to their multichannel design. Some of the top GPS watches use 12 parallel channel receivers to initially lock onto the satellites and maintain a strong lock in settings such as dense foliage or among tall buildings. In general, the common GPS watches today are accurate to within an average of 15 meters.

Most GPS watches generate data files that can be uploaded to a third-party software suite for postworkout analysis, through external sensors like wireless ANT+ protocol, usually by using a USB cable or Bluetooth technology.

SPEED-DISTANCE DEVICES (ACCELEROMETERS)

These devices are similar to GPS watches, but instead of using satellites to determine speed and distance, they use a motion sensor (accelerometer). Most commonly this is a foot pod attached to your shoe.

Because accelerometers do not rely on GPS signals, they are popular for their use indoors, usually on treadmills.

FOOT PODS

A foot pod uses an accelerometer, which measures the time the foot is in contact with the ground and counts the number of strides. With this, the foot pod calculates running pace, which gets transmitted to the watch.

The foot pod should be calibrated to each user, which accounts for individual running biomechanics and running shoes. Some athletes have reported as much as a 12 percent or more difference in calibration factors between racing in flats versus trainers.

GPS units or other speed-distance devices help to show the changes in grade (terrain) and the intensity of the effort athletes are putting forth. Both of these variables (grade and intensity) contribute to the physiological demands of running on terrain that is not flat.

In chapter 1, we discussed training with heart rate, showing the pros and cons while on the bike. The same basic principles apply with running, as heart rate is not an output-based metric. Remember, HR has a linear response to an increase in intensity, but it will only increase up to $\dot{V}O_2max$, which is the maximal volume of oxygen the body can utilize. This is due to an athlete's $\dot{V}O_2max$ being limited to a large extent by the cardiovascular system's ability to pump blood. Once we reach that limit, HR can no longer increase to match an increase in intensity.

Long before GPS watches, most runners used the distance covered and the time it took to determine pace, which was the primary method for tracking training load and training intensity. This basic approach works really well on flat terrain, but when examining the intensity and training load generated by varied-pace running on rolling or hilly terrain, there is a lot that can be missed.

Simply using distance and time to measure the quality of intense running works really well on a track, but what if you are not doing all of your intervals on a track? What if the other runs in your training are on hilly courses?

Some of the most important runs in your training are recovery runs. Using distance and time to accurately measure intensity and training load while on open or uneven terrain is simply not as accurate as we would like it to be, which can lead to overdoing a recovery run without knowing it.

KEY TERMS FOR INTERPRETING DATA

Here are some key terms to help understand and interpret the data that GPS devices, accelerometers, and foot pods provide.

AVERAGE PACE (AP)

Average pace, **AP**, is simply distance covered on a run divided by the time it took to complete it. If you use English units, you'll likely use minutes per mile, or min/mi. If you use the metric system, you will likely express this as minutes per kilometer, or min/km. In some examples we will even use kilometers per hour, or kph.

This is a simple measurement, but it plays an important role because most athletes already use this as a key metric to judge how their training is going. This is the exact approach this book is about! Follow the data from these key metrics and see how your training is going. If it isn't improving, then you need to address the training you are doing, before it is too late to fix it in time for your key event. Nice and simple, are you getting faster or not? Are you improving the fitness you want to improve?

NORMALIZED GRADED PACE (NGP)

As discussed in chapter 1, Cycling Technology, normalized power is a value that helps see what the true output or toll on the body is, had the effort been steady and consistent. In cycling, there are periods of coasting, stops and starts, tailwinds, and more.

In running, athletes don't have any coasting, but they can certainly have periods of uphill and downhill running, depending on the course they run. Athletes running with a lot of uphill or downhill on a course have a different toll on their body than those who run on a flat course at the same pace.

Normalized graded pace is calculated by recognizing the GPS coordinates that the run file covered, and what the elevation profile was of those points, or by using the accelerometer data that indicates incline and elevation changes while running (McGregor 2008).

One of the downsides of NGP for running that GPS units can't account for is running with a tailwind or headwind, which will affect the output and the recorded intensity of the run, without an ability to consider how those two factors affect the training stress on the athlete. Does this matter? If you are constantly training in windy areas, it could.

Also, there is indoor treadmill running to consider, where GPS data will read that the athlete is not moving at all. In this instance, the athlete needs a foot pod attached to the shoe to calculate the pace and how the incline on the treadmill might affect it.

If an athlete were running on a thick, sandy beach, the GPS couldn't really calculate the NGP, because it can't account for how the sand affects the effort to run at that pace.

Another downside is that sometimes we run on structures that can't be accounted for, such as a bridge. If you run across a bridge over a big canyon, the GPS file will show the change in elevation to be the canyon (big drop, followed by big rise), even though you ran nice and easy over the bridge.

The best advice for maximizing use of this technology is to avoid running for long periods in thick sand, into a headwind, or with a constant tailwind and avoid bridges spanning large canyons. If you can, use a foot pod to help calculate not only indoor run paces on treadmills but also to help with gathering cadence data from your runs.

INTENSITY FACTOR (IF)

The intensity factor of a run is just the quotient of normalized graded pace and run FTP, or NGP/rFTP. This helps define the relative intensity of a run workout. This becomes very important, considering that interval sessions vary greatly in intensity or even the variance of the run course.

PEAK PACE (P)

As discussed in the cycling chapter, the best average power an athlete can produce for a given amount of time is the athlete's peak power. The best average pace an athlete can produce for a given amount of time is the athlete's peak pace. The terms were called *critical power* and *critical pace* (CP) for many years, and you might still find them called that, but now coaches use *peak power* or *peak pace*, or simply P.

Peak pace is expressed with a number after it that represents the time period it is referring to, in minutes. If we were to discuss an athlete's best output for 1 minute, we would express this as P1. If we wanted to refer to the best output for 30 seconds, we would express this as P.5. I don't track below 30 seconds, because it becomes very difficult for the GPS to accurately record pace changes for such short durations consistently, and there is little correlation in training for long-course triathlon between these shorter metrics and actual performance.

An important run pace metric for a half Ironman athlete would be P60 or P90, because this is a race-specific value. An Ironman athlete would want to look more at run peak pace values of P120 or possibly even P150 (even though you won't find that value common, if you like it, you can use it). A more common peak pace value tracked is 30 minutes, since athletes tend to have a lot of 30-minute samples to track and compare throughout the year.

A pace file is much the same as a power file, only instead of watts being the output metric, pace or speed is used. Time or distance is put on the x-axis, and pace or speed is measured on the y-axis. And just like we can do with a power file, we can look at cadence, altitude, GPS coordinates on a map, and even heart rate data. See figure 2.1 for an example of a pace file. You will notice many of the same metrics we saw in the power file, but these are based on pace as the main output metric instead of watts.

EFFICIENCY FACTOR (EF)

As discussed related to cycling, in running, heart rate also plays an important role with other metrics. Again, it isn't that HR is useless, it's just that it needs an output metric to give it context. When we take the NGP and divide it by average HR, we get speed or pace per beat, or what we call efficiency factor (EF). As the athlete's aerobic fitness improves, if we track the aerobic intensity workouts, we should see an increase in this value, either because the NGP goes up for a given HR, or if NGP stays the same, the HR to maintain that effort goes down. All are signs of fitness improvement.

DECOUPLING (PW:HR OR PA:HR)

Much like EF, there is another way to measure aerobic economy of an athlete on the bike and the run. In long-course triathlon, aerobic endurance is critical, and the relationship of output to HR, and how much HR drifts or rises over time at a constant aerobic intensity, tells us how aerobically fit or economical the athlete is. If an athlete is maintaining an effort at or near the aerobic threshold (AeT), then this effort should show a HR that is relatively stable, not climbing during this effort to higher rates. The inverse should also be true, that for a given aerobic range HR, the athlete's output of power or pace doesn't decrease dramatically.

When we look at this relationship over a period of time, such as 4 hours on the bike at zone 2 watts for an Ironman athlete, or 2.5 to 3 hours on the bike for a half Ironman athlete, then we can get some measurement of the athlete's aerobic bike fitness, expressed as a percentage of variance between the two, labeled as Pw:HR. We can do the same for runners with pace data compared to HR, with Pa:HR.

If the athlete doesn't keep this value under a certain percentage for a given time specific to his or her race, then we know the athlete needs to continue working on aerobic fitness if the athlete's goals are any higher than a midpack finish. If the

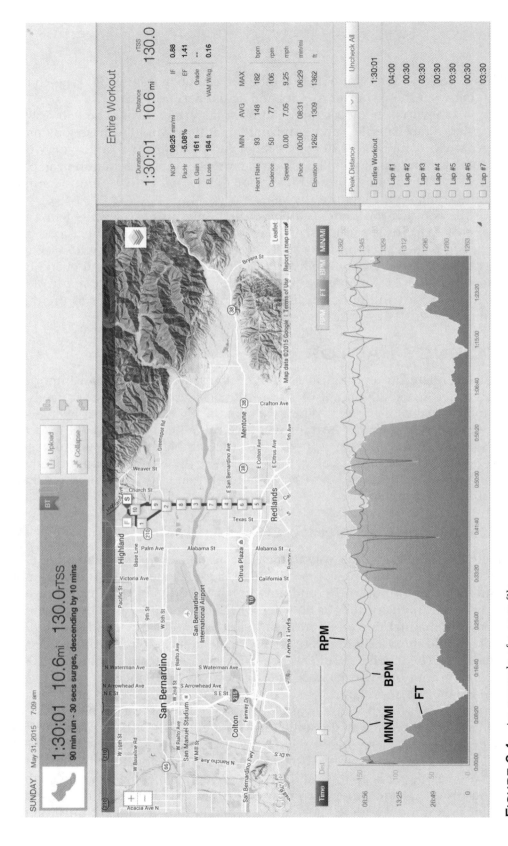

FIGURE 2.1 An example of a pace file.

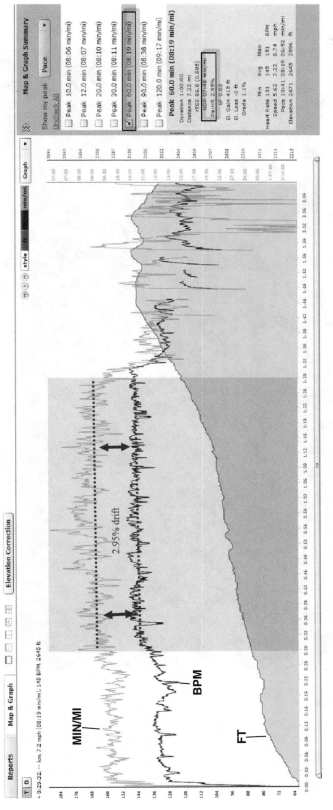

FIGURE 2.2 An athlete who has done a 2-hour run, with 1 hour steady at the zone 2 aerobic heart rate.

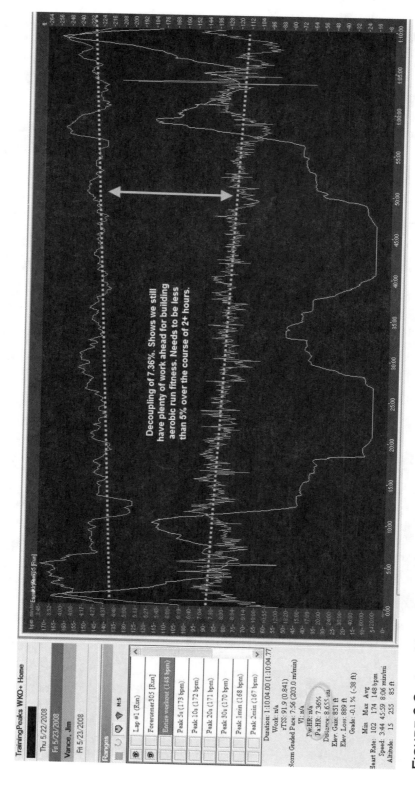

FIGURE 2.3 An athlete who is lacking the aerobic run fitness.

athlete can't show this level of aerobic fitness for those race-specific time periods, how can we expect that athlete to have the aerobic fitness to do really well in a race? We can't.

In figure 2.2, we have an athlete who has done a 2-hour run, with 1 hour steady at the zone 2 aerobic heart rate. This athlete is training for a half Ironman race, and you'll notice when we highlight the trend of the two lines, there is a drift of 2.95 percent between the two lines. If the lines were perfectly parallel, the percentage would be zero, and these lines would be considered coupled. Since they are breaking apart slightly, they are decoupling, in this case by 2.95 percent. This shows very good aerobic run fitness for 60 minutes. The next time this athlete does this run, it might be for 75 minutes, or 90 minutes, and we will see if he or she can still show the aerobic fitness for that time period.

In figure 2.3, we have an athlete who is lacking the aerobic run fitness he needs relative to his goals, as Pa:HR decouples by more than 7 percent over just a short 70-minute period, and the athlete is focused on an Ironman. He needs to get this to 5 percent for 2 hours. More on the specific ranges relative to goals soon.

SUMMARY

Running technology is exploding, using GPS technology in cooperation with HR monitors for HR data, and foot pods for cadence data and indoor training tracking, to help athletes and coaches better measure run training load and intensities and improvements in fitness. These files are similar to power files, but use pace as the main output metric instead of watts. Much like with a power file, we can gain a lot of insight into the athlete's aerobic fitness level and how well the athlete is on track toward personal goals by using other metrics like Pa:HR and EF.

3

SWIMMING TECHNOLOGY

There is water in every lane, so it is OK.

Ian Thorpe, five-time Olympic swimming gold medalist for Australia (on being in lane 5 for a final)

The above quote shows how sometimes as athletes and coaches we may make simple things more complex than they need to be. The past two chapters have helped to prove the value of technology in cycling and running training, so it would make sense that technology would be valuable in swimming as well. For the most part, that is true, because any data can help us better see trends in an athlete's performance, but there are a lot more limitations on the data from swimming, especially when using it to judge performance during training or racing or to estimate training stress.

For example, swimming in open water is not the same as swimming in a pool, so trying to gain insight on how they might be similar or compare to each other involves so many variables that it is impossible to equate. This is due to several components. Are the currents pushing with or against the athlete, or even from the side? Is the swim in a flat bay or lake or in large surf at the beach? The buoyancy difference between saltwater and freshwater can also affect speed and effort, as can the temperature of the water and whether the athlete wears a wetsuit. If the athlete is swimming in the open water in a pack of other athletes, the draft benefit must be considered.

Of course, most athletes don't swim perfectly straight in the open water, and therefore in a 1-km swim course, the athlete actually might swim 1.1 km, meaning the athlete's time for the course might seem slower. And many times, it is not uncommon for open-water courses to be measured inaccurately.

Just the difference between training pools that athletes swim in, the depth of the pool or its temperature, can affect how the athlete performs on the day, be it training or racing. If an athlete is consistently training in the same pool year round, this can eliminate a number of variables and make the data from the technology more useful for insight on performance and training.

Most of the technology used for swimming is no different from that used in running, commonly a wristwatch that has an accelerometer in it and, if swimming in open water, can use GPS to help the athlete track speed and distance in the water. Because the wristwatch uses the motion of the arm, it is likely ineffective at assessing or even acknowledging kick sets with a board, because an athlete isn't moving the arms very much during kick sets.

Considering all the variables that must be accounted for, sometimes it is just the simple metrics we should be concerned about. So what are some of the metrics that can be used for insight?

AVERAGE PACE (AP)

Just as in running, these wrist units can use GPS and accelerometers to provide feedback on how an athlete's average pace is improving for intervals.

If an athlete has a specific test set in the pool, the average pace for that specific test set can be very valuable feedback for how the athlete's swim performance is progressing. Usually, swim pace is expressed in minutes per 100 yards or per 100 meters. However, most training analysis software programs don't allow for this unit, when comparing over multiple days, or they take the distance swam and divide it by the total time for the workout, meaning the rest periods are included, which throws off the actual pace swam.

CADENCE (RPM OR SPM)

In swimming we also have rpm, which are just the cycles the arm makes per minute. Some might express this as strokes per minute, or spm. What's the right cadence to hit? Cadence is a topic of much debate, especially in swimming, but in general it depends on the athlete's ability and goals, which are discussed further in this book.

Perhaps one of the best insights from swimming technology is tracking the trend between swim cadence and swim pace, allowing the athlete to see if an increase in cadence is actually helping or hurting the athlete. Swimming is so technique dependent; it is not the fastest cadence or hardest effort that makes a swimmer faster than another. There is such a concentration to swimming required to keep good technique, and of course, racing in the open water with hundreds or thousands of other athletes around you doesn't make it any easier.

In figure 3.1, you can see an actual swim file from a wrist unit that gathered data on speed and cadence.

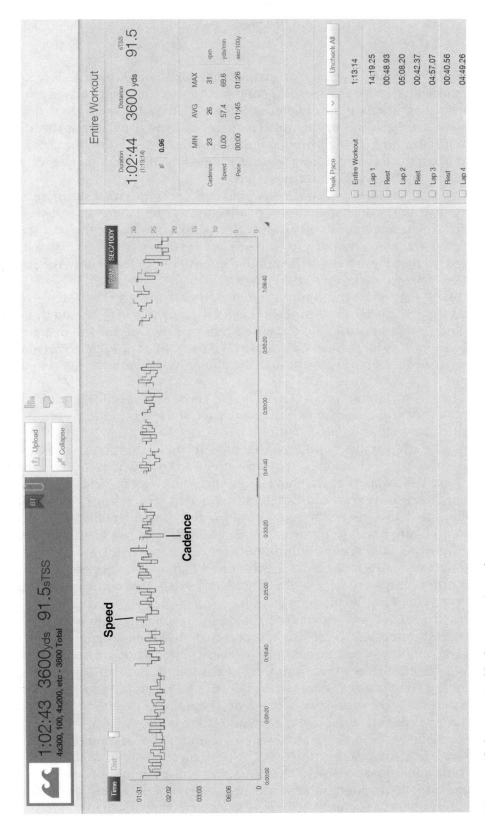

FIGURE 3.1 A swim file from a wrist unit.

Can much be gained from looking at a swim file? Some information can be gained, especially if there is a specific goal the athlete is looking to achieve within a session, such as maintaining a higher or lower cadence, or if trying to determine at what point in the workout the athlete really began to tire. Also, if the athlete is consistently training in the same pool, intervals recorded by the unit can help to give an accurate account of how fast the athlete actually swam in the set, to be recorded in a training log and later reviewed.

But in general, athletes and coaches should look for trends in performance, like swim pace over the course of a season, relative to cadence. In figure 3.2, we have tracked this athlete's average swim pace per day, in kph, for the length of the season, and plotted the average cadence for the session. Realize that this is average, not normalized, so this doesn't show the relative intensity of the sets, only the pace of the entire sets, from warm-up to cool down.

You'll likely notice the trend of the cadence increasing for the athlete. This is because as the athlete got closer and closer to race events, we increased the race-like sets and simulations, hoping to get the athlete prepared for the demands of the competition. This increase in cadence helped show that the athlete was making the efforts to do the sets effectively, and the ability to hold a higher cadence was improving.

Given the technical aspects of swimming, we know that cadence doesn't necessarily mean faster swimming, and the average pace of the sets in those periods isn't exactly much more than in other periods.

So with all these variables and challenges to the validity of the data, should an athlete even use this technology or pay any attention to it? The answer is yes, but athletes should be aware that changing pools, including a lot of kick sets, or swimming a lot of open water can add variables to the data, which must be considered when using the data to assess training decisions and improvement. In the case of the athlete in figure 3.2, it is important to also consider the rest and recovery and speeds or times actually achieved during the sets.

If an athlete uses GPS to measure the distance of an open-water swim, and perhaps assess the ability to swim straight or tendencies to veer to a side in swimming, this is a great use of this technology as well.

Some swim coaches and athletes use HR when prescribing swim workouts, but many of the HR monitors on the market can't currently send a signal through the water, so HR can only be assessed during recovery periods, and with the chest and monitor above the surface of the water, so measuring EF and Pa:HR isn't effective at this time for swimming. Taking samples of HR and recording those in a log is a possibility but not necessarily any better than simply recording times achieved in race or goal-specific sets to see if the adaptations are happening.

In the end, the best assessment tool when it comes to swim training is a test set that matches the demands the athlete will face to meet personal goals, conducted semiregularly and under consistent circumstances (same amount of rest and recovery heading into the workout, same warm-up, same recovery within the test), with the results recorded in a training log for evaluation and comparison to previous tests.

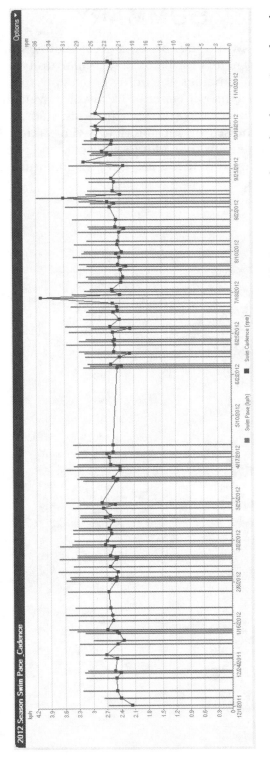

FIGURE 3.2 Average swim pace per day, in kph, for the length of the season, with the average cadence for the session plotted.

SUMMARY

Though technology for swimming can be a great tool, it still lacks the accuracy and reliability of power meters for bikes and similar units for run training. This is caused by a number of variables, including pool depth, pool environment consistency, open-water currents, saltwater or freshwater, wetsuit or no wetsuit, and temperature of the pool or open water. Specific skills, such as cadence and overall pace changes through the season, or ability to swim straight in open water, are useful for analysis. Regular sets that address the goals and plan for an athlete, and recording the times achieved in them, are still probably the best tool for assessing swim fitness progression.

PART II

PLANNING YOUR TRAINING

4
ASSESSING TRIATHLON FITNESS

You must believe and adhere to the principle of unending improvement and the setting and achieving of even higher goals.

Joe Vigil, Olympic running coach

The principle of unending improvement is becoming more and more important in the sport of long-course triathlon because the depth of competitive fields has increased, the volume and intensity of training required is very risky, and the improvement of coaching and training technologies allows for more athletes to train more effectively. If athletes aren't continuously improving, they are soon left behind, and this trend will only continue.

The power of the data that come from training technologies like power meters and GPS, and its value for making training decisions, cannot be understated. Power meters and GPS are vital tools for athletes and coaches seeking continual improvement. The higher your goals, the less you can afford to plateau or have a setback in your training, because every day and every training session matters. This is the heart of this book, to help you interpret the data from these tools to achieve and maintain continual improvement.

Can we really, truly improve without end? Well, Mother Nature may have some things to say about this concept, but in general, no matter your current fitness level, elite or beginner, you can get better, the only question being just how much better. An elite athlete is looking for that extra tenth of a percent of improvement and exploring everything from equipment and wind tunnels to the peak nutritional and recovery methods. A beginner can improve simply by continuing to train consistently. So, yes, continual improvement is always available.

The process of continual improvement begins with understanding the athlete's goals, assessing the athlete's strengths and weaknesses, and then looking at the metrics that represent these, which will be closely followed after training decisions are made.

STEP ONE: SET GOALS

The most common questions I as a coach receive from athletes deal with wanting feedback about what training they're doing or what I think they should be doing. What may surprise many is that the answers are rarely ever the same, even for athletes who are doing the same event. Each athlete is different, and most importantly, the goals of each athlete in conjunction with individual abilities lead to different answers.

The first and most important question that must always be asked is, What are your goals? Are they clear and set? Can you measure them? Have you prioritized what is most important for you to accomplish? You can have more than one goal, but knowing which goals are most important is vital. For example, two athletes of similar ability might be doing the same half Ironman, but for one it is a peak event for the season, while the other is using it as a tool for a later performance, such as a full Ironman. The approach and training these two athletes do for that event is not, and shouldn't be, the same.

So what are your goals? If you can't answer that question, then there is no point proceeding with other questions about specific workouts, race equipment, race schedule, strategies, coaching, or anything else you're trying to decide. Why? Because the answer that makes the most sense should be the one that most closely matches the goals you have set. Someone may ask me if he needs to get a disc wheel for a few thousand dollars for his upcoming half Ironman. The answer will greatly depend on if your goal is to finish with a smile on your face, move up in your age group, go for a World Championships spot, win your age group, or win the race overall. It makes no sense to spend thousands on race wheel sets if you just want to finish with a smile.

Whether you should do a race when battling a slight injury, continue with a workout when clearly tired, or invest in coaching or massage all depend on what your goals are.

I get people who ask me what I think about all of these training questions, and 100 percent of the time my answer is that it depends on your goals. Some people quickly and easily respond to me with clear and concise goals, but others stare at me with a look of bewilderment. If you tell me your goals, I can give you some advice that will probably help. If you have no goals, then I have no idea if the advice I give could help or hurt.

Make sure the first decision you make for your season is to set your goals and then prioritize them. Write them down, so you can easily refer back to them, even if that means writing them on a poster on the wall. Any time you have a question, go back and see which decisions will be in support of those goals and are necessary for achieving them. Your goals are the standard for which all training and racing decisions should be judged.

Set your goals and make sure they are measureable and realistic. For example, saying you want to "do well" isn't measurable. Setting a goal to qualify for Kona or to finish within the top 15 finishers or the top 10 percent of your age group is measurable.

Make sure the goals are realistic. If you're not competitive in your age group, thinking you're suddenly going to qualify for Kona is probably not realistic, at least not right away.

Remember, goals don't have to be short-term only; there can be a long-term approach (and hopefully there is). Olympic hopefuls work on a longer-term goal and must address the fitness needed to achieve that goal, which can take years. Perhaps you will work on building more aerobic fitness this year, in preparation for your first Ironman next year. Again, your goals are the standard for which all training and racing decisions are made.

STEP TWO: DETERMINE WEAKNESSES

Once you've determined your goals, the next step is to assess what the limiting factors are for accomplish them. These limitations are any attributes that would prevent the triathlete from reaching those performance goals, either basic aerobic fitness, anaerobic fitness, muscular endurance, or specific skills and abilities. When these attributes are known, a coach can more easily determine how much time is needed to address them.

Triathletes new to the sport may spend an entire season training only on basic skills and fitness. Because these triathletes may be lacking in very basic physical attributes, such as basic aerobic fitness, simply training consistently with easy to moderate aerobic sessions can bring about steady improvement for many months and possibly the entire season.

Triathletes who are competing at a high level, those who are elites or trying for the World Championships in their age group, can't afford to have glaring weaknesses. The higher the goals of the athlete, the better the competition becomes and the more important it is to address weaknesses. If you have a glaring weakness, it will be exposed against top competition.

Determining weaknesses should include race course considerations. For example, if the goal is to qualify for the 70.3 World Championships, and you're a strong cyclist but a weak runner, then if racing a course that doesn't have a challenging bike course to help maximize your bike prowess, you'll need to address your running in training more.

Many times determining weaknesses is easy and clear with an athlete having one or two significant weaknesses. The hard part is determining how to address them. However, generally athletes have either a speed, endurance, or technique weakness that needs to be addressed in training.

If you are unsure of your weakness, go back and look over past results, comparing your individual disciplines to the performances of those who beat you. For example, if you got 10th place in your age group, and 7 athletes who finished ahead of you swam faster, 5 rode faster, and 2 ran faster, you can see that the swim and bike are your weaknesses.

SPEED WEAKNESS

The definition here of a speed weakness is neurological fitness, or the ability of the brain to send the signal to muscles and then complete the movement. Run cadence is a great example; some athletes can maintain a cadence of 90 steps per minute or more, and others struggle to hold 75.

This is also related to fast-twitch muscle fiber, or high-force movements, such as short-duration power outputs on the bike (e.g., peak power for 5 seconds, 30 seconds, or 1 minute) or similar peak durations for running.

ENDURANCE WEAKNESS

The definition of an endurance weakness is when an athlete hasn't built the aerobic engine and economy needed to be successful in the discipline. This is usually common in athletes who are new to the longer distances of half and full Ironman.

TECHNIQUE WEAKNESS

Technique weakness is probably easiest seen in the swim, where movement skill is generally more important than fitness, as a very fit athlete with poor skill will not be a good swimmer. However, pedaling and run skills can also be greatly improved, resulting in dramatic improvements in performance.

Once you have identified the weaknesses that could prevent you from achieving your goals, the next step is to figure out the metrics to follow using technological tools to assess how the progression and improvement of the weaknesses goes.

An athlete or coach might feel that addressing an endurance weakness can provide the repetitive movement opportunity to fix a technique weakness. There is some validity to this idea; however, it is not a simple more-means-better formula. Prescribing the right amount of endurance training that allows for improvements in both endurance and technique weaknesses is a balance that must be found, and following the appropriate metrics can help dial in this balance for each individual athlete.

TESTING FOR WEAKNESSES

So how can one go about finding personal weaknesses if the athlete is not sure? The first and most important metric to find is functional threshold power (FTP) for both bike (bFTP) and run (rFTP).

Determining bFTP

How do we calculate bFTP for an athlete? This can be done in a lab, but that can be expensive, and many athletes don't have access to those resources. Instead, athletes should use a field test, which can easily be repeated throughout the season, if necessary. Once you have this value, you can begin to track and better understand your training.

For calculating bFTP, the key is simply having a power meter on your bicycle. Here are the three common field tests I do with athletes:

1. 30-minute solo time trial. The emphasis here is on *solo*, where an athlete does an all-out 30-minute interval on a flat stretch of road, and takes 100 percent of the average power value for that 30-minute interval. The reason it needs to be done alone and on a flat stretch of road is because competition and climbs inflate the number.

2. 30-minute trainer time trial. This is similar to the previous test, only done on a trainer. The results of this are usually a little lower than out on the road, but if you are consistent with this test, this test will be fine.

3. 20-minute trainer time trial, minus 5 percent. This test estimates bFTP quite well and is probably a bit easier mentally than the 30-minute version on the trainer. After the 20-minute TT, you take 95 percent of the average power for the interval.

Which test you choose to do doesn't matter as much as being consistent with the follow-up testing you do. If you do a 20-minute trainer TT test in the winter, then you should do that in the summer months as well, even if the weather is better.

Most software programs will calculate power zones for you, but you will need to choose which zone system you want to use. For this book, we use Allen Coggan's power zones.

Once you know your bFTP, you can compare this value with your mass in kilograms to get watts per kilogram (w/kg) at bFTP. Based on your goals, you can determine how this value compares with that of others in your age and category group who qualify for the World Championships in Kona and for 70.3 (see table 4.1 for males and table 4.2 for females). These values should help show if making the World Championships is a realistic goal.

TABLE 4.1 Male w/kg Ratios at FTP and General FTP Range Needed Based on Goals for World Championships

Age/category males	w/kg at FTP	Watts at FTP
Under 40 qualifier	4.0+	290+
Over 40 qualifier	3.75+	270+
Over 60 qualifier	3.0+	200+
Elite 70.3 event champion contender	4.55+	330+
Elite Ironman event champion contender	4.8+	350+
Elite podium contender at World Championships	5.0+	370+
Finisher at any event, non–World Championships	2.5+ (varies)	150+

TABLE 4.2 Female w/kg Ratios at FTP and General FTP Range Needed Based on Goals for World Championships

Age/category females	w/kg at FTP	Watts at FTP
Under 40 qualifier	3.9+	230+
Over 40 qualifier	3.7+	220+
Over 60 qualifier	2.8+	160+
Elite competitor	4.0+	240+
Elite podium contender at World Championships	4.25+	275+
Finisher at any event, non–World Championships	2.4+ (varies)	130+

Determining rFTP

One of the most common and best run field tests in order to calculate rFTP is to have the athlete do a 30-minute hard run alone on a flat course, preferably a track. The average pace and HR for that last 20-minute period of the run effort is fairly indicative of your rFTP and lactate threshold heart rate (**LTHR**) for running. Usually, cycling LTHR is approximately 7 bpm below this run LTHR value, meaning you can set your HR zones based on these values. If you do the 30-minute bike TT test, you can use the same protocol of taking the average HR for the last 20 minutes to estimate bike LTHR.

You're probably asking why we only focus on the last 20 minutes to determine LTHR. The reason is because HR lags behind effort, taking time to respond to the effort being put out. This is why we use power and pace, because from the first moment we can tell what the effort and intensity are.

Other ways to estimate rFTP include an actual performance from a recent hard effort (such as a race) of a 10K or 15K run. However, this depends on the time it took the athlete to complete the distance. Usually, if the 10K time was more than 45 minutes, the athlete can use the 10K pace. If the athlete is faster than 45 minutes for the 10K, then using a 15K pace or even half marathon (if the athlete is fast enough) will work well. Again, the idea is to estimate output for one hour and to be consistent. As you improve from season to season, you might change the method used to estimate rFTP. In fact, advanced athletes can probably estimate their rFTP simply from recent run training and how they feel at certain intensities and paces. I was once able to estimate a half marathon time for myself within 30 seconds when I was racing professionally.

Based on your goals, you can determine how this value compares with that of others in your age and category group who qualify for the World Championships in Kona and for 70.3 (see table 4.3 for males and table 4.4 for females). These values should help show if making the World Championships is a realistic goal.

For calculating run HR zones, I recommend Joe Friel's run zones based on threshold HR from the run test. Table 4.5 shows how Friel's run HR zones break down.

TABLE 4.3 rFTP of Males Qualifying for the World Championships

Age/category males	rFTP (kph)
Under 40 qualifier	15.5+
Over 40 qualifier	14+
Over 60 qualifier	13+
Elite 70.3 event champion contender	17.5+
Elite Ironman event champion contender	17+
Elite podium contender at World Championships	18.5+
Finisher at any event, non–World Championships	10+

TABLE 4.4 rFTP of Females Qualifying for the World Championships

Age/category females	rFTP
Under 40 qualifier	14.5+
Over 40 qualifier	13+
Over 60 qualifier	9+
Elite 70.3 event champion contender	15.5+
Elite Ironman event champion contender	15+
Elite podium contender at World Championships	16+
Finisher at any event, non–World Championships	10+

TABLE 4.5 HR Zones for Run Training by Joe Friel

Joe Friel HR run zones	% of LTHR
Zone 1	Less than 85%
Zone 2	85% to 89%
Zone 3	90% to 94%
Zone 4	95% to 99%
Zone 5a	100% to 102%
Zone 5b	103% to 106%
Zone 5c	More than 106%

My recommendation for long-course triathlon training is that you always use power zones for training on the bike, and when the time is right, you pay attention to HR zones for the run. The reason for this is consistent metrics, providing reliable data to base training decisions on.

Determining sFTP

For the swim, a test to determine sFTP is helpful. Swimming a 1000-meter/yard time and taking the average pace for this distance is fine. Make sure it's completed solo, in a pool you swim in normally. Depth and structure of pools, as well as lane lines and other people in the water, can affect the pace, so try to get this completed in the pool you use regularly. Do not attempt to establish sFTP based on open-water swim times because there are too many variables and distance accuracy issues.

Once you have sFTP from a 1000 meter/yard time trial, you can use most software suites to determine your pace zones. However, paying attention to swim pace zones isn't going to be necessary, because this is mostly a tool to help you better understand your swim training tendencies, have a benchmark for improvement, and be able to track swim training stress score (sTSS) as needed.

STEP THREE: EXAMINE METRICS FOR WEAKNESSES

The value of the technological tools really begins to shine when you can identify the key metrics needed for improvement and achieving specific goals and get objective feedback on whether those weaknesses are improving. The bigger challenge is choosing which weakness and metric to track, prescribing the training to improve it, and determining when to begin. I'll discuss the *when* part in the next chapter.

Once you've determined the biggest weakness or limiter, then you need to determine the metric that correlates to it, so you can track whether the training is actually improving it. This metric is to be tracked through the periods in which you focus on improving it but also beyond in order to make sure you maintain the improvement through the season or as long as possible.

TESTING

Metrics are great for tracking, but the best and most important metric is a test result. If you have a test set, the comparison of one test to another should hold heavy weight, as long as the testing is done under the same conditions and approach each time. For example, a test workout in a big-volume week compared with a test following a few light or recovery days is not the same. Make sure the lead-up to both tests is the same. If the tests are races, then the same race-week protocol should be followed. There is no better test than a race, especially since motivation is high, and the result is directly measured against that of the competition.

Table 4.6 helps distinguish which metrics help identify weaknesses as well as how to track the progress via the corresponding metrics for each discipline of the sport.

TABLE 4.6 Metrics for Identifying Weaknesses and Tracking Progress

	Swim	Bike	Run
Speed metrics			
rpm	X	X	X
P5 secs		X	X
P12 secs		X	X
P30 secs	X	X	X
P1 min	X	X	X
P6 mins	X	X	X
P30 mins	X	X	X
FTP	X	X	X
w/kg		X	
Endurance metrics			
P30 mins	X	X	X
FTP	X	X	X
w/kg		X	
Pw:HR		X	
Pa:HR			X
AeT power (zone 2 steady state power)		X	
AeT pace (zone 2 steady state pace)			X
Z1 run pace			X
EF		X	X
AP/wk		X	X
CTL (chronic training load)*	X	X	X
Steady blind ride*		X	
Envelope pace*			X
Technique metrics			
SWOLF	X		
rpm	X	X	X
Envelope pace*			X

*See specific sections in this chapter for more info.

Realize this is just a list for general use. You can also create your own metrics, such as a common run loop around your neighborhood or a hill you like to climb on your bike, where you can compare the times for these efforts over the course of the season or from seasons past. When I was racing XTERRA triathlons, I would use Black Mountain in San Diego as an off-road climb to determine fitness levels throughout the year, doing the climb twice with an easy descent in between for recovery. Was this official? No, but it meant something to me as an athlete. And I could also isolate the effort into an interval for comparative purposes for many sessions and seasons to come.

I would also run a 10K loop from my door, along the bay and Pacific Ocean, and would compare the time for each run frequently. Ryan Bolton, a 2000 Olympic triathlete for the United States, is a coach who leads an elite run training group in Santa Fe, New Mexico, which includes many of the top male and female Africans racing the U.S. marathon and half-marathon circuit (his top female, Caroline Rotich, won the Boston Marathon in 2015).

Ryan has his athletes do a tempo run workout on a tough road called Buckman Road, which happens to sit at an elevation of more than 7,000 feet. Buckman Road may not mean much to you or me, but to Ryan it is an excellent metric he can use to estimate very precisely what an athlete's marathon time would be.

The important thing is that you have a metric that matters to you, because you probably haven't used a power meter for your whole biking life, or a GPS your entire running career, but you know what fast is to you. And when you can break through with that metric, your confidence will soar, and your satisfaction and motivation for training will likely improve as well.

Now imagine when you start looking at more metrics from data you've collected for years. You can probably guess how much you're going to improve your daily training.

You will notice in table 4.6 that some of the metrics overlap, showing themselves in more than one group, which is common, because energy systems overlap as well. You don't use one energy system or one muscle group alone when doing a certain discipline; you just use some more than others.

Let's take FTP for example, which appears in the speed metrics and the endurance metrics. It is a 1-hour output, but efforts less than 1 hour, such as 30 minutes, should affect it as well. If you're an athlete who has done nothing but slow and easy rides for years, you might consider efforts at FTP to be intense and therefore speed oriented. Many athletes have a low FTP but great endurance and ability to hold near their FTP. If they are going to improve their endurance, efforts at or below FTP are important, and because it is more intense than Ironman or even 70.3 efforts, it could be considered a speed weakness that needs to be addressed.

Table 4.7 from Andy Coggan helps show how different training intensities overlap, where the more checks per square, the greater the adaptation from training that energy system or intensity (Coggan 2008).

You'll notice in table 4.7 that Z6 training actually has a training effect across all areas of fitness, and training in Z4 (FTP) and Z5 ($\dot{V}O_2$max) affects many areas of fitness effectively also, but slow and easy Z1 training has little effect on these fit-

TABLE **4.7** Expected Physiological/Performance Adaptations Resulting from Training at Zones 1–7

	Z1	Z2	Z3	Z4	Z5	Z6	Z7
Increased plasma volume		X	XX	XXX	XXXX	X	
Increased muscle mitochondrial enzymes		XX	XXX	XXXX	XX	X	
Increased lactate threshold		XX	XXX	XXXX	XX	X	
Increased muscle glycogen storage		XX	XXXX	XXX	XX	X	
Hypertrophy of slow-twitch muscle fibers		X	XX	XX	XXX	X	
Increased muscle capillarization		X	XX	XX	XXX	X	
Interconversion of fast-twitch muscle fibers (type IIb -> type IIa)		XX	XXX	XXX	XX	X	
Increased stroke volume/ maximal cardiac output		X	XX	XXX	XXXX	X	
Increased $\dot{V}O_2$max		X	XX	XXX	XXXX	X	
Increased muscle high-energy phosphate (ATP/PCr) stores						X	XX
Increased anaerobic capacity (lactate tolerance)						XXX	X
Hypertrophy of fast-twitch muscle fibers						X	XX
Increased neuromuscular power						X	XXX

Adapted, by permission, from H. Allen and A. Coggan, 2010, *Training and racing with a power meter*, 2nd ed. (Boulder, CO: VeloPress).

ness adaptations. In fact, this table helps illustrate how variance of workouts and training intensities can still build the athlete as a whole.

When you have established what your weaknesses are, and begin to plan how to address them, table 4.7 can help you determine the zones of training you want to target to help improve the performance and metric.

You might have noticed that rpm is listed in table 4.6 as a metric across all three sports, for both technique and speed. This is because you generally must have good technique and neurological fitness to hold a high cadence effectively for longer durations. Elite triathletes have been shown to maintain high cadence off the bike, suggesting excellent neurological fitness (speed) and technique. A range of 90 to 100 strides per minute has been shown in higher-performing runners, and running off the bike in long-course triathlon racing means running in a state of fatigue (Dallam 2013). So if you have high-level goals, and your run cadence is low, it is likely something that needs to be addressed for improvement of both speed and technique. The effects of this technique-based training could be the surge in performance you need.

In swimming, one can hold a high rpm and not necessarily be fast or do it with good technique. Usually in a race, triathletes increase swim cadence, especially at the beginning, meaning an increased neurological demand must be addressed in training to be successful. Tracking rpm and comparing the changes in that number to pace can tell an athlete and coach a lot, especially over the course of a season or many seasons.

In cycling, some athletes are gear mashers and need to work to raise their cadence, a speed and neurological fitness skill. Other athletes need to figure out how to get better economy with their pedal stroke, making it smoother and engaging the pedal throughout more of the stroke, a technical skill that must be developed. Understanding the rpm at which you are most effective and efficient is an important concept that can bring you closer to your goals. But you must train and study the output at these different cadences to know which ones are the most effective.

POWER PROFILE

Watts per kilogram (**w/kg**) is relative to outputs at certain time intervals. One can use a power profile chart to determine the cycling weakness for an athlete as well, based on the athlete's peak power outputs for different time intervals compared to the athlete's mass in kilograms and that of peers.

The following three power profiles show the w/kg of different athletes, in order to better assess the athletes' areas of weakness. Power profiling helps assess how the w/kg metric compares with cyclists in the differing categories (Category 5 is novice; Category 1, pro, is the highest level). If you look at a power profile chart with data covering the entire length of a season, you can get some good signs of where your weaknesses might lie.

The athlete in figure 4.1 clearly is strong in the 5- to 60-minute range but lacking in performances of less than 5 minutes. A training assessment and protocol might find this athlete needs to work on shorter-term outputs.

Similar to the athlete in figure 4.1, the athlete in figure 4.2 is lower in outputs of less than 5 minutes. However, the output is low across all time spectrums, so power is a weakness to address. There are a number of options, but probably this athlete has never addressed high-intensity short sprinting in training. Or perhaps general preparation across all time intervals is best.

The athlete in figure 4.3 is relatively strong across most time intervals, so the question is whether any specific area actually needs to be addressed. This athlete

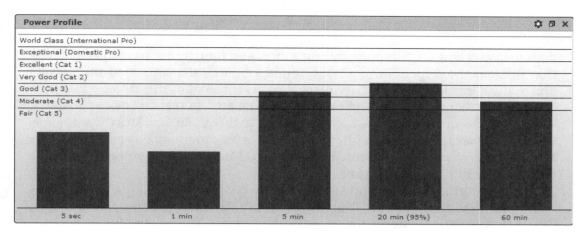

FIGURE 4.1 This athlete is strong in the 5- to 60-minute range but lacking in performances of less than 5 minutes.

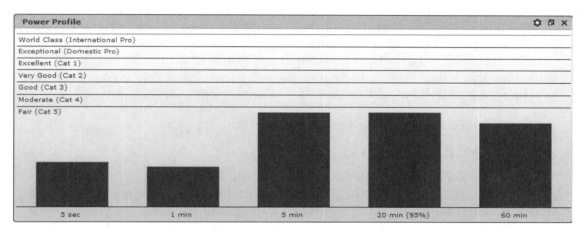

FIGURE 4.2 This athlete is lower in outputs of less than 5 minutes.

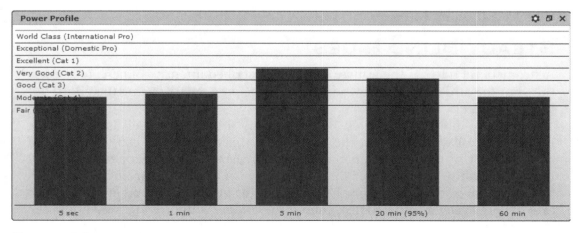

FIGURE 4.3 This athlete is relatively strong across most time intervals.

does really well in the 5-minute output range, and it might be good to assess why that is. Does the athlete have a background in sports that provided the needed preparation for this 5-minute interval? What is the goal of the athlete, and how can you use that success at 5 minutes to help the athlete reach personal goals?

The athlete in figure 4.4 is clearly strong at threshold but lacks the higher-intensity power in the shorter intervals. The shorter-duration peak power outputs are the clear weakness and must be addressed if the athlete is going to raise the performance at FTP in the future.

So if you notice your 1-minute power is not very good, it is likely a speed weakness (poor neuromuscular force and slow speed). To address it in training, watch the P1 metric and the metrics closely related, P30secs, P5secs, and P5.

Does this mean your power profile chart should have 1-minute w/kg outputs at as high as FTP? No (that would be impressive though), but realize that as a long-course triathlete you spend the majority of training time at aerobic intensities below threshold, and if you want to improve, you need to address skills and abilities you tend to ignore for a good portion of the year (or for some of you, all year). If the goal is to get faster overall, this is something you will need to address. If the goal is to be competitive (qualify or podium at the World Championships), then you must be a good all-around athlete and address these. If the goal is to just finish, you likely won't need to address this, nor will you even care.

DECOUPLING FOR POWER (PW:HR) AND PACE (PA:HR)

The Pw:HR and Pa:HR decoupling metrics are critical for analyzing the aerobic fitness of a triathlete specific to the disciplines of cycling and running. If a triathlete hasn't reached the threshold of having an appropriate value for the specific time intervals, then we can assume the athlete is not aerobically fit enough to move into race-specific training, since the general aerobic fitness required is lacking. Depending on your goals, you should try to achieve the decoupling values discussed in chapter 9, Base Phase.

STEADY BLIND RIDES

A steady blind ride has the athlete ride at a prescribed intensity of perceived exertion, but the athlete is not allowed to look at the power data during the effort, but must go by feel.

The steady blind ride, which I use with my athletes, in itself isn't a metric (more of a test workout), but the result from this type of ride can be compared as a metric. This type of ride helps an athlete reestablish a baseline perception of intensity because while riding blind the athlete isn't riding according to numbers but instead focusing on how he or she feels. If the athlete rides this at a consistent rate of perceived exertion (**RPE**), then if the athlete is improving, we should see an increase in the power outputs for this ride. This will be a key preparation session in this book, especially for Ironman training.

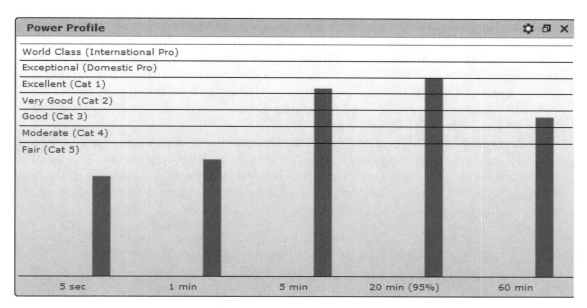

FIGURE 4.4 This athlete is strong at threshold but lacks the higher-intensity power in the shorter intervals.

ENVELOPE RUN PACE

Envelope runs are something I created as well and are runs conducted at an effort level in which the athlete must stay relaxed and easy and make the pace get faster by changing technique, not effort.

Envelope runs are another test workout metric introduced here, for both endurance and technique. As physical as running is, running fast also requires a mental focus on the technical aspects that must be honed and refined just as athletes do for physical fitness. But how do we focus on and learn about the mental side of running hard? How do we handle pushing the pace and maintaining the intensity? Many times we hear about an athlete's ability to be mentally tough and tolerate pain, but how does one do it? The answer is simple: train for it.

Mental toughness is not really an ability to tolerate pain but rather an ability to focus on the things that will keep you going fast when you inevitably fatigue.

You can train to be mentally tough by including envelope runs in your regular training regimen. An envelope run starts off easy, then works to a quick pace right on the edge between comfort and discomfort. At this point the athlete should try to push the envelope of comfort and speed, hence the name. Now instead of focusing on the pain and discomfort of the run, the athlete focuses on economy and speed, trying to maximize speed and pace for the energy used.

To be clear, this is not a tempo run. Tempo runs are hard efforts at or above lactate or functional threshold pace, intending to raise an athlete's threshold pace. An envelope run is a subthreshold, moderate effort designed to let athletes experiment with technique for economy, specifically the mental focus needed to go faster with ease. If a runner can learn to go faster while maintaining the same intensity, those same skills and actions can be applied at faster, harder intensities like races and tempo runs. In a race, it is very difficult to just go harder because you're already running near your max. In every race, from sprint to Ironman, there is a point at which there is no such thing as going harder. The athlete is maxed out. This is the point in the race when you need to be able to gain speed with ease, because you can't work any harder.

What types of technique and form items should athletes experiment with when trying to go faster without going harder? This is an important question, because it is here where athletes will learn the key things to focus on when they reach those difficult points of a race. The main technical aspects athletes need to experiment with are the following:

- Forward lean. What happens to the pace when you lean forward? How does it compare to when you lean back or stand up tall as you run?

- Cadence. What happens to the pace when you increase the cadence of your footsteps, taking shorter and quicker steps? How does it compare to when you slow down the cadence and take longer strides?

- Head position. How do small adjustments in your head position affect your pace?

- Eye position. Where do your eyes focus? What happens when you focus closer in front of you or farther away?

- Relaxation. How does releasing the tension in your shoulders, neck, and arms affect your pace?

- Foot strike. How does the position of your foot when it lands on the ground affect your pace? Change to a different foot strike to compare with other positions. Can you hear your feet? What happens if you land them softly?

Once athletes begin to experiment with the different technical aspects of their run form, they can begin to see what their tendencies are and learn how to improve on them to be faster come the tough parts of the race. This run will force runners to take inventory of their body and take an active, rather than passive, role in the pace. Now they are focusing on how fast they can go for how they feel.

For example, most runners are too upright when they run. As they get tired, they stand even more upright, slowing down. Simply adding a small amount of forward lean changes the center of gravity for them and increases their cadence and speed. For this run, focusing on leaning forward when tired will make athletes faster for the same energy output, and they will clearly see it.

Envelope runs are completed on the edge between comfort and discomfort because they force athletes to balance the economy of the movement and see how small changes in technique affect their speed for a given effort. They also teach athletes to focus while under a bit of discomfort because they are pushing the envelope of comfort, much as will happen in a race but without the physical stress on the body afterward. Most runners will find these runs are on the mid to high end of their endurance pace, approximately HR zones 2 to 3.

Because this run is subthreshold, it can be performed up to a few times per week in your regular training routine. It fits especially well between hard workouts, when another day of rest is too much, but you don't want to kill yourself before your next key workout. It offers a great balance of endurance, speed skill, and focus work.

Because this run is completed on the edge between comfort and discomfort, it prevents athletes from going too hard, inadvertently turning easier days into harder efforts. Though athletes may feel this run after the first couple of times, the body should adapt appropriately within a few attempts.

Envelope runs are best done for a minimum of 40 minutes, because it takes a while for the body to warm up, and athletes should be starting these runs off easy, working into the pace. These runs can last from 2 to 3 hours but are not recommended for lengths beyond that.

Athletes should use a speed-distance device, such as a GPS watch, and a heart rate monitor and record the data of the run but not pay attention to it during the run, letting the pace happen. Focus on the feel and take inventory of your body, noticing changes in pace. You can briefly check the watch to see pace changes for feedback on technique variances, but don't let the watch control you. Remember, this is a run for experimentation and focus on technique. If you are holding yourself back with the watch, then you are not experimenting and focusing on the technical aspects.

Over the course of many months, the improvement in the pace of this run can help show the mental, technical, and physical benefits the run training has achieved. It also helps athletes better assess their technique and the changes they need to work on for all runs.

CHARTING THE PROGRESS

Chapter 6, Training Analysis Software, will help to show you how you can chart the progress, but there are always certain segments of data that must be isolated and compared separately with similar workouts, in order to achieve reliable information to base your training decisions on. For example, you wouldn't take a half Ironman race power file and compare it with a recovery ride power file at zone 1 to 2 watts. They are not the same thing.

Table 4.8 shows how you can isolate aerobic workouts and track how you are progressing through the season. You can see that I separated each discipline and tracked the metrics specific to aerobic fitness development, because this was this athlete's clear weakness for the goals he had. I have isolated all the aerobic sessions, and the other key metrics for this athlete, and begun tracking the progress. If your training analysis software allows you to tag certain workouts to track, this can become even easier for you.

The athlete has seen excellent improvement in his EF, Pw:HR, Pa:HR, FTP, and swim test through the early training periods. As a coach, I can be confident that the training stimulus this athlete is under is the correct amount. When I begin to

TABLE 4.8 Isolating Aerobic Workouts and Tracking Athlete Season Progress

Bike

Date	EF	Pw:HR	Time	FTP	Steady ride blind - NP
1/5/2013	1.26	11.16%	3:45:00		
1/6/2013				240	
1/12/2013	1.31	10.35%	5:43:00		183
1/19/2013	1.3	7.77%	4:08:00		198
1/26/2013	1.37	4.43%	4:28:00		197
2/9/2013	1.32	3.51%	5:35:00		198
2/12/2013	1.16	3.78%	0:45:00		
2/16/2013	1.37	6.10%	5:19:00		206
2/19/2013	1.13	3.01%	0:45:00		
2/23/2013	1.37	3.75%	6:04:00		197
2/24/2013	1.39	4.81%	7:30:00		189
2/28/2013				263	

Run

Date	EF	Zone 1 pace	Time	Pa:HR	AeT pace	FTP	Envelope
1/3/2013		10:01	0:46:00	6.29%			
1/4/2013	1.18	10:04	0:46	7.81%			
1/7/2013	1.21	9:56	0:46	8.36%			
1/9/2013	1.21	9:58	1:30	9.31%			
1/11/2013	1.18	10:00	0:45	7.18%			
1/13/2013	1.18	9:51	0:30	3.93%			
1/16/2013	1.22	9:50	1:30	3.75%			
1/18/2013	1.23	9:41	0:45	6.36%			
1/20/2013	1.2	9:42	2:09	0.85%			
1/23/2013	1.25	9:31	1:35	1.10%			
1/24/2013	1.24	9:29	0:46	6.77%			
1/25/2013	1.25	9:31	0:50	6.20%			
1/30/2013	1.24	9:29	2:00	1.47%			
1/31/2013	1.16	9:43	0:44	5.89%			
2/1/2013	1.23	9:27	1:00	9.33%			
2/3/2013	1.22	9:36	1:27	-1.72%			
2/8/2013	1.33		1:01	-2.67%			8:24
2/10/2013	1.27	9:10	2:10	2.48%			
2/13/2013	1.31	8:53	0:30	6.54%			
2/17/2013	1.26	9:24	1:51	1.88%			
2/26/2013	1.28	9:18	0:30	6.57%			
2/27/2013	1.29	9:06	0:40	5.89%			

Swim

Date	Test - avg 100
1/4/2013	1:31
2/28/2013	1:27

see these values no longer improve, or even begin a trend of decreasing values, it is clear a change is needed in the training stimulus. Sometimes this can mean more recovery is needed, or a recovery period not recovering from other sessions that might be harder than they should, or other times it might mean that the athlete is missing workouts and actually not doing enough training to maintain improvement.

You might be wondering what the swim test is or should be. Honestly, I rarely give two athletes the same swim test, because I think it is important that athletes choose a swim test they enjoy and believe is important to them that represents the demands of long-course racing and their goals. For example, some like to swim a straight 1500, 2000, or even 4000. I have had a number of athletes do a series of 100 repeats on a certain interval. The important thing is it must represent the race goals of the athlete, so a midpacker might be a 1500 or 1000, or even 2 or 3 times a 1000, with a set amount of rest or on a certain interval. If the goal is trying to make the front of the pack, then a test that simulates the fast start and then tests the strength of the athlete will help show if the athlete is improving and ready for the race demands.

USA Triathlon (USAT) has a swim test set for their junior elite triathletes that consists of a 200 dive start at all-out effort with 1 minute of rest, followed by an 800 push start at all-out effort. Because of the years of data for this set, USAT can accurately predict the potential performance of the junior elite athlete in race competitions. The demands of the test represent the specifics of junior elite racing fairly well, which is a 750-meter swim, with a maddening sprint start and then the ability to show the strength that one can stay with the leaders even if one's first 200 is excellent.

SUMMARY

Coaches and athletes with high goals must commit to the concept of unending improvement. The best course of action for improving performance begins with setting goals to understand what needs to be accomplished with the training. The next step is to assess the weaknesses of the athlete, based on a review of results and metrics from the past if available, as well as initial testing, and select the weaknesses to address in training that are likely going to be the biggest limiting factor for accomplishing the goals. Once you have the skills and metrics corresponding to them, you can begin planning and executing the training, tracking the progress of the metrics for those skills and abilities you are addressing, and working to create unending improvement.

5
PLANNING THE TRAINING YEAR

Fail to plan; plan to fail.

Benjamin Franklin

Lack of a plan is one of the most common mistakes triathletes make, from elite to beginner. Many triathletes simply train according to peer pressure. Whatever their training buddies are doing, they are going to do it too. If there's a group ride every Saturday, they will be joining it no matter if the group ride has zero correlation to the skills and energy systems the athlete will use on race day of a half or full Ironman.

Many athletes will repeat the same group workouts, day after day, week after week, month after month. In North America, it starts off usually as the daylight hours get longer and the temperature starts to warm up, and athletes are super-excited to train hard and get in every group session they can. For the first three months or so, they continue to improve, and they are loving it. Come the fourth or fifth month, they begin to plateau, and the frustration of no more improvement begins. They push harder, and they rest more. Training becomes random based on trying to find the one workout that seems to be proof that it still works. They can't understand how the training worked so well for a while and why it wouldn't just keep improving indefinitely.

It seems ridiculous to even think that you could do the same training over and over and expect to always improve, but many athletes think just that. This is why periodization is so important and a plan to change the training stress over the course of a season must be present. With no plan, there is no destination or pathway that can be effectively determined, tracked, and achieved.

A general definition of periodization is changing the stress according to different time periods, with the training changing its focus from general ability development to race-specific development over the time frame of the season or buildup to a big race.

For example, base training is the time to address the general abilities an athlete will need to perform on race day. This might include general turnover work and cadence improvement but also basic aerobic fitness development. After all, it is an aerobic endurance sport.

Come the specific preparation period, the main goal of all sessions is to better prepare the athlete for the specific intensity and demands of race day. This considers the athlete's goals, strengths, and weaknesses; course demands; and the competition demands brought by the quality and attributes of the athletes in the field.

In Joe Friel's Training Bible series, he uses the following training period names:

- **Preparation.** This is basically getting the athlete ready to train. This provides the break-in time, where the athlete can get to a healthy state of being ready to train seriously. This may last as little as one week, or if the athlete is really behind, due to a return from serious injury, or the athlete is a beginner just getting off the couch, it could last weeks or months.

- **Base.** Friel breaks this phase into three parts, but it is mostly aimed at developing the general abilities of the athlete to achieve goals. This is the time the athlete should be addressing the most basic weaknesses, like those outlined in chapter 4, Assessing Triathlon Fitness. This is also where the athlete sets the foundation for the body to be able to handle the load and intensity of the workouts in the build phase.

- **Build.** Friel breaks this phase into different parts as well, but this whole time frame is devoted to race-specific preparation. Whatever is going to happen at the main goal event needs to be addressed here. If the course is hilly, the athlete is training on a course with similar hills, at the desired power outputs for race day. If it is going to be hot, the athlete is training in the heat. If the strategy is to attack a certain part of the race, then that attack is practiced and trained here in this phase.

- **Peak (Taper).** Some might include this in the build phase, but I feel it's important to be addressed as its own phase, because the goals change from simply representing race demands to trying to do that while also shedding fatigue. How much fatigue you need to shed is entirely individual, based on the importance of the race, the history of the athlete, and the length and demands of the race.

- **Transition.** This is dedicated to the off-season or downtime for the athlete. This might last a few months or be as short as a week. Rest and regeneration are the goal, and the athlete is hoping to have the body and mind ready to start training again for the next phase of the season or for a full season.

Other coaches use different terms, but the concept is the same, breaking the time periods up to meet the needs of the body to perform and achieve the goals set.

PERIODIZATION

The concept of periodization has been around for many years, and despite many claims against it, all that has happened is the definition has changed. In general, periodization just means recognizing the different periods of time and how the training must change over different time periods for it to be truly effective.

Any coach or athlete claiming that periodization is worthless, or a thing of the past, doesn't understand its definition and just believes traditional periodization models are the definition. And any coach or athlete who doesn't change the training stress over the course of time is just doing the same workouts over and over and is not improving.

Friel made linear periodization popular with his Training Bible book series, because it is a simple and effective method for most all amateur athletes. Linear periodization simply takes training as building an aerobic base, building volume with lighter amounts of intensity, and then dropping volume and increasing the amount of intensity in the training in the weeks leading up to the race. You can see in figure 5.1 how the amount and type of stimulus on the body changed as the days and weeks progressed.

But there are different ways of planning the season, some of which are the exact opposite of linear periodization, such as reverse periodization, shown in figure 5.2.

Reverse periodization starts with lower volume and more relative intensity and as the season goes along, begins to add more volume while decreasing the relative amount of intensity. Athletes in colder climates with early season peak events might find this type of periodization planning effective because this allows them to do less volume in the colder winter months, before starting higher-volume, race-specific training in the weeks leading into the peak event. In fact, this type of model

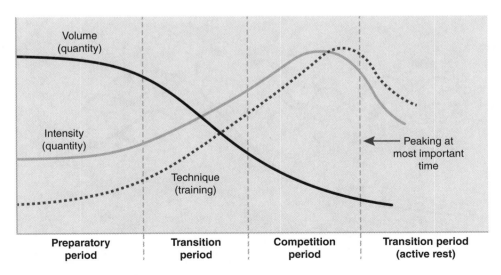

FIGURE 5.1 Linear periodization model.

allows athletes to address speed and technique weaknesses in the colder months, with shorter-duration but effective workouts for their weaknesses, before getting into the race-specific volume required for long-course success, especially Ironman.

Undulating periodization, shown in figure 5.3, involves changing the volume and intensity consistently but in varied patterns, in order to create a variance to promote adaptations even faster. Again, variance of stress and stimulus are what the body responds best to. This is an especially effective model for athletes who have varied schedules due to work demands, family commitments, and anything else that would cause a need to vary the volume of training.

Block periodization is a model brought to light by Vladimir Issurin, where athletes focus on only a small number of abilities and invest their training time on

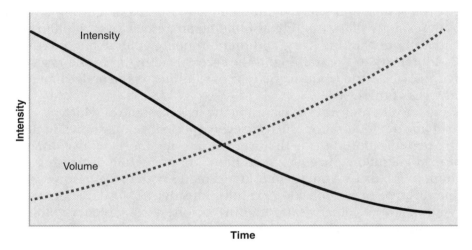

FIGURE 5.2 Reverse periodization model.

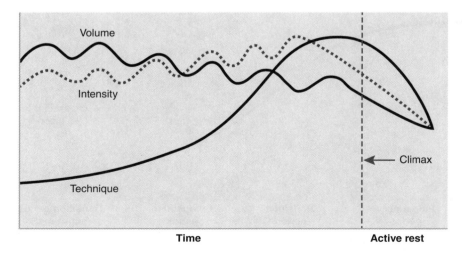

FIGURE 5.3 Undulating periodization model.

building those, one after another. The belief is that you can only truly gain a lot of headway with a focus on building a couple of skills or energy systems and sacrificing others until a later time when it is better to address them. These periods tend to last three to six weeks. Figures 5.4*a–b* from Issurin help illustrate what the block periodization model looks like.

There are other models, but the idea is that in each model the training stress changes over time in an attempt to prevent plateaus.

These models sometimes get intertwined and used in combination with others. You can follow one of these models, combine a few, or use none of them. The great thing about data is you can be creative and unique in your approach to training, and if the data continue to show you're improving toward your goals, it is hard to criticize what works.

Planning your training year isn't very complicated, because periodization isn't very complicated when it comes down to it. All you need to do is change the training

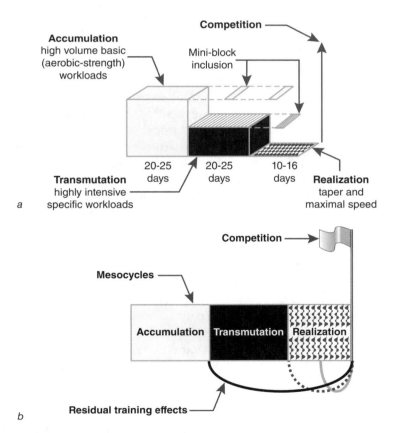

FIGURE 5.4 Block periodization model.

Figure 5.4*a* Adapted, by permission, from V.B. Issurin and G Lustig, 2004, "Klassifikation, Dauer und praktische Komponenten der Resteffekte von Training," *Leistungssport* 34(3): 55-59.

Figure 5.4*b* Adapted, by permission, from V. Issurin and V. Shkliar, 2002, "Zur Konzeption der Blockstruktur im Training von hochklassifizierten Sportlern," *Leistungssport* 32(6): 42-45.

stress as time progresses, moving from general to specific as the peak race date nears, no matter the model you follow.

One of the biggest criticisms of traditional periodization has been that it is too structured, with little flexibility. It also doesn't take into account other demands in life, like work, holidays, and family commitments, and so following periodization strictly is difficult.

The traditional model might set up a training year and plan for 16 weeks of base work, followed by 12 weeks of specific preparation, and then the race. This time prescription doesn't take into account an athlete's individuality and strengths and weaknesses. Here is where technology has moved periodization into a new era.

What if the athlete doesn't need 16 weeks of general preparation work? If the athlete is a veteran long-course triathlete, a traditional linear model of high-volume base training is likely not needed. The athlete hasn't lost much aerobic base from one season to the next, so why go back and build it like the athlete did the first time?

What if the athlete is new to the sport and actually needs about 24 weeks of consistent aerobic and general ability development? If the prescription was 16 weeks long, then the athlete fell short of really improving, because another 50 percent was actually needed.

Metrics from technology now can let us see where the athlete is weak and spend more time developing those weaknesses. Instead of a long ride or long run, when the data show the athlete is not in need of these sessions, get the athlete to do some quality sessions to address speed weaknesses. Instead of a junk mileage session, give the athlete a session that works on technical weaknesses.

One of the key markers is 12 weeks out from the race. This is usually a time when training needs to be switched to better represent the race demands, but if the athlete is ready for specific training 16 weeks out, a head start on it might lead to the breakthrough needed. These changes and decisions are where the real gains happen for an athlete. Training sessions that meet the biggest needs of the athlete, and give the most improvement, that are repeated time and again, instead of the general prescription of X number of weeks of general development, are where the breakthroughs really happen.

If an athlete has met the metrics that show sufficient ability, then the amount of time left should be devoted to areas that will yield the biggest return in training. Trying to get that last tenth of a percent of aerobic fitness, instead of the next 1 to 2 percent you can gain in another skill or ability, is the smarter investment.

Next are some guidelines and metrics that will help you know when the athlete's ability is sufficient and it is time to move on and begin working on other abilities. Realize that these change from athlete to athlete, based on age, gender, and goals.

PLANNING GENERAL PREPARATION

General preparation, usually called the base phase, is any amount of time up until 12–16 weeks before the race date. This general preparation can be weeks, months, or even years if the plan is more long term. The more time an athlete has in this period, the less risk is needed to get the fitness required. Many athletes raise the training stress too quickly and get injured. A longer time frame allows the training stress to be introduced in smaller amounts, keeping injuries to overuse or overtraining less likely.

PLANNING SPECIFIC PREPARATION

Specific preparation, usually referred to as the build phase, begins 12–16 weeks out from the race date and lasts up to the race date. The variance in this is based on how fit the athlete is when approaching this time frame. The fitter the athlete, the sooner you might start this period, but beyond 16 weeks begins to risk early plateaus prior to race day. Remember, the goal is to hit the race just before the plateau. This keeps the athlete mentally fresh and physically ready.

What do you do if you have more than 16 weeks of time left and you feel like you're ready for specific preparation? Good question. If you're about 17–18 weeks out, and you are certain that you can begin specific preparation without peaking too soon, mentally and physically, then use the time to your advantage and begin the specific prep sessions, but be sure to be generous with your rest and recovery periods. Time is on your side, so don't take needless risks. This will likely allow the adaptations to take effect and prevent injury or early plateaus. But you must be sure to track the data and metrics to make sure there isn't a premature plateau or peak before the race.

Actually, you can begin training specifically for the race from a numbers stand-point even many months out from the race. If the goal is to prepare for a certain training stress score (TSS) value for a race, you can begin preparing for the race by creating training sessions at those TSS values. These sessions won't necessarily have intervals at race intensity, but the TSS to be achieved on race day is perfect general preparation for teaching the body to better perform at that stress level. For example, if you want to ride 180 TSS points in your 70.3 race, you will want to have even long, easy rides in the general base period yield a 180 TSS. This begins to prepare your body for that level of stress, even if easy instead of at race intensity.

There are still a number of subjective aspects of these guidelines to be considered. For example, an athlete who is a very fast runner might not need to reach the higher end of the run chronic training load (**CTL**) or can make up for not reaching the w/kg for bFTP. A strong rider might not need to reach the bike CTL goal in order to still perform very well, so that rider might focus on run training more.

There are also age and gender considerations to be made; masters athletes and females might have trouble reaching the higher ends of these values.

Course considerations must also be made if the race the athlete is attempting to peak at is a course that demands more bike preparation or run preparation.

Here are some CTL metrics and guidelines to achieve as a whole for the season.

BIKE CTL

The question many have when they train for an Ironman event is how high their bike CTL should get. The answer to this question is (like almost all training questions) related to your goals for the event. For example, if your goal is to simply finish the race, then a lower CTL is fine, but if you're trying to qualify for Kona, or win your age group, then you likely need a much higher CTL. If you're a pro, trying to earn a paycheck, or win the race, you should probably be even higher than what the top age grouper is achieving. If you're trying to win Kona as a pro, then you likely need an even higher CTL.

If you're looking for a bike-only CTL value to achieve in your training, the number is likely going to be related to your functional threshold power (FTP) value. Why? Because usually the higher the FTP of the athlete, the higher the performance goal. Table 5.1 shows the peak bike CTL recommended values for athletes according to their goals.

TABLE 5.1   Peak Bike CTL Recommended Values for Athletes According to Their Goals

Athlete	Bike CTL
Ironman finisher	15–25% of bFTP
Kona age grouper qualifier	20–30% of bFTP
Kona elite qualifier	30+% of bFTP
Kona elite podium	35–40% of bFTP

There are five important things to keep in mind with table 5.1.

1. This is just a guideline for peak CTL values, mostly for seasonal planning purposes. Because of that, there will be people who don't fall into these guidelines, but I do find a majority of athletes do. I don't find much need to list a midpack athlete, since that athlete varies the most in terms of background and training styles. The higher the FTP, the faster the athlete is in general. I know an athlete who got second in his age group at Kona recently, and his CTL only reached 18 percent of his FTP, which was 330 watts. This athlete was obviously able to get more speed from his aerobic endurance efforts than the typical rider, because riding at zone 2 during a race will obviously be a higher speed for a typical rider than for an athlete at an FTP of 280 or lower, since that athlete's general aerodynamic differences are minimal.

2. Your swim, bike, and run skills will also play a role in whether you achieve these goals. Again, this is a guideline for your bike training, in order to know how much is enough or provide a range of what might be enough.

3. I have only listed long-course Ironman CTLs here, because the ranges for 70.3 athletes are not much different, only where an athlete falls in that range might change. The competitive level of 70.3 racing has been rising considerably, and most of the top Ironman triathletes are also some of the best 70.3 triathletes.

4. The course an athlete races for a goal event is a big determinant of the value the athlete should achieve as well. The Kona elite qualifier and elite podium categories are course-specific to Kona. The Kona age grouper qualifier is general for all courses, since age groupers qualify at many different individual races. There is a big difference between qualifying at Ironman Lanzarote and Ironman Florida.

5. Your FTP will likely (and should) improve throughout the season. For some it will improve more than others. This means your initial CTL value goal will likely change a little, so give yourself a range or be prepared to adjust it as the season goes along.

How can you use this information? Look at the end of your past seasons to see what your FTP values were, the peak CTL value you achieved, and what your goal was for the event to determine how well you lined up with these. You can then use this information to better assess your training, set new or different bike CTL goals for your upcoming events, and use your goals to help motivate you in your training.

It's important to recognize though that CTL doesn't win races, performances do. No awards or Kona slots are given for those who had the highest CTL in training. Don't get hung up on CTL. Make sure you are seeing the performance gains you want in your training first and foremost. It's all about balancing training stress. This is just a guide to better understand your training and how to progress or target the future, so you can improve fitness.

There are many possible approaches, because of different skill sets, training time availability, and the personal training and performance histories of individual athletes. My hope is you'll look at your past CTL/FTP ratio in your training and racing and use it as a benchmark to make better training decisions in the future, whether that is to raise or lower your bike CTL.

RUN CTL

When it comes to running well in Ironman, much of it is determined by how you ride and your bike fitness. For example, if you ask a top marathon runner to ride a 112-mile time trial before the run, the athlete likely will not run well, despite an impressive run ability.

This is proof that though there is a need to prioritize the bike training, you still need to determine the right amount of run training to supplement it, especially as the goals for the event go up.

So what is the peak CTL for run training an athlete should achieve? Much like bFTP was used to determine the bike CTL, we use rFTP to determine a guideline for run CTL. This CTL should be tracked separately for running, in a running-only performance management chart (**PMC**), and be based on the athlete's ability and goals.

The range is much simpler because the rFTP is measured in kilometers per hour (kph), and the CTL is a multiple of this, from 1.5 to 5.5, based on the goals of the athlete (see table 5.2).

TABLE 5.2 Peak Run CTL Guidelines (rFTP in kph as CTL)

	Finisher	Midpacker	Kona/70.3 World Championships qualifier	Elite
Run CTL Ironman	(1.5+)x rFTP	(1.5–3)x rFTP	(2–5)x rFTP	(3–5.5)x rFTP
Run CTL 70.3	(1.3+)x rFTP	(1.3–2.5)x rFTP	(2–4)x rFTP	(3–5.5)x rFTP

If your race goal is to finish, chances are you're dealing with a high injury risk, due to lack of training history, and the fact that most of your run leg might be a walk has the CTL value as conservative.

If you're a Kona or 70.3 World Championships qualifier, then your run speed is likely pretty good at rFTP, and based on your bFTP, you either train to ride hard and hold on or ride well enough to run down the field.

If you're an elite, you likely have a solid rFTP but also have the time and dedication to reach the highest levels and must take risks in training to gain those critical few extra percentages of fitness. This can mean the difference between contending for the podium and being at the back of the elite pack.

Obviously, the faster the athlete, the lower these ranges can be because the athlete's speed allows for potentially less training in order to achieve goals. Athlete individuality must always be considered with these ranges, but they help give an idea of where athletes need to aim.

SUMMARY

Planning the training year has to consider the athlete's strengths and weaknesses as well as personal goals. Choosing which training periodization model to follow, and the guidelines for peak CTL values for bike and run, help to give a road map to better drive training decisions.

PART III

HIGH-TECH PERIODIZATION

6
TRAINING ANALYSIS SOFTWARE

We're entering a new world in which data may be more important than software.

Tim O'Reilly, founder and CEO of O'Reilly Media, who popularized the terms *open source* **and** *Web 2.0.*

Many athletes and coaches seem to shun software and data in endurance training. Athletes ask me for advice on equipment all the time, from wheel sets to frames to wetsuits, but usually my response is to ask them if they use a power meter for their cycling and a GPS or similar device for their run training. Sometimes the response is that these items cost too much, but the irony is that the athlete is asking me about frames and wheel sets that cost thousands more. This happens very often.

I once sat on a committee of coaches where athletes asked us questions, and I spoke of the need for tools to collect data and software to analyze the data to make sure the training was effective and appropriate. One coach on the committee said the technology was all gimmicks and toys and not worth it. Ironically, the coach said this after closing his laptop and turning off his iPhone. Somehow technology has helped this coach in his daily life, but he couldn't see how it could possibly help him coach athletes better. Is it laziness? Perhaps, but I have a feeling coaches like him won't be around much longer because they will get swallowed up by athletes and coaches who embrace technology to do their craft even better.

Can you imagine not using technology in your daily life? No smartphone and no e-mail or video calls with family and friends? How about imagining not using technology in your career? Can you name a person who doesn't use technology in a daily job? I bet it would be hard to find someone. Even if people don't use it themselves, the industry they work in has likely been positively affected by technology in some manner. In this coach's case, I doubt he would say that carbon fiber bikes, triathlon wetsuits, or better wheels and more aerodynamic bikes are gimmicks. Software that helps us analyze data for the effectiveness of training is the next technological breakthrough in sports. And the time for this breakthrough is now.

USING TRAINING ANALYSIS SOFTWARE

I have been using training analysis software since the early 2000s, when I realized it was important to get objective feedback on how my training as an elite triathlete was going. The insight gained became invaluable information. It takes a small investment of time to learn, but once you begin to understand the metrics, and what they represent, you'll begin to see your training in a whole new light.

I once heard coach Joe Friel describe using a power meter as reminding him of being a grade-school student with poor eyesight. When he got glasses, suddenly the world wasn't fuzzy anymore. He never knew things could be clear and in focus; he simply thought everyone else saw things the same way he did—fuzzy. Data from training, and training analysis software, helped make the world of training and racing a lot less fuzzy. Right now you might not think this is necessary, but much like Joe, maybe you never knew the world wasn't fuzzy.

The analysis provided from the charts and graphs in this book will likely bring a lot of clarity to your vision of training and racing.

PERFORMANCE MANAGEMENT CHART (PMC)

The biggest and most important analysis tool for training is the performance management chart, or PMC for short. The real benefit to this chart is that it helps us see the overall fitness picture over a long period of time, with a record of activity and how the athlete responded to the training stimulus. In the chapters on tapering and postseason analysis, this becomes even more valuable. In fact, it can even help us to foresee training and fitness, which will be discussed in other chapters. The PMC is based almost entirely on training stress scores.

TRAINING STRESS SCORE (TSS)

The training stress score, or TSS, is the basis of the performance management chart, looking at different time frame averages of TSS in training, the differences of these averages over time, and how the differences affect performance and preparation. Three important lines make up the base of the PMC: chronic training load (**CTL**), acute training load (**ATL**), and training stress balance (**TSB**). Each of these lines and its value is based on the TSS achieved in your training.

Remember, TSS is based off FTP, and the metrics just mentioned are based off TSS, so it is important that FTP is correct and current in order for the TSS to be accurate.

KEEPING FTP CURRENT

TSS is an excellent tool for better understanding, monitoring, and prescribing the correct amount of training stress the body is under, or what you want or need it to be under, in order to achieve your goals. However, since TSS gauges intensity and stress on the athlete based on what the athlete has set the rFTP and bFTP values at, it is only as accurate as these values allow it to be. If the FTP values, one or both, are not accurate, then TSS is not useful information to base any training decisions on. It is important that you keep your FTP values accurate.

How can I better monitor my FTP values to keep them current and correct?

Some analysis software helps do this for you, monitoring the files uploaded to the athlete's account and comparing these data with the FTP values set in Athlete Settings. This can help many athletes who may not have good experience monitoring or understanding when their FTP might have changed. Here's how one company, TrainingPeaks, calculates a need for a change in FTP or LTHR:

- Heart rate threshold: Peak 60-minute *or* 95 percent of peak 20-minute heart rate (whichever is higher) is greater than the currently set threshold.
- Power threshold: Normalized power peak 60-minute *or* 95 percent of average peak 20-minute power (whichever is higher) is greater than the currently set threshold.
- Pace threshold (run only): Peak 45-minute average pace is faster than the currently set threshold.*

Can I change my FTP values on my own?

Yes, you can. In fact, the more experience you have, the more likely your intuition on your FTP and fitness level is accurate. But I would caution you from raising it if you have little data to support a change but just happen to feel good one day. You might feel horrible the next and need to change it back or, worse, make it even lower. Don't get caught up in an excited emotional roller coaster of training; wait a couple of days to be sure.

*Source: TrainingPeaks, 2008, Thresholds 411. [Online.] Available: http://home.trainingpeaks.com/blog/article/thresholds-411 [August 25, 2015].

CHRONIC TRAINING LOAD (CTL)

If we take a look at an athlete's daily average TSS over a long time period, generally set at six weeks, we can get a good idea of the athlete's fitness, or chronic training load (CTL). This value gives us an idea of how hard the athlete has been working over the period of six weeks and is pretty indicative of the athlete's fitness level relative to potential. If the athlete's six-week daily average TSS is high, it indicates a high level of fitness.

Two athletes with the same CTL won't necessarily finish near each other, but relative to potential performance in Ironman or 70.3 racing, CTL is pretty accurate in determining how well they will do among their peers in their age group because there is a strong correlation between long-course triathlon performance and CTL.

CTL is a six-week (42 days) rolling average that takes the TSS accomplished today and the 41 days before it and averages that score. CTL is measured in the units of TSS per day (TSS/day). In figure 6.1, you can see the CTL increasing over time for an athlete through the season.

ACUTE TRAINING LOAD (ATL)

Acute training load, or ATL, is a short-term training stress score average over seven days. It takes the TSS from today and the previous six days and averages those values. You can see in figure 6.2 that it's a little bit higher than the CTL line. This is what we commonly refer to as fatigue, which makes sense. If an athlete has had a long-term training stress score average of, say, 25 TSS/day, but in the last seven days has averaged 75, you would probably assume that athlete is relatively tired just due to taking on a bigger load, three times what the athlete is used to on a daily basis. Expanding on figure 6.1, figure 6.2 is the ATL line plotted with the CTL.

You'll notice the bigger spikes and valleys with the ATL line, since the sample size is much smaller, one week instead of six weeks. A day off, with low TSS, or a single harder session, with high TSS, makes a bigger difference in the average.

One of the other things you can see in figure 6.2 is that the bigger the spike in ATL, the more CTL rises. This makes sense, because the more and harder you train, the more fitness will rise. It's a basic principle of training: you must provide a stimulus and stress the body with fatigue in order for fitness to improve. This requires training, represented by TSS in this case. Of course, the opposite is true as well: when ATL or fatigue drops, fitness drops. This makes sense also, because low stress means the body's fitness level is not being stimulated or stressed, resulting in low TSS, and therefore after a while fitness level drops. We know you can't get fitter without training, otherwise whoever sat around the most would win the most races.

TRAINING STRESS BALANCE (TSB)

So now that you see the spikes in ATL, indicating the level of fatigue, and the spikes in CTL, indicating the level of fitness, you can see there are times when ATL

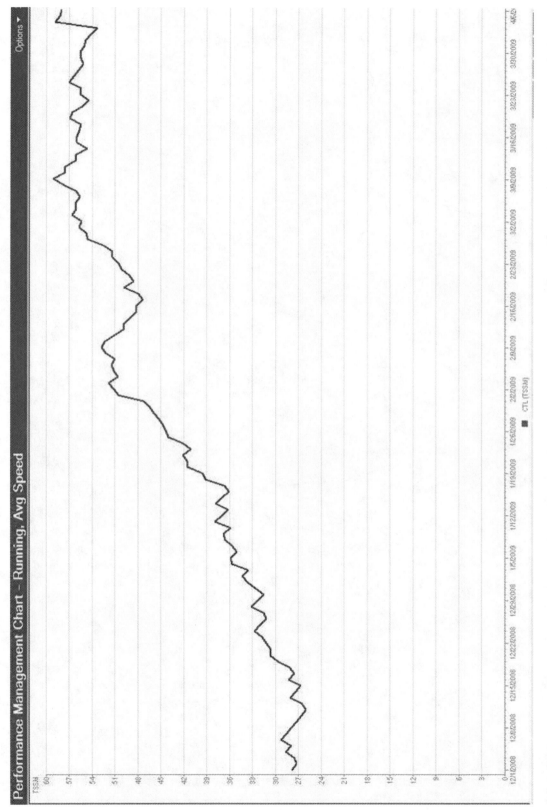

FIGURE 6.1 CTL increasing over time for an athlete through the season.

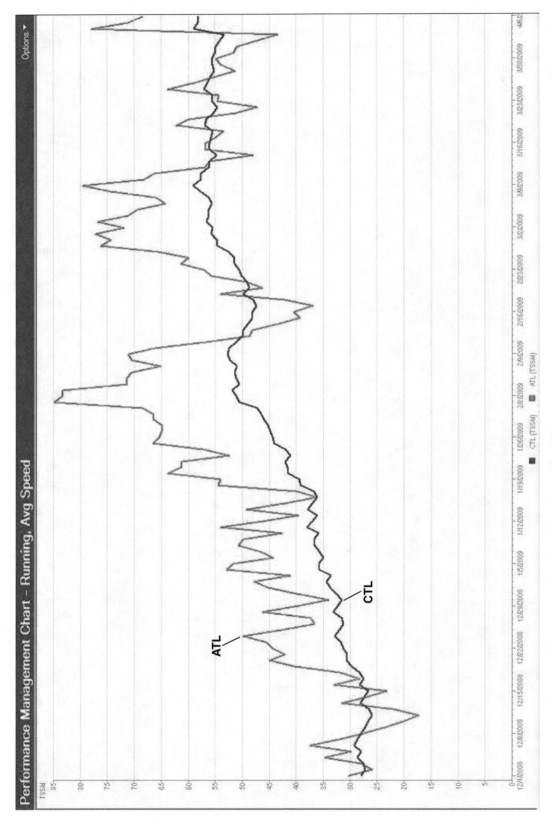

FIGURE 6.2 The ATL line plotted with the CTL.

is small and times when ATL is large, relative to CTL. When ATL is small, training stress on the body is low, and the body becomes more rested. When ATL is high, the body is fatigued, under some duress. How much duress depends on the spike of ATL, relative to CTL. In simple terms, this means how much training stress or fatigue there is relative to the fitness level of the athlete. We can graphically show this relationship with another line, called training stress balance, or TSB, as shown in figure 6.3.

This TSB value represents the CTL value minus the ATL value in TSS per day. In simple terms, it means how much fatigue the athlete is carrying. If ATL is higher than CTL, it is going to give us a negative value in TSB. This would indicate that the athlete is not ready for optimal performance due to carrying some fatigue from the training.

When this difference of CTL minus ATL is positive, the athlete is much more rested and more capable of performing well. In some cases, the athlete might actually be too rested; remember that it takes training stress to create and hold fitness. If training stress is low for too long, and TSB is very high, then the athlete will quickly lose fitness if this trend doesn't change. In chapter 11, Tapering and Peaking, we discuss how to use this balance of TSB to peak perfectly for your race events.

TSB is *not* representative of fitness, only of restedness. You can be very fit but in no condition to race, such as the day after an Ironman. You would never think you are able to go hard and fast the day after such a physically demanding event. And as mentioned, you can have high TSB just from sitting around and getting out of shape for months, but that doesn't mean you are ready to race.

TRAINING SPECIFICITY WITH PMC

One of the criticisms of the PMC has been that CTL isn't specific to long-course triathlon training. Though it isn't specific by itself, CTL and long-course high performance are related, and there are ways to enhance the PMC to make it very specific to long-course triathlon and seeing the training response you want to see. It also does an excellent job of showing you if your training is not specific, and if you're not seeing the training response you want to see, so you can adjust your training protocols. The trick is in tracking the intensities and metrics that are specific to what you are training for, for example, tracking peak or mean maximal outputs.

BIKE AND RUN TOP PERFORMANCES

Remember, if the training is truly specific to the race demands over the course of weeks leading into the race, and the race demands are identified in certain metrics, it makes sense that if those metrics are improving, you are doing the right training. If those metrics aren't improving, then you're doing something wrong.

If you take some of these peak power and peak pace outputs for these time intervals listed and track them within the PMC, you can really begin to see how the training is going.

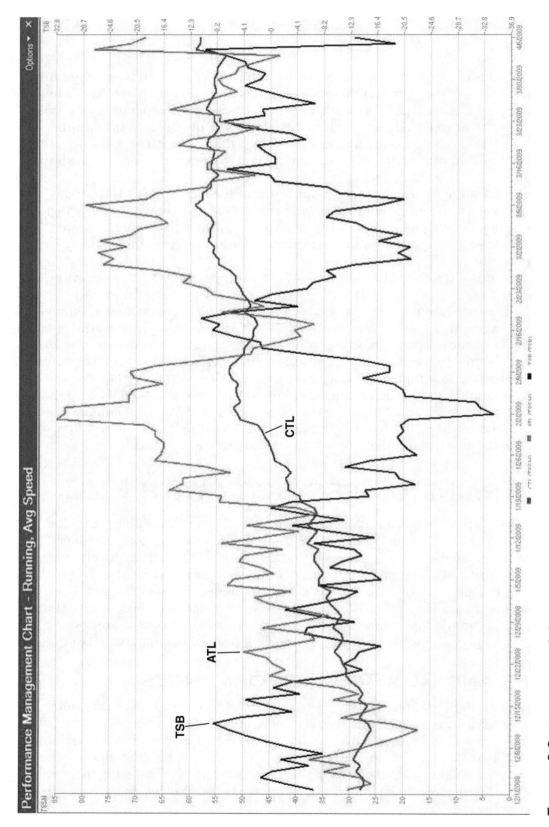

FIGURE 6.3   Training stress balance.

P6 – This value is very representative of an athlete's V̇O₂max, so seeing the 6-minute power output on the bike go up is a good sign that the athlete is getting fitter. Is it specific to Ironman or 70.3? Not really, but maybe in the general preparation phase you'd want to see how it is doing. You can track this for both bike and run.

P30 – We track this value because there are a number of samples within the season to choose from, especially during the build phase, when training is supposed to be specific, which can be tracked for both bike and run training.

P60 – This output value helps us see if FTP is likely going up or, at the very least, the athlete can hold closer to his or her FTP for longer.

P90 – This is an excellent peak pace metric for running for 70.3.

P120 – This value is very important for Ironman run training and very important and specific for 70.3 bike training.

P180 – Some athletes might do a number of three-hour runs (though this is not recommended by me), so they might be tracking this output. For the Ironman bike, this becomes a key number as well, especially for those athletes who can't necessarily get in two long rides during the week, who maybe max out at three hours, due to career and family responsibilities.

P240 – This is about the highest Ironman value worth tracking, and only for the bike, because no athlete should be doing four-hour runs. As you can imagine, athletes are on the bike for more than four hours in the race and in training usually go up to six hours. These rides usually contain a warm-up and cool down, so tracking the meaty portion of the ride, the peak four hours, is the best tool for seeing how the progress is going.

Combine these metrics with the ATL load on the athlete, and you can begin to fine-tune your training regimen to dial in the exact amount of stress the athlete can tolerate within the mesocycle.

Figure 6.4 is an example of how the outputs help show the specific improvement athletes want to see as they head into their big races.

In all these output cases, if the specific metric is improving, the athlete is responding well to the training. If for some reason the athlete shows a decrease in output once, it might be due to some of the following:

- Sessions too hard prior to coming into the workout
- Outside stress, such as family or job
- Poor recovery focus from the last sessions, such as poor sleep or poor diet
- Injury or sickness, small or big
- Different course, especially during a run session, and perhaps slower pace due to more uphill or even a change to training at altitude

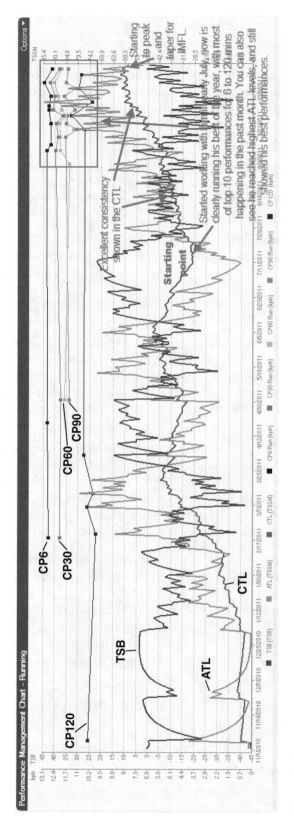

FIGURE 6.4a Positive training responses.

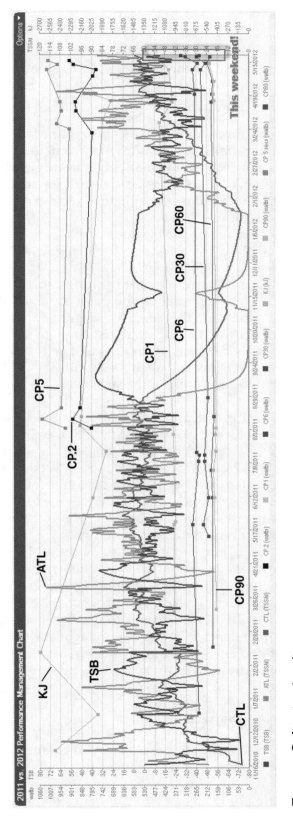

FIGURE 6.4b *(continued)*

- Conditions, such as wind for the run or heat and humidity for both run and bike sessions
- Lack of consistency in training

If the athlete has two or three consecutive samples either at a plateau or decline in outputs, with or without one of the reasons just listed, then you must consider whether the athlete is not fully recovered, either from multiple sessions being packed together too closely or, if a single session, such as longer race-specific sessions, carrying too much TSS to allow the athlete to recover within the time given before the next specific session.

It might also mean a need to put in a bigger recovery period, such as two to five days of light training, to allow the athlete to shed fatigue and absorb the fitness gains before starting back.

If the sessions or structure hasn't changed through this time period, then it could also be that the athlete has reached the point at which the training stress prescribed is no longer producing the desired change, and it becomes necessary to figure out how to change the training stress to stimulate more fitness improvements. This could be trouble if it happens in the build period because it may have overcooked the athlete. If it is just a plateau, a couple days of lighter training or total rest and adjustment to the timing of the sessions or the total load on them is likely all that is needed.

If this decline is happening over three samples, in the key metrics in the build phase, you need to consider some block of rest or light training, possibly up to five days. This is more than a plateau, and overreaching can quickly become a hole the athlete cannot climb out of in time to perform at the level desired.

It is important to recognize that though an athlete may follow an exact training schedule or prescription of specific workouts from one year to the next, that athlete may not respond the same way, positively or negatively, as the previous time. I find that a number of athletes recycle a training plan from a previous season, thinking it worked well the first time, but they are not the same athlete as they were that season. They have different daily stressors at work and home and possibly different sleeping patterns, sometimes it is a different time of year, and of course, the older the athlete the more age becomes a factor in recovery ability.

This is another reason why it is important to use training analysis software to monitor how training is going, even if you're confident the training decisions are the correct ones. If nothing else, seeing improvement and performance gains is a big boost of confidence to the athlete, and confidence is one of the biggest performance enhancers there is.

SINGLE-SPORT PMC

Triathlon is especially complex, because athletes are balancing three sports, not just one. Many athletes will look at a combined PMC, which includes all swim, bike, and run workouts. This is a great way to view the overall load the athlete is under, but it misses seeing the independent sport development.

I would suggest athletes create three main PMCs:

- Bike and run PMC – This takes all TSS from bike and run workouts, helping to see the overall load of the athlete.
- Bike PMC – This takes only TSS from bike workouts, helping to see the specific bike fitness and development.
- Run PMC – This takes only TSS from run workouts, helping to see the specific run fitness and development.

It is within the single-sport PMCs, for bike only and run only, that we include the race-specific metrics mentioned previously, to track their specific development. This is where the PMC becomes an incredibly insightful tool.

Note that it is very challenging to continue to improve in all three sports at the same time. Yes, it is ideal and should happen for a majority of the season. But as you begin to take more risks in training load, it is not always possible to continue improving in all three at the same time. What tends to drop or plateau usually depends on your personal history as an athlete. If you were a runner before coming to triathlon, then you might find that swimming begins to fall off as overall training load increases. For a swimmer, the opposite might be true. This is the beauty of the challenge of triathlon!

ESTIMATING TSS FOR SWIMMING

You probably noticed that one key sport was missing from the PMCs just listed—swimming! As mentioned in chapter 3, the data that can be collected have limitations, and these can be amplified if an athlete is training in different pools, bodies of open water, different water temperatures, or currents; wearing a wetsuit or not; or doing kick-based, technique-based drill sets or hard sets. Even getting accurate data can sometimes be a challenge.

Trying to create a PMC based on all these variables really adds to the challenge of gaining insight from the data. If an athlete is swimming in the same pool, each and every time, under the same conditions, then this chart has more value. However, if you don't have a data collection tool for swimming, you can likely still estimate TSS from your session, to help you better estimate training load from your swim sessions, while checking your times and paces as you do the workout. But the problem then becomes estimating TSS from swim sessions accurately.

One of the best skills you can develop is predicting your TSS postworkout. If you finish a workout and can guess closely the value of your session's TSS, without looking at the data file first, then you're becoming very much in tune with your training intensities. This becomes especially helpful if there is a malfunction with the technology, such as a dead battery, a lost or corrupt file, erroneous data, or accidental deletion. It also helps an athlete better understand when he or she is pushing too hard in training or when to push harder.

Swimming is one of the hardest sports in which to estimate TSS. And remember, all TSS points are not created equal. A one-hour all-out bike effort is 100 TSS points, the same as a one-hour all-out run and one-hour all-out swim. Obviously, you can bounce back fairly easily from the swim set compared to bike or run, and the bike is certainly easier on the body than the run effort, due to a lack of weight bearing.

So what should a swim TSS be, if an athlete wants to track and estimate it? Here are a few guidelines:

1-hour easy swim: 30 to 45 TSS

1-hour hard swim: 75 to 90 TSS

1-hour all-out swim: 100 TSS

With these in mind, I would suggest an athlete collect and track the data for several weeks and months and look for trends, but put the majority of weight for swim training decisions on paces and performances in the pool or open-water events. As with all statistics, sample size is key. Give yourself some time to get a sample size large enough to draw some conclusions from, which is likely a full season.

There is still some great information that can be gleaned from devices that track swim pace, cadence, and more in another chart I like to use that measures swim pace w/rpm by session (figure 6.5).

OTHER TRAINING METRIC CHARTS

You may be asking what other metrics and simple charts besides PMCs are useful over the course of a season. Great question! The PMC is just one tool, and I use a number of charts besides it. Here are the key metrics and charts I use to track athlete progress through the season and even compare multiple seasons.

SWIM PACE W/RPM BY SESSION

Since we were just talking about swimming, let's talk about tracking swim training and performance, where we can see it visually. The best chart I find, outside of peak swim paces within the PMC, is tracking the swim pace in min/km (kph is also useful but is a bigger unit so it's harder to see improvements) and average cadence per workout session (figure 6.5). These tend to best show if the trend of swim pace is improving and how it relates to cadence in the water.

PEAK 30 MINUTE BY WEEK (P30/WK)

In this chart, athletes are simply taking the peak 30-minute output from a seven-day period and plotting it on a chart. This should be done in two charts, one for watts and one for pace, in kph or a similar run metric. It can also be done with swimming.

The great thing about this chart is that athletes will have many 30-minute samples every week throughout the season. By isolating the best output each week, we can see if the athlete is really getting faster and fitter, even if 30-minute output isn't specific to long-course triathlon. Chances are, the athletes will be doing similar workouts to represent race intensity, so a steady increasing trend in P30 should still happen, at least during the build phase. Figure 6.6 is an example of what this chart might look like.

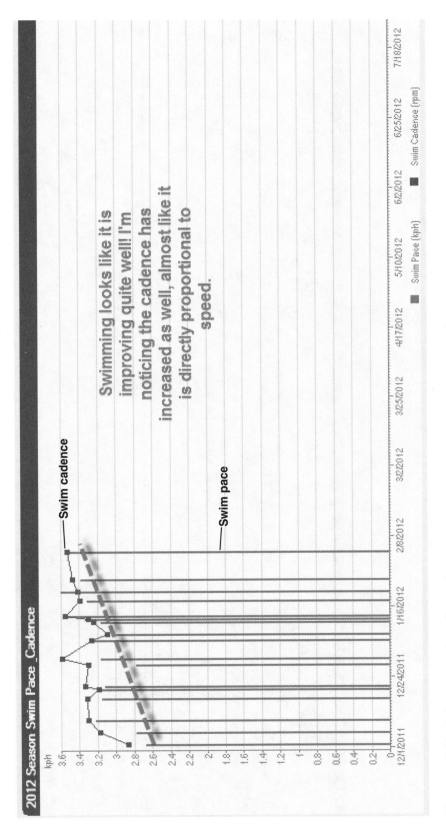

FIGURE 6.5 Swim pace w/rpm by session.

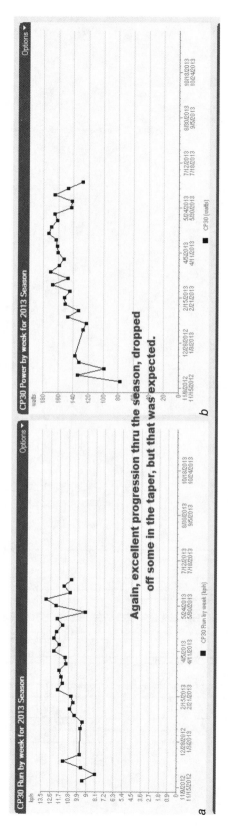

FIGURE 6.6 P30/wk charts for (*a*) run and (*b*) bike.

TSS PER WEEK FOR SEASON (TSS/WK)

Figure 6.7 really helps show the load of training the athlete is under, on a weekly basis, and the general trend of training throughout the season, in terms of load, on a progressive basis. Athletes can also compare weeks of training directly and even isolate different weeks to see if they were able to hold a higher load and perform better. Conversely, they can see if they didn't perform in a certain week, if perhaps the increase in load was more than the previous trend. There are many benefits of seeing the data presented this way, since trends can be much easier to see than in a typical PMC.

AVERAGE WATTS PER WEEK (AP/WK)

Figure 6.8 is the average watts for *all rides* in a single week for an athlete. This includes easy rides, hard rides—everything. Some may question why easy rides are included since they are not race specific, but if an athlete is getting fitter, he or she might very well be riding at higher watts even on easy rides, meaning all rides are improving.

As with all charts and data, sample size must be considered. If an athlete only rides once or twice per week, or has a week where only one ride has data available, then that will bias the chart. But again, you're wanting to see positive trends, so don't put too much weight on a single week; look at the overall picture.

AVERAGE RUN PACE PER WEEK IN KPH (AP/ WK KPH)

Just like in figure 6.8, in figure 6.9 we are just tracking run pace instead of watts for *all runs* in a week, for each week of the season. This allows us to see how the athlete is improving in run fitness over the course of the whole season. If the athlete is really improving, then even easy runs will be at a faster pace than earlier in the season.

If you've been working to improve your cadence, you can even track rpm/wk, along with AP/wk, to enhance the information gained from this chart.

MEAN MAXIMAL POWER CURVE

Figure 6.10 allows you to see your best outputs on the bike for many time ranges, such as 30 seconds or 3 hours, for whatever date range you want to inquire about. One of the best ways to use this chart is to have two lines where one represents the current season and the other represents all the past seasons combined or recent seasons if you're an older athlete with many years of data. This allows you to see how you compare to yourself historically and where your weaknesses are that you might need to address.

You can also compare the same weeks leading into your big race last year with how the weeks look heading into it this year. This works for any other time periods you want to compare.

Mean Maximal Pace Curve

This does the same thing as the mean maximal power curve but uses pace outputs instead of power. When you can isolate and see areas where you're faster or slower than seasons past, you have some crucial feedback and motivation for your training (see figure 6.11).

Multiple Workout Analysis

When you have either a test workout or a race-specific workout you will repeat over the course of a number of weeks, sometimes the best chart isn't really a chart at all, just an assessment of the numbers from each session. If you can compare the sessions against each other specifically, that can glean a lot of valuable insight as to whether you are improving in the specific metrics, especially if you feel like conditions might have played a role in performance.

Summary

Technology and software programs help nearly every one of us in our daily lives, from home life to our careers, and now technology can clearly help in analyzing training and guiding training decisions. There are numerous charts to help us do this, but the most important one is the performance management chart (PMC) where we can analyze swim, bike, and run together, or separate them into individual analysis charts, and enhance the analysis with overlaying the specific performance metrics for the goal events.

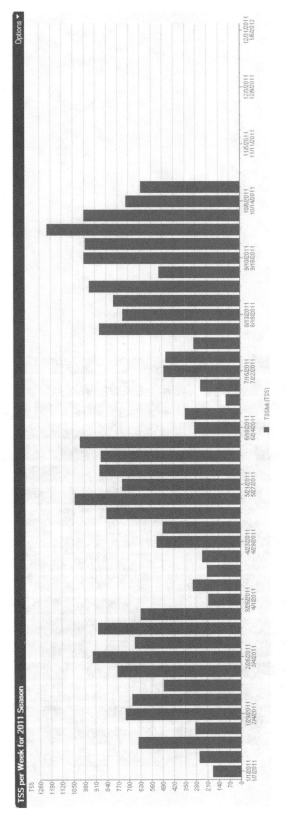

FIGURE 6.7 TSS per week.

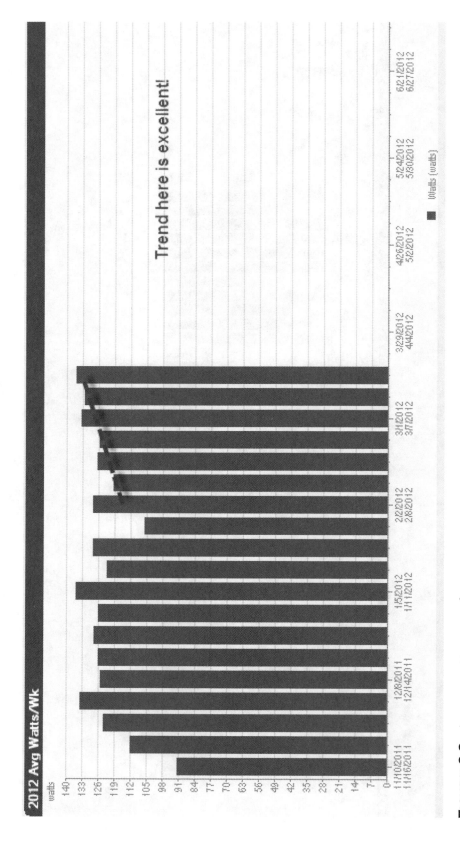

FIGURE 6.8 Average watts per week.

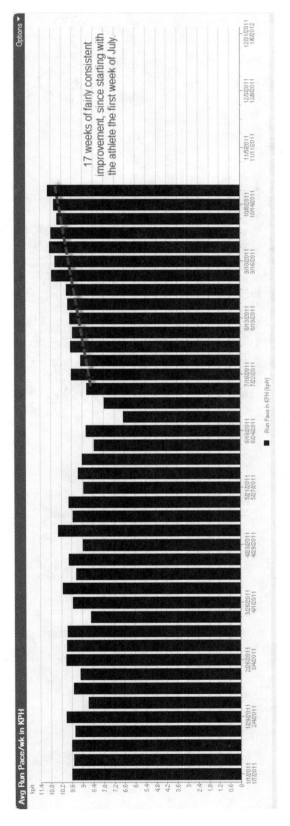

FIGURE 6.9 Average pace per week.

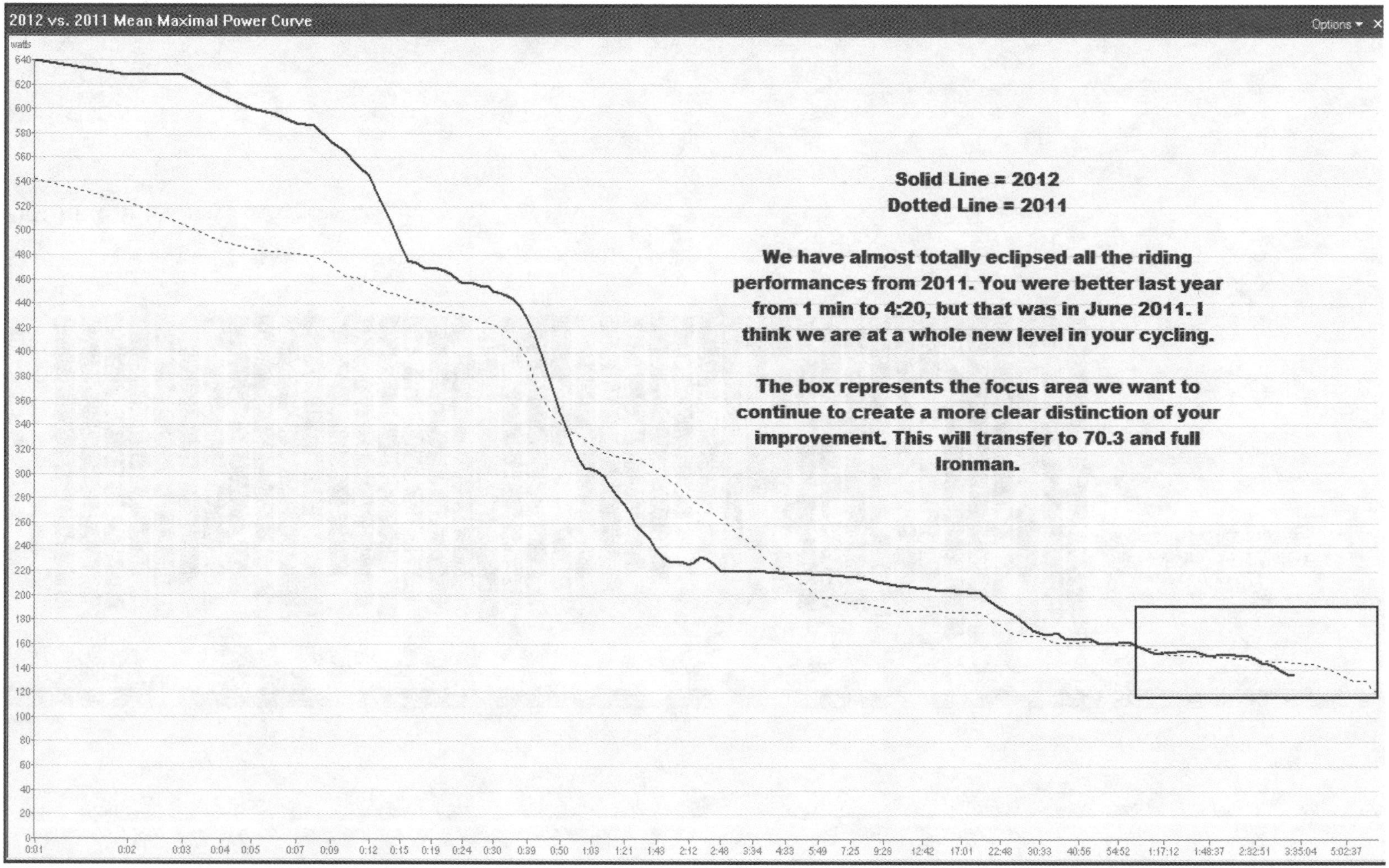

FIGURE 6.10 Mean max power curve.

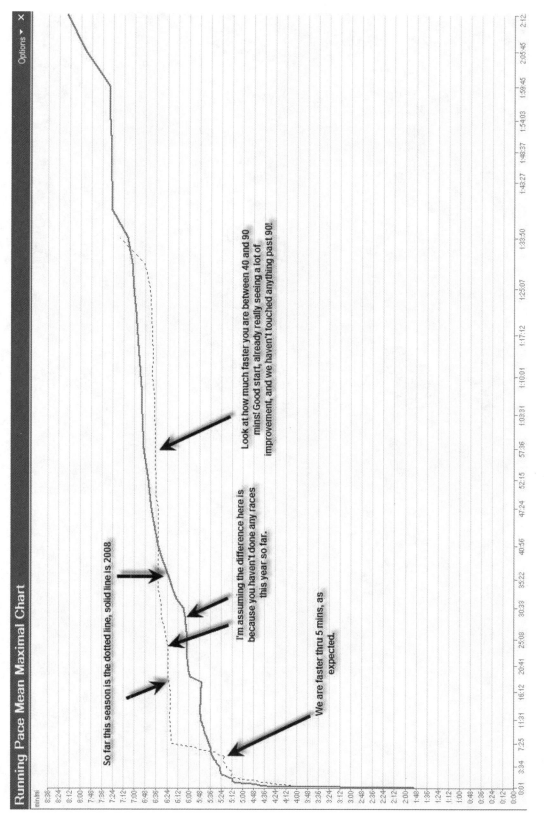

FIGURE 6.11 Mean max pace curve.

7

STRESS-BASED PERIODIZATION

In God we trust. All others bring data.

William Edwards Demming

Training for triathlon can be one of the most complicated things to master in perhaps all of sport, especially as the goals and competitive levels get higher and higher. Think about all the variables that can affect it, from those in our control to the randomness of sicknesses, non-sport-related injuries, stress, crashes, race mechanicals, and more.

It's no wonder the chapter-opening quote discusses God and faith; I have seen plenty of athletes who use prayer to try to help their performance. It makes sense that with so many things seemingly out of our control, we have to use our faith that the things we can control are good enough to help us achieve our goals.

If you look at the top professional triathletes in the world, especially those chasing the Olympics, many of them train with a coach and some training partners on a daily basis. They travel to remote places in the world to train without distraction, with a group of similarly minded and skilled athletes who can push them. They have a coach watch all their moves to help keep them doing things technically excellent and also for telling them when to slow down and not push too hard.

In the world of elite endurance sports, we call this a daily training environment, or DTE for short. Not many athletes in the world can commit to a DTE that involves travel around the world, with everything devoted to training and racing, and eliminating almost everything else to be the best at the sport. Not many athletes want to give that level of commitment, since the sport is their escape and an outlet to be competitive and healthy. They have families, responsibilities, careers, and more.

But that doesn't mean athletes don't want to work hard or try their best to maximize their training time and commitment to the sport. They are fascinated with the challenge of long-course triathlon and want to compete at a high level, while still trying to balance all of life's demands, stressors, distractions, and more.

Ask many triathletes what their biggest challenge is with doing triathlon, and they will likely tell you time for training. The time commitment to compete in a 70.3, or even just complete one, is enormous. The time commitment for a full Ironman is no less than 10 hours per week, just to finish. If your goals are well beyond finishing, you definitely need more time than that.

This time challenge only adds to the burden of getting training right, because there can't be mistakes in training. And with limited training time, but a lot of time spent away from training involved with other variables in daily life, it becomes even harder to get the training right. Overreach in a workout, and you might lose a few following quality sessions because you're too tired or possibly injured or sick.

But with applying numbers to efforts and intensities, you eliminate a lot of the guesswork. You don't have to take the big risks in your training. In fact, you can dial in the perfect training stress nearly every time, whenever you need, based on your goals and history.

You can also track the numbers and prescribe fitness based on the numbers, instead of postscribing workouts to determine what happened. Once you know what event you're training for, much like you can do with an annual training plan and breaking the year into cycles, with stress-based periodization you can begin to plot the road map to where you want to go. The road map and periodization cycle is written out by numbers, to define the load.

Traditionally, athletes set up their annual training plan (ATP) with the load distinguished by volume of hours trained. This is not a good gauge of training load because intensity, and the amount of training at specific intensities, is the biggest determinant of training success and stress load.

As mentioned in previous chapters, volume is a very overrated metric, and the more you use TSS to track your fitness, the more you will find that to be true. What you are training for in long-course triathlon is not the Tour de France. It's not multiple long days of four to six hours in the saddle, going very hard for 21 of 23 days. That test requires a large amount of volume on a daily basis.

Long-course triathlon is a single-day event. Your ability to peak for that one day, making sure everything comes together, is the key to success. Come race day, you are all in. You have to get it right, and the numbers of stress-based periodization, using TSS to help plan and execute training, are what help you maximize training on that day.

APPLYING STRESS-BASED PERIODIZATION TO TRAINING

So what does stress-based periodization look like, by means of application?

1. Setting a CTL goal for the season
2. Knowing the specific TSS you want to achieve on race day
3. Prescribing workouts based on meeting that specific TSS on race day and the CTL goal for the season

You will want to refer back to chapter 5, Planning the Training Year, where we set some guidelines for determining what CTL number might work for the athlete, based on an athlete's goals and bFTP and rFTP. For example, let's take an age-group triathlete who wants to qualify for the 70.3 World Championships, who has a bFTP of 280w and an rFTP of 16 kph. According to the guidelines, the bFTP should be from 20 percent to 30 percent of the bFTP and two to four times rFTP in kph. Let's say this athlete has a lot of time challenges and knows the results won't be on the high end of these numbers, and the athlete is a strong swimmer. We might go with 20 percent of bFTP, which is 56, and three times rFTP, which is 48. Adding 56 and 48 gives us 104 for CTL.

When you know what CTL value you want to achieve for the season, based on your history, your strengths and weaknesses, and what you feel will get you to the next level of performance you seek, you can begin to plan your weeks accordingly. You can divide the peak CTL by the number of weeks to determine the average needed per week to reach it.

Goal combined bike/run CTL = 104

Number of weeks until race day = 14

Starting bike CTL = 33

Starting run CTL = 22

Starting combined CTL = 55

Total combined CTL to gain = 49

49/14 weeks = 3.5 per week change in combined CTL

Of course, you'll need to determine how much you want to raise your bike CTL each week and how much to raise run CTL. Realize again that 1 bTSS does not equal 1 rTSS, because the weight-bearing aspect of running makes it much harder on the body.

So how does a change of 3.5 in CTL per week look in terms of risk in training? That depends on the starting point of the athlete's CTL. Table 7.1 helps illustrate the CTL ramp rates and the training risk associated with the different rates. For the athlete in the example, that is somewhere in the low to moderate risk for training.

TABLE 7.1 CTL Weekly Ramp Rate and Risk Assessment per Sport

	CTL of 45 or less	CTL of 70+
Low risk	4 (9%)	6 (9%)
Moderate risk	6 (13%)	8 (11%)
High risk	8+ (18%)	10+ (14%)

Let me be clear, table 7.1 is intended to be a total amount of CTL raised in each sport or discipline of triathlon. You will find athletes who go above these values regularly, and they tend to be very successful, elite triathletes or those with a life-long history of endurance training, able to handle the loads.

Next, you need to know what your goal TSS is for race day. For the bike, this is quite easy. Table 7.2 shows the TSS range for most athletes on the bike at 70.3 and Ironman distances.

TABLE 7.2 Bike TSS Range for 70.3 and Ironman Races

Race	Bike TSS range
70.3	170–190
Ironman	270–300

Once you have the values for the bike portion of the race, you know what the bike workouts in your training that are specific, or even in the general preparation phases, should be achieving in terms of TSS, to better prepare you.

What about the run? Good question! The run is quite varied, based on the speed of the athlete and how well he or she paces the bike. I wouldn't try to simulate the TSS of the run in a race during your training, mostly because the speed of an Ironman marathon isn't really that fast in and of itself. The fact that it happens in the heat of the day, after a 2.4-mile swim and 112-mile bike makes it seem fast though. For a 70.3 half marathon, athletes should be able to run within 5 percent of their open half marathon time though, so that should help to give you some numbers to work with for pacing and understanding the TSS.

Once you have your weeks planned for CTL ramp rate, and know the TSS you want for specific workouts that simulate the race stress (the foundational workouts), you can dial in the training stress per day, within each week. With a goal TSS for the week, you can figure out what the main foundational workouts can be, in terms of TSS for those days, and then just figure out the balance of the rest of the days in the week and plan for those numbers on those days. For example, if you only tracked bike and run, your week might look like this:

TSS goal for the week = 550 TSS [(550 / (7 days) = 78.57 TSS per day)]

Monday – Rest, 0 TSS

Tuesday – Run 1 hr, 60 TSS, and easy spin, 30 TSS

Wednesday – 1 hour bike, 45 TSS, plus swim

Thursday – Run 1 hr, 60 TSS, plus swim

Friday – Bike trainer set, 80 TSS, plus swim

Saturday – 70.3 base training ride, 180 TSS (3 hours at 60 TSS intensity)

Sunday – Long, zone 1 aerobic endurance run, 90 mins, 90 TSS

TSS total for the week = 545 (-5 from goal TSS)

Bike TSS for the week = 335 (47.9 TSS per day)

Run TSS for the week = 210 (30 TSS per day)

TSS avg/day for the week = 77.9 TSS

Use this example to set the training load for the week, and now you can see how the numbers for the week compare with your CTL. Remember, the ramp rate of your CTL is not going to be the difference between the training week you plan and your current CTL, because CTL is a six-week rolling average. So the training week you prescribe would only account for one-sixth of the CTL value.

Using the PMC, you can actually prescribe workouts in the future and see what the ramp rate will look like if you tweak or adjust the training for the weeks ahead. You can use this foreseeing tool to see if the training you plan looks like it is within the guidelines listed in table 7.1. It can also help to plan the foundational workout days (highest TSS) and help to set the training load you want to achieve and balance high-TSS days with the rest days. Figure 7.1 shows how the planning ahead looks, with dotted lines for the future 21 dates, in the PMC.

Let me be clear that you want to prescribe training as you feel you need it, *not* according to the numbers planned per week, so don't just go out and do random training to achieve some number. Plan the session you need, but use the scores to help balance the right amount of stress for the session to accomplish your goal of adaptation and consistency of training.

Once you get to the specific training phase (build phase), you will see a bigger jump in TSS and CTL, as intensity per hour will increase, since you'll be simulating race specificity much more often.

This type of training example is not designed to tell you to do a certain number of days at a TSS score, followed by others at a different score. The art of training and racing comes in fine-tuning the numbers per day for the individual and his or her goals. Some athletes will handle bigger days every week, while others will need to spread the TSS out more over the course of the week.

But the purpose is to get you to better determine what training stress is best, on the right day. If you can dial that in, you will find yourself handling the training load you prescribe and bounce back from it very well. If you're looking for confirmation that you are prescribing things correctly, you need to track your peak values for the metrics you are focused on improving during that time frame, along with the ramp rate for the athlete. Figure 7.2 shows how you can get reports on your ramp rates for CTL, in real time, as well as updates on how the last 28, 90, and 365 days have gone, so you can compare if the training is too aggressive for your history or too conservative.

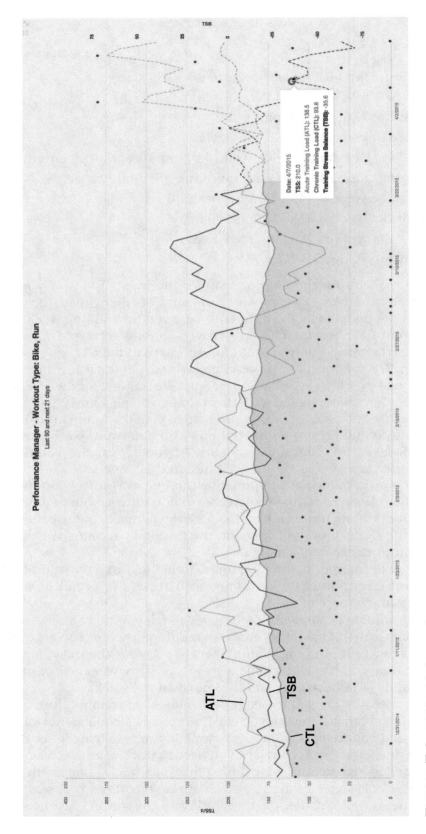

FIGURE 7.1 PMC with future dates.

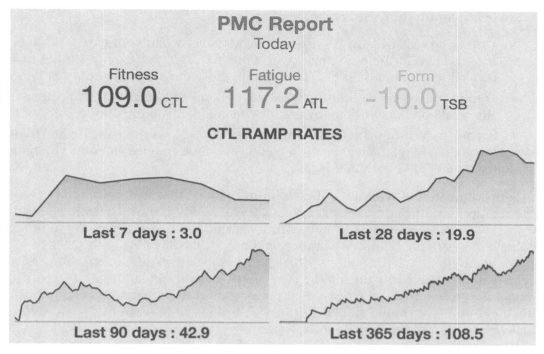

FIGURE 7.2   CTL ramp rates.

Some people claim that TSS monitoring ruins or takes away from the art of training. I disagree. I believe it only enhances the art, because the training decisions the artist determines should be based on the data. If you don't make the decisions based on the data, and instead on tradition or a timeline, then you are making decisions that have nothing to do with how the athlete is actually responding.

If you hear that an athlete has done really well with 50-hour training weeks, you might be curious to try it, since you're hearing it works. But if you look at the data for that individual athlete, it might not be an accurate statement, or the athlete might have an entirely different background from you. No matter what everyone else is doing, or what you heard worked well for a certain athlete, make training decisions based on your individual goals, needs, and history.

One of the hidden benefits of stress-based periodization is that athletes can get a better sense of self, training according to their stress levels and making decisions that help them balance the load, instead of just following random training guidance. In the end, it doesn't ruin training; it enhances it well beyond what an athlete could expect.

Some athletes don't like guidance that seems too calculated, figuring that they have to follow it perfectly or it is not good guidance. But it's better to know where you want to go, and how you stand versus that, than just randomly guess. Athletes invest too much time, energy, and money to be guessing and going on faith.

Some important things to remember:

- Your build CTL will always rise more aggressively than your base CTL, so be conservative in the base phase with your CTL ramp rates, and should that go well, you can raise the CTL ramp rate more during the build phase.

- Your foundational workouts should not regularly exceed the TSS for the specific goal you are working toward, or you are likely taking unnecessary risk.

- If your bTSS from the foundational, race-specific workouts is higher than the goal bTSS you have, but you feel is easy enough on your body, you may have your bFTP set too low.

Your foundational workouts, the workout sessions that will best prepare you, should represent the stimulus for race day. If you're doing a race-specific intensity workout, the TSS should be in line with what you'll try to achieve. If you're *not* doing a race-specific intensity workout, it should still come *close* to the TSS.

For example, a 70.3 bTSS ride is 170 to 190 TSS usually. Your main training ride, even if slower and easier during the base phase, should still fall in the 170 to 190 range, if you want to use stress-based periodization to prepare. Once you reach the build phase, it should still be 170 to 190, but it will be a shorter session with higher intensity, mimicking the race watts.

If you're an Ironman athlete, it can be hard to do an easy ride with 270 to 300 TSS, without spending a number of hours on the bike, which you don't have available, especially if riding indoors on the trainer during the winter. However, once you head outdoors, and begin longer rides, you should hit these numbers and progressively increase at the race-specific intensities, maxing out at this range of TSS.

Your transition runs should grow as well, to simulate what you're trying to accomplish pace-wise off the bike. Now you are gaining confidence, running off the bike from workouts that represent the specific training or performance stress you are preparing for.

Summary

Now you can begin to see how the numbers correlate and become a guideline for training prescription, not just postscription, and week-to-week progression. We can now define the training stress and racing specificity more accurately and raise the probability of success with each workout you do.

8

TRANSITION AND PREPARATION PHASES

Rest when you're weary. Refresh and renew yourself, your body, your mind, your spirit. Then get back to work.

Ralph Marston

Athletes should and usually do take a period of rest, referred to as the off-season or transition phase, where training ceases or becomes unstructured, light activity (Friel 2009). This usually follows a peak event, where the athlete has invested much time, emotion, and energy into the race, making the rest a welcomed period by the athlete.

There are no real goals of the training, other than to not lose too much fitness and not gain too much weight. The main purpose of the period is rest and regeneration, recovering from a long season in order to be fresh physically and mentally for the next season or phase of training.

Following this rest period, athletes usually aren't ready to simply jump back into a full-on high-training mode. There must be an adjustment period. This is where the preparation phase begins, helping to prepare the athlete for the more serious training days, weeks, and months ahead (Friel 2009).

TRANSITION PHASE

How long the transition phase lasts is entirely athlete dependent, based on the demands the season has placed on the body, as well as the age, training history, and mental resiliency of the athlete. The transition period is easily seen in a performance management chart (PMC), because it is characterized by a steep drop in CTL, since the level of stress on the body is very little and sometimes nonexistent. Figure 8.1 represents the drop of CTL in the transition phase quite well.

Reviewing PMCs from past seasons can help determine what a typical drop in CTL might be for an athlete. Table 8.1 provides some guidelines of how much CTL should or can drop based on the athlete type and a guideline for the intensity of the workouts during this phase, based on intensity factor (IF).

Realize that these are guidelines from the CTL at the final race of the season, assuming this was your peak event. The drop may be more if the athlete sustained an injury in his or her final race event or preparation, which necessitates extra rest.

It should also be noted that athlete type in table 8.1 is not necessarily based on the CTL value the athlete reaches but more on the type of recovery and resiliency the athlete shows. Remember, the purpose of this book is to help identify the individual needs and specific characteristics of the athlete, not use general guidelines applied to a large population.

Some athletes recover very quickly, while others need more recovery on a regular basis. Some are mentally strong and show great motivation and resiliency all the time, while others see their motivation wax and wane throughout the season. This is likely correlated with an athlete's CTL in his or her training and peak event preparation, but not necessarily. There are plenty of high-CTL-achieving athletes who need an extended break, because the training load takes a large toll on them, just as with lower-CTL-achieving athletes.

Table 8.1 also doesn't explain the TSS one should look to achieve on a daily basis because that is relative to each athlete, based on his or her peak and starting CTL. Remember, these are guidelines, and how an athlete treats the transition phase will make a big difference in how much CTL is lost. For example, some athletes might not want to work out at all for an entire month (or longer), others will want to get out and do some light activity each and every day or maybe have a moderate TSS every few days sprinkled into the easy sessions, while others will fall somewhere in the middle of this.

Another important factor of individual differences is that an athlete might be in one of these categories one season and the next he or she is in a different one. As athletes improve, their ability to recover improves as well, so perhaps they move up a category after the next season. In figure 8.2 we have an athlete who required a huge loss of CTL one season but the next season needed about half the loss before being ready. This might also be common if the athlete has a peak Ironman event one season and the next season his or her peak event is a half Ironman (70.3), which takes less of a toll on the body.

There is also the reality of how the end result of the season or peak race might affect the athlete. If the athlete had a breakthrough performance, he or she might be very motivated to keep the transition short and get back into training for the next season. Conversely, if the result of the peak event was poor, or the athlete was eager for the season to end, then he or she might want to take an extended break, perhaps longer than in past seasons.

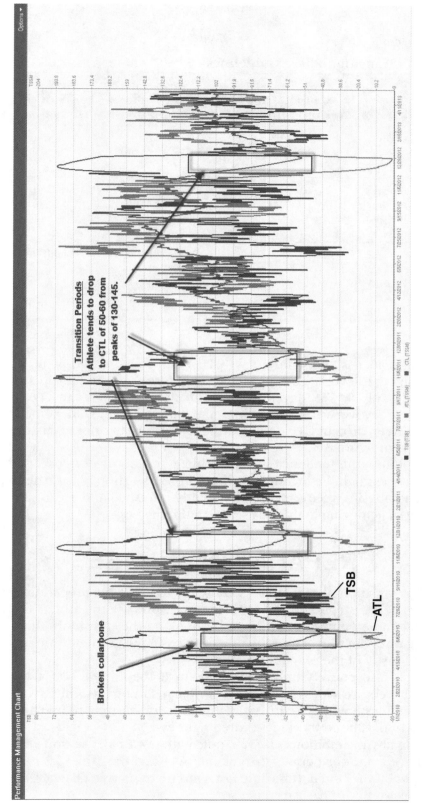

FIGURE 8.1 In this PMC, the athlete's bike and run TSS and CTL are combined. This athlete typically drops to a CTL of about 50 to 60 TSS/day.

TABLE 8.1   Transition Phase Guidelines

Athlete type	% of CTL loss during this phase	Number of weeks of transition phase	Intensity factor of workouts in transition phase
Very resilient, strong at recovery, motivated	10–20%	1 after half 1.5–2 after full	0.68 IF or lower
Normal athlete, peaks and valleys of mental fatigue, needs normal recovery time	20–50%	1.5–2 after half 2–3 after full	0.65 IF or lower
Extreme peaks and valleys, needs extended mental and physical recovery time	50–65%	2–4 after half 3–6 after full	0.60 IF or lower

In general, the idea is to lose fitness, or CTL, but just enough. How much is lost will depend on what level the athlete achieved before. You can imagine that if an athlete has a CTL of 180 TSS/day, it will be difficult to maintain a level of training that will provide recovery and still maintain a relatively high CTL. Some training will prevent a steep drop in CTL, but an athlete must be sure not to rush back too soon, as shown in figure 8.3.

It is best to know the tendencies of the athlete and his or her goals going forward. Though one might be inclined to shorten the transition phase, the athlete's motivation and physical recovery need to be fully refreshed and accomplished, or the likelihood of achieving high goals set forth diminishes.

PREPARATION PHASE

Following the transition phase, athletes are ready to begin the preparation phase. The main goal of the preparation phase is to simply prepare the athlete to train at a high level at some point down the road. How long the transition phase lasted and how long until high-level training must begin are the key determinants of the length and intensity of the preparation phase.

This phase is also entirely athlete dependent. If the athlete had a very long season, it might require a longer transition period, meaning the athlete comes into the preparation phase with less fitness and needs a longer time to prepare for the training ahead, so as not to become injured right away.

If the athlete has an ambitious race schedule with some early season key events, it might require a shorter period, such as one week. If the athlete is a beginner coming straight off the couch, this could last a month to six weeks, where the main goal is just consistency of basic training sessions.

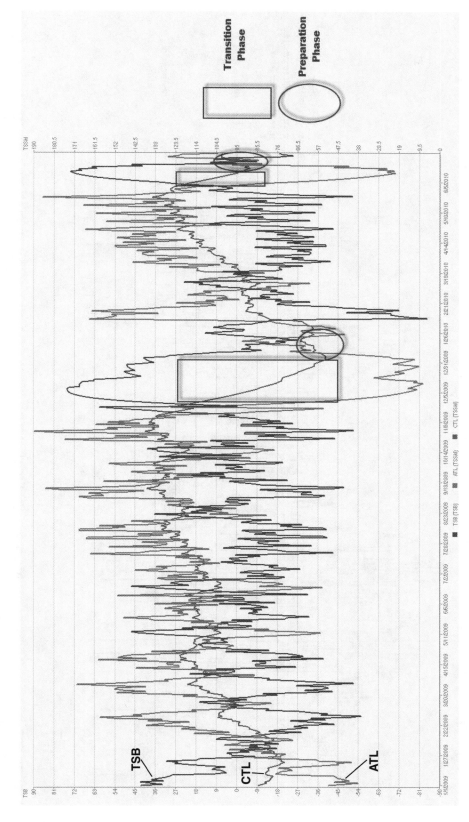

FIGURE 8.2 This athlete required a huge loss of CTL one season but the next season needed about half the loss before being ready.

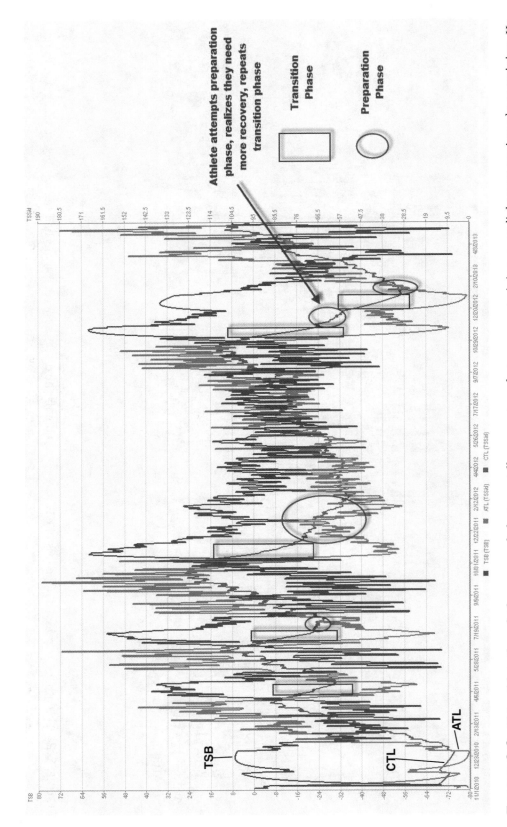

FIGURE 8.3 This athlete thought he was ready but mentally was not ready to resume training, even light preparation phase training. He took another break before beginning again.

If the athlete has planned to reach a certain CTL, the general amount of CTL gained in this period is not significant and probably shouldn't be a focus. However, if the athlete has a goal CTL to reach, and doesn't want to exceed a certain amount of CTL gained per week with training that is too easy, then the athlete needs to pay attention to the lowest value to which he or she can allow CTL to fall to during the transition period, before beginning the preparation phase. This becomes tricky because using CTL to determine the amount of rest an athlete gets is not necessarily in line with what the athlete needs. For example, a CTL value doesn't tell us how well the athlete's motivation has returned.

Also, trying to gain CTL here might be difficult if the athlete takes a long time off or decides to ease back into training. The athlete might find, as you can see in figures 8.1 and 8.2 that just slowing the drop of CTL can be the goal, due to the high CTL the athlete ended the season with and if the transition phase was short. Table 8.2 provides guidelines for the preparation phase.

One of the things that stands out in table 8.2 is the IF cap for each athlete type. The lower end is different, but the higher end is close to the same. Usually, a beginner is going to have such a low bFTP and rFTP that achieving higher IF values isn't hard to do.

A word of caution also: with a longer transition phase, the athlete will lose a lot of fitness, and bFTP and rFTP will likely need to be reset to more accurate values. If not, then training at what used to be an IF of 0.65 might now be a 0.85, leading to potential injury or early fatigue. You can test for FTP values early in the preparation phase, but the intensity of these sessions usually makes them too hard for the goals of the period. It is better to end this phase with testing instead (more on that later). Instead, estimate the loss based on perceived exertion of the sessions. Even if you are off slightly, if the sessions are easy aerobic work to build back into training, you can still avoid injury and see improvement. The more experience you have with data and TSS, the more likely you will be able to estimate the intensity, TSS, and IF for a session with just your perceived exertion. This will provide guidelines as to what your current rFTP and bFTP are.

The execution of training in the preparation phase should yield consistent improvement, without a need for much intensity. Remember, the intensive training is ahead; the goal now is simply to prepare the body to handle that intensity

TABLE 8.2 Preparation Phase Guidelines

Athlete type	Number of weeks of preparation phase	Peak intensity factor and guidelines of workouts in preparation phase
Highly fit, strong, under 40, or elite	1–2	0.69–0.75 IF
Moderately fit or masters athlete	2–4	0.65–0.72 IF
Beginner	4–6	0.60–0.72 IF

without injury. Depending on how long you have been off from training, and your activity level during the transition phase, the best thing to do is simply aim for consistent, relatively easy workouts and look for an increase in the outputs of those easy efforts first. In figure 8.4, you'll notice this athlete is seeing his or her average pace increase for all runs in the week. The pace is this athlete's easy, aerobic pace.

In figure 8.5, we've isolated the best 30-minute sample from each week (the peak 30 minutes or P30) for run pace. You can see the trend improving, and this comes from just basic aerobic training, increasing the volume a little each week to get the athlete back and ready for more intense training.

Once an athlete begins to see this increase plateau, or feels like he or she is prepared for the next phase of training, the athlete can end this phase. This is the point of tracking data through the phases, making sure things are going according to plan and letting the data help guide the training decisions. When the coach and athlete see the performance trends they want, or recognize those they don't want, they can avoid wasting training time and change the training stress appropriately.

Figure 8.6 is an example of a high-level age-group triathlete who, after taking a season off, came back to training. The athlete did little training and started with a CTL of 7, for the bike and run combined. I've highlighted how this athlete has increased his CTL each week and the percentage that increase represents. You'll notice that at first he increased 100 percent. Sounds like overtraining, but in truth, the athlete's fitness was so low to start that a conservative increase of 7 CTL in one week represented 100 percent.

You'll notice the range of increase in CTL is 7 to 12, and though this is a Kona-qualifying triathlete, he came into this season very unfit. You may find that historically you are a fast responder to training, and can handle more of an increase, or you may find that this is too large for you. If you have data from past seasons, you might be able to determine what has historically been your tendency of training or CTL loss in the transition phase or TSS and CTL increase you can handle during the preparation phase.

Figure 8.7 maps out the season for this athlete, with the TSS achieved each week and where the athlete had his transition and preparation phases in conjunction with his peak race events.

You'll notice that in each of the transition weeks, this athlete chose to train very little, achieving a TSS high of 70 in a transition week, which is only 10 TSS per day. That's not much training at all, demonstrating that this athlete liked to rest a lot. You'll also notice that the first time the athlete used two weeks of preparation, while later in the season used only one, because the athlete was plenty ready for training and just needed to recover from an Ironman event.

Finally, you should end the preparation phase with a little time for resting and testing. Take a few light days—two should be plenty—and set up the testing you will do through each period, for each of the disciplines. If you've identified the testing you will do from chapter 5, Planning the Training Year, to look for progress in certain areas of weakness, execute those tests in the final week of this phase. The timing is important here, because you need a good baseline to determine where you are at and to see if the training protocol you have set forth is actually working.

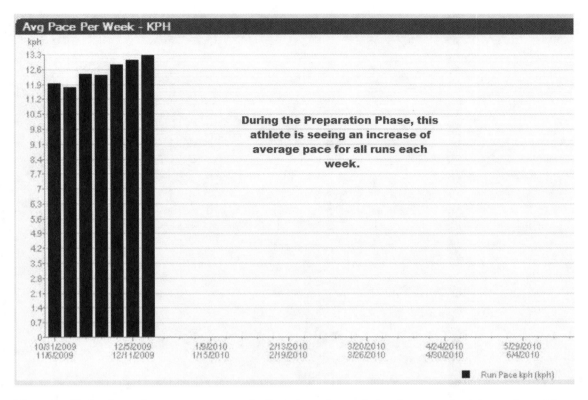

FIGURE 8.4 Here the average pace of all runs each week has increased without the athlete trying to go faster.

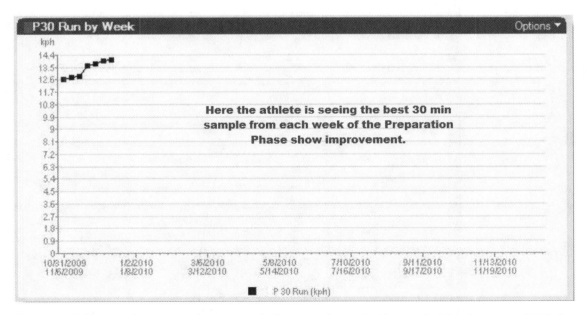

FIGURE 8.5 The best 30-minute sample from each week (the peak 30 minutes or P30) for run pace.

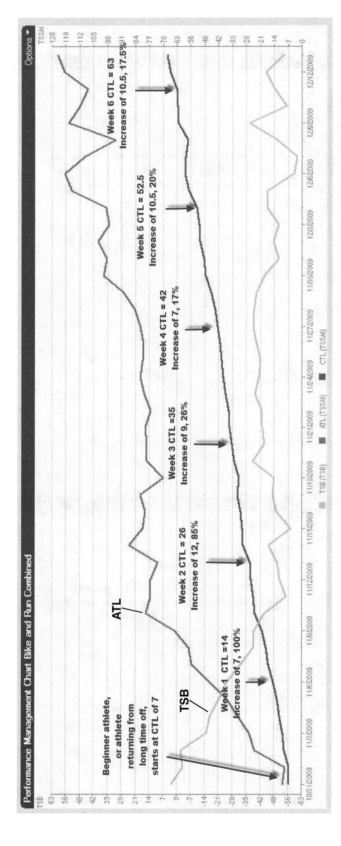

FIGURE 8.6 An example of a high-level age-group triathlete who, after taking a season off, came back to training.

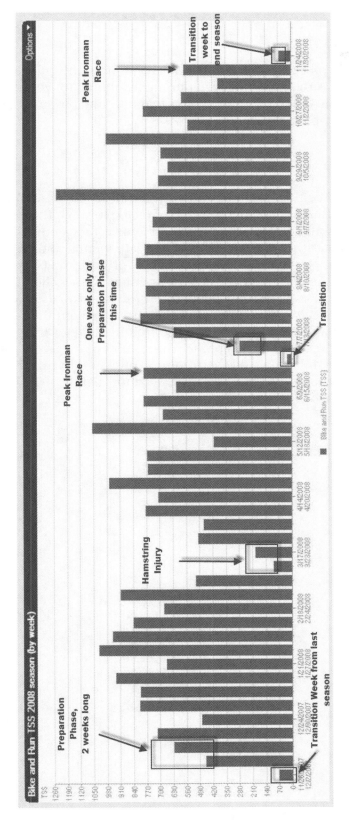

FIGURE 8.7 Athlete's season mapped out.

These sessions are more intense and are an exception to the guideline IFs listed in table 8.2. As long as the guidelines are normally adhered to, you will likely come out of the transition and preparation phases mentally and physically ready to begin the hard training for the season.

SUMMARY

Each season should either begin or end with a transition phase to help the body and mind recover from the toll of training and racing through the many weeks and months of the season. This phase may include some activity, but it is not a time for actual training. After the athlete has had adequate mental and physical recovery from the transition phase, he or she can begin to prepare the body for the harder training ahead in the season, with the easy training phase called the preparation phase. How long these phases last depends on the individual athlete—his or her race schedule and goals—but the goals of the phases remain the same for all athletes, to be rested and ready for the intense training load of the season. Making sure athletes leave the preparation phase with a series of tests to assess their fitness level is key to assessing how well their training protocols in the phases ahead are providing the fitness results they want and need for their goals.

9

BASE PHASE

As much as 80 percent of race day fitness comes from the base period.

Joe Friel, Olympic coach, best-selling
endurance training author

The quote here helps illustrate just how important the base training phase, or basic, general preparation, is to performance. In fact, it is probably better described as the general preparation phase, because the basic, general skills need to be developed before any great performance or specific abilities can be developed. This phase usually begins a new season and is all about preparing the body with the basic abilities required to perform well, such as the following:

- Basic aerobic conditioning and moving efficiently
- Technical skills of swimming, cycling, and running
- Basic speed or ability to move fast

In Joe Friel's *Triathlete's Training Bible*, he uses a triangle to show the three basic skills athletes need to focus on in this period. The triangle consists of the following:

- Aerobic endurance: the basic ability to perform at an aerobic intensity for long periods
- Force: the ability to apply a high amount of force in movements
- Speed skill: the ability to complete the movements in a technically proficient manner at a high rate

These skills and abilities are improved most effectively with steady and consistent training throughout this period.

For some reason, most triathletes have thought of this period as just doing long and easy-paced workouts and building volume. Yes, that would help with endurance, building the aerobic engine needed, but this approach doesn't address an athlete's ability to apply a force or develop speed or technical abilities.

What skills and abilities are holding you back? Chances are they are an ability to run fast, produce higher watts on the bike, or swim faster. It's hard to become faster if, in general, you are slow in your training. For example, if you want to run a three-hour marathon off the bike (7:00-min/mile pace), it is hard to think you will get there if you are a slow-cadence runner (low 80s or less) and your best stand-alone mile time is 6:00 minutes. You need to address getting your cadence faster and lowering your mile time. This is certainly not specific training for an Ironman or half Ironman, but it is an important, general premise you need to develop to make that goal time happen.

If you can accomplish improving these basic abilities, you will find an overall increase in your fitness level (chronic training load; CTL) with an increased base, which the more race-specific training will be built on.

Regarding periodization, the base phase is usually the first real training phase of preparation for an event or race season. It can last anywhere from four to twelve weeks depending on the athlete, past racing and training experiences, and the athlete's goals. An athlete preparing for his or her first Ironman-distance triathlon will need a longer base period than an athlete who has competed in 10 or more Ironman-distance races, completing two of them in the prior season.

If you are new to the sport of triathlon, your primary goal is to increase your overall level of fitness in a triathlon-specific fashion. If this is you, then simply building your endurance and strength while swimming, cycling, and running is your primary goal. Speed skills are also important, but this is mainly learning to do the movements and be technically proficient, using these sessions to balance out the training load.

If you are moving up to a longer distance, let's say from an Olympic-distance event to a half Ironman–distance event, extending your endurance from one to two hours on the bike up to three hours or more is the goal. The same applies to swimming and running, simply building your endurance or ability to hold an aerobic intensity for a long time.

TRAINING DURING THE BASE PHASE

Your goal in the base phase is to train your basic abilities, such as endurance, force, and speed. These three abilities create the foundation on which the higher-intensity training will be built as you progress through the season.

I have found that as many triathletes get older, they simply do more aerobic work, logging lots of long rides and runs during this phase and building volume as if the aerobic part is what is really holding them back. Because the triathlete has likely been doing this for years, there is little need to make aerobic fitness the primary focus of this period. Yes, it must be addressed, or maintained if it is high, but the other general abilities need to be addressed if the athlete is serious about getting faster.

ENDURANCE

Endurance is easy to understand; it is your ability to delay the onset of fatigue and reduce its effects over a longer period of time. This is essentially the size of your gas tank. It is generally understood that an endurance- or aerobic-based workout takes place under your anaerobic threshold.

The spectrum of intensity, from easy to all-out effort, is represented through heart rate, watts on a bike, pace on a run, and even perceived exertion, through a series of zones. In chapter 1, we described the zones via power, and in chapter 4, we described Joe Friel's pace zones. One commonality in these zones is that usually an aerobic endurance effort is classified as a zone 2 effort or intensity. These workouts put more stress on the slow-twitch muscle fibers that contract more slowly but have the ability to recover quickly, which allow them to work for extended durations.

These endurance-based workouts produce the following desired physiological adaptations:

- Increased blood plasma volume
- Increased muscle mitochondrial density
- Increased lactate threshold
- Increased muscle glycogen stores
- Hypertrophy of slow-twitch muscle fibers
- Increased muscle capillarization
- Interconversion of fast-twitch muscle fibers from type IIb to type IIa
- Increase stroke volume/maximal cardiac output
- Increased $\dot{V}O_2$max

Remember, endurance training is very specific to the event you're training for and your goals. If you are preparing for an Ironman-distance event, you will need to be able to ride for about five to six hours, whereas that would not be the best use of your training time if you were preparing for a sprint-distance event.

The key to making the most of your endurance-based training is to be consistent. The long workouts are required, but they must be accomplished consistently to maximize the physiological adaptations.

Aerobic endurance can be measured and tracked by using a HR monitor with your power meter and GPS. Metrics such as efficiency factor (EF) and aerobic decoupling (Pw:HR for cycling, Pa:HR for running) and your zone 1 aerobic paces will help to give you an idea of whether your focus should be on this basic skill or on the others. If you're performing well with these, work to maintain these skills only, while working instead to address force, speed skill, and muscular endurance. Metric thresholds to help you know if you're performing well with endurance are listed later in this chapter.

FORCE

When we speak of force, we mean muscular force, the ability to overcome resistance, whether it be water, wind, or elevation. Force workouts also serve to strengthen the slow-twitch muscle fibers, ultimately allowing them to generate more power, which allows for faster paces at an aerobic intensity.

The most effective way to improve force is simply to train in ways in which the athlete must overcome the force of gravity. Hilly courses, or hill repeats on the bike or while running, will certainly improve the ability to apply force. However, one might also consider that force should be relative to the individual. If you compare two individuals who produce the same force, but one is lighter than the other, the lighter person has greater force production, relatively speaking. It might be that your force is not a weakness but your mass is. Consider that when choosing training strategies to develop better force production.

There really aren't any specific metrics within a GPS system to help you see if your muscular force is improving, but there are ways to measure it in training, especially by tracking any weight room numbers, such as the weight or mass lifted in movements like squats, presses, and pulls.

With a power meter, you can measure torque, but that is hard to track and can be a bit cumbersome to use as a basis for training decisions. But if you are doing a lot of sprint sessions in the base period, such as short hill repeats or surges, and seeing your peak watts or paces go up for short durations (5 to 30 seconds), it is likely that your muscular force is improving. It is also probably true that your speed skills are improving if this is the case.

SPEED SKILLS

Speed skills are a combination of technique and efficiency. The term itself can be a little misleading; it does not refer to the pace or velocity you maintain while swimming, cycling, or running. Speed skills are an athlete's ability to move more effectively, at a higher rate or turnover. This refers to skills such as a hydrodynamic position and high stroke rate while swimming, maintaining a higher cadence while cycling, and leg turnover while running.

The largest and most measurable benefit of working on speed skills is your economy, which refers to the amount of energy expended to maintain a given pace. As your economy improves, you will be able to maintain a given pace at a lower energy cost.

Much as with improved muscular force, short durations of peak power and pace, from 5 to 30 seconds, signal a clear improvement in speed skills. Considering that this is not specific to long-course triathlon, this is the best time to address this.

Most triathletes tend to ignore this type of training, but this is what most of them need during this phase, especially if they have high goals, since much of the year or season is spent on race-specific aerobic intensities.

Another key metric is cadence on the bike and for running. If an athlete can't hold 90 rpm on the bike or during training, then he or she likely will rely on a lot of force, meaning recruiting more fast-twitch muscle fibers, which won't perform for very long in long-course triathlon racing. Simple, easy rides and runs in the base period, trying to get your cadence to match what you will want to do on race day, or higher, is a clear and easy way to improve speed skills.

Foot strike in running and efficient pedaling strokes are usually improved with cadence-focused work, meaning you can measure the improvement of the technical abilities of these movements.

MUSCULAR ENDURANCE

For a more experienced triathlete, working on muscular endurance will come into play during the base phase. **Muscular endurance** is a combination of aerobic endurance and muscular force or, in simpler terms, your ability to maintain a high force output for a longer period of time.

For triathletes, this ability to maintain a given pace toward the end of each segment of the race is key, especially considering fatigue is cumulative throughout the entire event.

If you've found that you have excellent aerobic endurance, according to the metrics, and you have high peak outputs of pace and power for short durations but tend to not be able to perform well at holding sub-FTP (functional threshold power) intensities, then muscular endurance is probably where your focus needs to be.

If you're an Ironman-focused athlete, this is zone 3 power intensities, while for the half Ironman athlete, this is more like the higher end of zone 3 up to zone 4. Focus your interval training in these zones, and you'll likely see big improvements in holding higher intensities longer.

COMMON APPROACH TO BASE PHASE TRAINING

The classic method for laying out training has been a block model of training and recovery: three weeks up, followed by one week down or, alternatively, two weeks up, followed by one down. Prior to the advances in technology addressed in this book, this was considered to be the best and safest way to plan out training. With the current technology available to athletes of all abilities, this approach is outdated.

With the common approach to base phase training in mind, let's examine what the classic model consists of. It usually starts off with aerobic endurance workouts with some speed skills work. As the first part of the base phase progresses, the duration of the sessions increases with a corresponding increase in speed skills.

Once training moves on to the second 3/1 or 2/1 block, the aerobic endurance workouts continue to increase in duration with muscular endurance workouts being gradually introduced into the program in moderate amounts and intensities. Muscular force workouts also start to appear at this point as well, all of which are starting to take on a more sport-specific purpose.

As the base phase moves into its third block, athletes continue working on all four abilities with volume reaching its highest levels at this point. The intensities of the muscular endurance workouts also increase here along with an increase in overall muscular force workouts.

These methods are a good guide, but with the accessibility of current technology, there are more precise methods to determine not only the length of your base period but also the specific work-recovery ratio that works for the athlete instead of relying on the 3/1 or 2/1 model.

MONITORING METRICS DURING THE BASE PHASE

Earlier in the book, we discussed training metrics such as efficiency factor (EF), decoupling, training stress score (TSS), acute training load (ATL), chronic training load (CTL), and training stress balance (TSB). With these metrics, the old 3/1 or 2/1 model can be improved, based off your individual training performances.

Efficiency Factor (EF)

Tracking your EF in the base phase is a good place to start. Remember, EF is your normalized power (NP) or normalized graded pace (NGP) divided by your average HR for a given session. As your aerobic fitness increases, we should see an increase in the EF value, which is a sign of increased fitness.

When we see this number start to level out or plateau, we know we have reached a solid level of aerobic fitness, which is an indicator that we are either near or at the end of the base phase in terms of aerobic endurance.

Decoupling for Power (Pw:HR) and Pace (Pa:HR)

Another great metric to examine and track your progress through the base phase is decoupling. This is the relationship to an output metric (power or pace) to heart rate over time.

As you're tracking your decoupling through the base period, you are looking to see by what percentage your steady state aerobic sessions are decoupled. Once they are under a certain percentage based on your goals, you really want to start paying close attention. Once you have four data points where the percentage is really close, within 0.25 to 0.5 over the four data points, that is an indicator that it is time to move on from the base phase or that you only need to do workouts to maintain this aerobic fitness, turning your attention to the other skills so you can get more workouts devoted to them.

Acute Training Load (ATL)

As you progress through the base phase, you will want to see an increase in the peak ATL (fatigue) you achieve. Instead of guessing the training stress of a given session or a given week with the 3/1 or 2/1 model, we can now more precisely measure fatigue.

With ATL, we are looking for a particular percentage of increase in fatigue over a certain period of time before we want to add in some recovery, based on the individual athlete. If you've got data from past seasons that were successful, what was the typical pattern of ATL and the percentage of change from peak ATL to the next one? What if you lowered that percentage of change and were able to do four up, one down instead? Or instead of needing five days light, you only needed three? Imagine how many sessions you could add or, better, recover from, if you knew not to exceed a certain change in ATL based on your own history? Once you begin to know these values specific to you, you can dial in the training even better.

Chronic Training Load (CTL)

As fatigue increases through the base phase, we will see an increase in CTL, or fitness. We want to see a continued increase in fitness with fatigue throughout the base phase, as well as a slight leveling of CTL as we recover and reduce fatigue.

CTL in the base phase will not rise as quickly as in the build phase, but it should see steady, consistent increases. How high should CTL get in this base phase? It depends entirely on how long your base phase lasts and the type of training you are doing in it, what areas of weakness you put more emphasis on, and your training history. But if you look back and find a range in past seasons that worked well, that would provide the basis point to help guide the threshold you want to hit.

Training Stress Balance (TSB)

In conjunction with the increase in fatigue, we will expect to see a corresponding decrease in TSB. This makes sense because if you go out for a four-hour ride on Friday, you wouldn't expect to race well on Saturday.

The value this metric provides in the base phase is giving you a floor. A floor is a negative value of TSB that you do not want to achieve, or go beyond, or you are likely to become injured or sick. If you go back and look at your past seasons, and look at where you got sick or injured, you likely had a very low TSB just days before. As much as we look at by what percentage we can raise ATL, we want to know the TSB value to avoid while doing so.

UPDATED APPROACH TO BASE PHASE TRAINING

As you've seen, with the current technology and metrics, the more classical models of base training are simply a guide. You now need to take a closer look at the following:

- Goals as a triathlete
- Specific needs in training
- Triathlon history
- Strengths
- Weaknesses
- Desired outcome

If you are a finisher, your base phase will look very different from that of a mid-packer or a front-pack competitor. Let's look at these scenarios more closely.

FINISHER

For the purposes of this book, we'll call a finisher someone who ends up in the bottom one-third of the results. These are athletes who are new to the sport, moving up in distance, or simply participating in triathlon for fun or health benefits.

For a finisher, the base phase will mostly be guided by EF and decoupling. Aerobic endurance sessions will be prioritized and speed skills included, working primarily in zones 1 to 2, with steadily increasing duration. The duration should be guided using the TSS generated for each session and the corresponding ATL values. You will want to continue to keep an eye on the EF and decoupling values; as they start to move in the proper directions, it will be important to adjust the training. For example, when an athlete with a finisher goal reaches less than 8 percent Pw:HR for a two-hour steady state ride, he or she can begin to go two and a half to three hours, trying to maintain the same percentage over the course of four to five rides. Once you've achieved that, continue to add more time. A finisher might never actually vary from this training, basically continuing a base phase all the way to the race, since his or her aerobic endurance might be the biggest weakness, and with consistent training it can continue to improve.

The next type of workouts to add in are muscular force sessions as well as continuing to increase the duration of the aerobic endurance sessions. This will start to round out the basic abilities you want to solidify for the base phase. Continue to track EF and decoupling. As they plateau and get closer to the metric thresholds listed in table 9.1, that is an indicator to add in the muscular endurance sessions.

TABLE 9.1 Finisher Base Phase Metric Guidelines

	EF Bike and run	Pw:HR	Zone 1 run	Pa:HR
Ironman	Keep increasing	<6% for 4 hrs	Keep increasing pace	Varies based on run ability but track for continued lower percentage
70.3	Keep increasing	<6% for 3 hrs	Keep increasing pace	Varies based on run ability but track for continued lower percentage

Once these metrics are within the recommended ranges, it's time to move on to the build phase. This could take four weeks, eight weeks, twelve weeks, or longer depending on where you started and how long you spent improving these basic abilities.

MIDPACKER

For the purposes of this book, we'll define a midpacker as someone who finishes in the middle of the field, anywhere from the top 20 percent to 65 percent of the field. These athletes are competitive at a shorter distance but are moving up to long course or are still relatively new to long-course triathlon.

In general, midpackers need to identify what their strengths and weaknesses are, based on their racing and training history. If you are a midpacker and have just moved up in distance, aerobic endurance and muscular endurance will most likely be your limiters at the new distance.

If that is the case, you will want to follow the same basic guidance as for the finisher but with two caveats. First, you will want to start your base phase with aerobic endurance sessions and muscular endurance sessions. You have a track record of success in racing and training, so you are not starting from the beginning.

If you are a midpacker who has a couple years' experience at a given distance and really want to see what you can do in long-course triathlon, you will have to really dig into your previous racing and training results, because that is where the details are. Will your performance increase the most from an increase in aerobic endurance, the ability to go longer? Or is it muscular endurance, the ability to maintain a given pace for a longer period of time, that is holding you back?

Regardless of the answer, you will need to track your EF and decoupling; those have to be within the proper ranges before moving out of the base phase. Once you know the limiter, you can put more of an emphasis on it while still tracking the key metrics (see table 9.2). As a midpacker, who has not enjoyed an extended off-season, the base phase might only last four or eight weeks. Let the numbers be your guide.

TABLE 9.2 Midpacker Base Phase Metric Guidelines

	EF bike and run	Zone 2 Pw:HR	Zone 1 run	Pa:HR
Ironman	Keep increasing	<6% for 4 hrs	Keep increasing pace	Varies based on run ability but track for continued lower percentage
70.3	Keep increasing	<5.5% for 3 hrs	Keep increasing pace	Varies based on run ability but track for continued lower percentage

TABLE 9.3   Front Packer Base Phase Metric Guidelines

	EF bike and run	Zone 2 Pw:HR	Zone 1 run	Pa:HR
Ironman	Keep increasing	<5% for 4 hrs	Keep increasing pace	Varies based on run ability but track for continued lower percentage
70.3	Keep increasing	<5% for 2.5 hrs	Keep increasing pace	Varies based on run ability but track for continued lower percentage

FRONT PACKER

For the purposes of this book, we'll consider a front packer to be in the top 20 percent of the field (see table 9.3). If you are a front packer, you should look into your previous racing and training results to see where your strengths and weaknesses are and compare them to your goals for the upcoming season.

Muscular endurance, and all the weaknesses you've identified in speed and technical deficiencies to improve it, is the best place to start. What was the regression rate between given periods of your key races? Did your power output drop off dramatically between the first hour and the last hour of the bike? Did your running pace drop off dramatically between the first mile and the average pace overall of the run? If it did, chances are it's either a pacing or muscular endurance issue.

As discussed earlier, speed skills training, and a focus on shorter-duration peak power and pace values, as well as cadence on the bike and run, might be training that could use your attention and help you boost that aerobic fitness and muscular endurance to new levels.

As you start out your base phase, make sure to track your EF and decoupling, along with peak outputs, because that will be a guide for when it's time to move to the build phase. If you find the peak outputs for short durations and EF are plateauing, it's time to move on to the build phase. As a front packer, your base phase might only last four weeks instead of the classic eight to twelve weeks. Don't set a timeline; let the data and the improvement curve determine it as you go.

SUMMARY

As you can see, with current technology, an athlete's ability to track his or her progress in a far more precise fashion is very doable. During the base phase, make sure you track efficiency factor (EF) and decoupling, not only on the bike but on the run, along with the metrics identified as the weaknesses you want to address in this general training phase. If you're a front packer, looking to make a big competitive step, it is time to look at including peak outputs for shorter-duration improvement, while simply maintaining your high aerobic fitness. These will be the main guiding points that will tell you when it's time to move on to the build phase.

10

BUILD PHASE

You should always be able to answer the question: What is the purpose of this workout today?

Jack Daniels, from his book *Daniels' Running Formula*

The build phase of your training program is where you will see the first definitive shift from the general training of the base phase to a more race-specific dynamic. This phase begins about 12 to 16 weeks out from the key race event, with the typical build phase lasting anywhere from 6 to 8 weeks, but usually longer for more advanced athletes.

Regarding periodization, training in the build phase needs to continue becoming more and more race specific. Regardless of the periodization model you have selected (e.g., linear, reverse, undulation, block), the training has to become more and more race specific in order to be successful.

As mentioned previously, you have to look very closely at the demands of the race as well as your personal strengths and weaknesses. I have laid out the different training metrics in the previous chapters, and in this chapter, I show you how to use those metrics to plan and execute race-specific training based off of your abilities.

COMMON APPROACH TO BUILD PHASE TRAINING

Your goal in the base phase was to train your basic abilities, such as endurance, force, and speed skills. As discussed in chapter 9, these three abilities create the foundation on which the higher-intensity training will be built as you progress through the season.

Now that we are moving into the build phase, let's take a closer look at the more advanced abilities that are built upon the basic ability foundation.

MUSCULAR ENDURANCE

As discussed in chapter 9, muscular endurance is a combination of aerobic endurance and muscular force or the ability to maintain a given output (high force) for a longer period of time. In other words, this is the ability to maintain a given pace toward the end of each segment of the race, especially considering fatigue is cumulative throughout the entire event.

As said previously, a more experienced triathlete would most likely work on muscular endurance and high-intensity and speed skill sessions during the base phase, while a new or less experienced triathlete would most likely not. Now that you have transitioned into the build phase, muscular endurance work is going to be critical to your overall success.

ANAEROBIC ENDURANCE

Anaerobic endurance is an athlete's ability to resist fatigue at very high efforts with a high turnover (stroke rate and cadence). Therefore, anaerobic endurance is a combination of endurance and speed skills. Shorter events (such as sprint- and Olympic-distance events) require a high level of anaerobic endurance, which is physiologically manifested in that athlete's ability to tolerate and clear blood lactate. For longer events such as half Ironman– and Ironman-distance events, this advanced ability is far less important. It's important to discuss it here, because it is the typical approach, but this type of training is actually better used in the base phase, for long-course triathletes, because it is important but not specific to Ironman or half Ironman racing.

So you're probably asking, if it is not specific, and this is the specific phase of training, why is it listed here? Good question. Remember, this is the common approach to build phase training because most triathletes think of this type of training as a kind of sharpening of the aerobic intensity they do. The goal is to get you to challenge that way of thinking. Ideally you will use this type of training and work on these energy systems at the right time for you in your training. Of course, if the data show you that putting this type of training in your build phase does produce the response to the race-specific metrics you want, then no one can argue with the results. That's the great thing about data and analysis of training, the ability to challenge current thinking and use data to provide evidence of the effectiveness of it.

A typical anaerobic endurance workout will take place above your anaerobic threshold, commonly in zones 5 or higher while cycling and zones above rFTP while running. The physiological goal of these types of workouts is to produce a high level of lactic acid, with the physiological adaptation goal being an increased ability to clear it from the working muscles. Keep in mind that it can take two to three minutes for your heart rate to catch up to this intensity, while your respiratory rate can take 30 to 60 seconds.

There are two general types of intervals within the anaerobic endurance family. The first version, usually in zone 5, lasts three to eight minutes, with a recovery equal to the work interval in early build phase sessions and decreasing to half of the work interval as your training and fitness increase through the build phase. The overall duration of time spent in zone 5 for a given session is usually 30 to 40 minutes at most.

The second version of an anaerobic endurance session is shorter 30-second to 3-minute intervals, usually in zones 5 or 6. These intervals can be more complex; we have to consider the duration in order to determine the recovery time. The basic guidelines of recovery for these intervals can range from equal to the work, up to three times the duration.

With the shorter, near maximal effort intervals, let's say one minute or less, your body will produce large amounts of lactic acid. The duration of the rest interval will determine how your body deals with it. The overall time spent at these intensities can range from 10 to 25 minutes in zone 5 and 5 to 15 minutes in zone 6. Only experienced triathletes should push the upper limits of these ranges.

For longer anaerobic endurance intervals, ranging up to three minutes, we want to have an extended rest period, usually two to three times the duration of the work interval. With the longer work intervals, we can afford the short period of time it takes for our body to produce the desired lactic acid and still achieve the physiological benefits we are seeking.

POWER

Power is the ability to apply a tremendous amount of force in a very short period of time. Short and steep hills, fast swim starts, and sudden surges are situations where power is important. For most triathletes, especially long-course triathletes, this ability will rarely be called on in a race. Power, the combination of force and speed skills, requires a well-developed neuromuscular pathway. The development of the neuromuscular system is critical for athletes with high goals.

These types of intervals are at absolute maximal effort and usually last 5 to 10 seconds at most. These intervals rely primarily on the ATP/CP system, which is rarely used in triathlon, regardless of the race distance. ATP stands for adenosine triphosphate, and CP stands for creatine phosphate. Both are energy sources stored in most muscle cells and supply about 5 to 30 seconds of energy for intense muscular activity. The advantage of these energy systems is not that they last long but rather that they can deliver the energy needed by the muscle cells more rapidly than other energy systems.

One thing to keep in mind, now that you have progressed into the build phase, is to not neglect the basic abilities you have developed, such as aerobic endurance and speed skills. Your training must continue to become more and more race specific, which must include aerobic endurance.

If you are preparing for an Ironman distance, cutting out your longer aerobic sessions on the bike and run in favor of the higher-intensity intervals would likely be disastrous on race day. Like anaerobic endurance, it is likely more effective to use this type of training during the general preparation phase, because this is not specific to long-course racing demands but is still a critical basic skill that most triathletes don't address often enough.

UPDATED APPROACH TO BUILD PHASE TRAINING

Now that we have laid out the basics of the classic approach to a build phase, let's get into what more advanced technologies can tell us in terms of what we need to accomplish during a race and, therefore, what we need to accomplish in training.

Up to this point, you've seen the different metrics available that allow you to measure your output both during and after training. Now I'm going to show you how to use them to plan your training based on the event you are training for!

The first part of this chapter was spent hammering home that your training must get more and more race specific as you get closer to the race. So what exactly does that mean?

If you merely want to complete an event, it's simple: you need to be able to swim a given distance, ride a given distance, and then run or run and walk a given distance, within the time allotment. To a very large degree, that can be accomplished with base training, working solely on aerobic endurance. This ends up in the black hole known as long slow distance (LSD) training. There is good news: you don't have to get sucked into that black hole. There are more training options available to you. That's why you're reading this book.

If you want more than to just get through an event, then we need to dig deeper into the demands of the race.

To do this, you need to look at not only the race distance but the goal times you have. For example, if you want to ride an Ironman-distance bike leg in six hours, what are the actual demands of that? Knowing that and tailoring your training accordingly would be an advantage.

The two most important metrics you have available to you for this are intensity factor (IF) and training stress score (TSS). Whether you are going to ride the six hours on the bike at 0.75 IF or 0.60 IF makes a big difference in the TSS.

Remember, IF is your normalized power (NP) divided by your bFTP. Table 10.1 shows race data I have accumulated over time and my best recommendations for athletes of different abilities.

TABLE 10.1 Intensity Factor (IF) Bike for Different Athletes

	Finisher	Midpacker	Kona/70.3 Worlds Qualifier	Elite
70.3 bike IF	0.60–0.70	0.70–0.80	0.80–0.85	0.85–0.95
Ironman bike IF	0.60–0.65	0.65–0.75	0.76–0.80	0.78–0.83

Once you know your goal on race day, you can plan your training around those numbers. But this is only half of the equation. We also need to look more closely at the TSS that your goal time will generate on race day. Remember, TSS is the workload of a given effort. To do this, let's review the equation used to calculate it again:

$$\text{TSS} = [(\text{sec} \times \text{NP} \times \text{IF}) / (\text{FTP} \times 3600)] \times 100$$

The goal TSS will start to take shape as you define your goal. For this example, let's assume you want to ride 112 miles in 6 hours (21,600 seconds), your FTP is 250 watts, and you want to ride at 70 percent of your FTP (175 watts) as a normalized power (NP).

The equation now looks like this:

$$\text{TSS} = [(21{,}600 \times 175 \times .7) / (250 \times 3{,}600)] \times 100$$

If you executed this ride plan to perfection on race day, your TSS would end up being 294.

So what does that mean? Why should you care? That answer is one of the main reasons you're reading this book: to leverage technology to ensure your training is as exact as it needs to be. If that IF and TSS is your goal, you'll need to train to reach that TSS in your bike performances and run well off it.

Table 10.2 shows the TSS race data I have accumulated and my best recommendations for various levels of athletes.

TABLE 10.2 Training Stress Score (TSS) for Different Athletes

	Finisher	Midpacker	Kona/70.3 Worlds Qualifier	Elite
70.3 bike TSS	110–150	150–170	170–190	180–195
Ironman bike TSS	220–260	240–270	270–290	280–300

What is the point of all these numbers and ranges? Excellent question. The point is you must plan your training to better understand how the balance of these numbers and which part of the range best suits you to perform your best swim-bike-run on race day. Notice I said perform your best *swim-bike-run* race, not perform your best in one category only. So many athletes get hung up on trying to produce a power file they can boast about later, posting on forums and blogs. Remember, this is a triathlon, not a bike race. You are judged by where you place at the finish line, not at T2. Remember too, these are guidelines. You should use your training data and your own strengths and weaknesses to determine where you should fall within this range or if you are an outlier and can be outside of it.

If we continue with our example, you can see that a TSS of 294 is on the higher end of what a professional triathlete generates. Does this mean you should change your goal time? Maybe. It depends on your goals, strengths and weaknesses, and the course.

Now that we know our goal TSS on the bike, we need to account for the run leg of the event. Table 10.3 shows running TSS and IF race data and my guidance for athletes of all levels.

For the finisher, you'll notice that these metrics aren't really applicable because it is all about just getting to the finish line. If an athlete has a bike plan to get in before the cutoff, he or she should likely be able to walk and make the cutoff.

So what do the data in table 10.3 mean? Another excellent question!

TABLE 10.3 Run TSS and IF for Different Athletes

	Finisher	Midpacker	Kona/70.3 Worlds Qualifier	Elite
70.3 run TSS	N/A	100–120	110–130	110–130
70.3 run IF	N/A	0.75–0.85	0.85–0.90	0.90–0.97
Ironman run TSS	N/A	210–250	190–250	190–220
Ironman run IF	N/A	0.70–0.80	0.75–0.85	0.80–0.85

Now that you have some guidelines on the ranges for the bike and the run, sessions should be planned to achieve these numbers on the bike (IF and TSS) and run off the bike at the IF you want to hold on race day. One of the biggest questions athletes have is what pace is specific for them off the bike? What pace should they expect to run? Well, now you can dial in the pace you want to run based on these numbers and know what is realistic and what your competitors are likely doing.

If you really want to ride a certain percentage of your FTP (IF) on the bike in an Ironman, then you should be testing that IF in your training, doing the transition runs off the bike at the maximal goal IF you can realistically hold. If you can't hold it, then you need to make a decision:

1. Continue to try in your training to hold the IFs with the hope that a taper allows it to happen. (The odds are against you on this if it hasn't happened the closer you get to race day.)

2. Back off your run IF and try for a slower pace, while holding your high bike IF.

3. Back off your IF on the bike and see if you can hold the higher run IF.

The challenge of the training now is figuring out which strategy and numbers work in your favor, based on your strengths and weaknesses, and planning the training to meet that perfect strategy.

Can you go higher than these guidelines? Sure, but there is a lot of risk involved. There is no point, though, in thinking you are going to ride the IF of a pro at the event when your bike split is 30 or more minutes slower than the pro's. This only adds to the TSS your body experiences, meaning you are wasted. You might be able to hold those watts, but your run will be nothing more than a slow jog or walk.

You can also guess that if you're simulating Ironman or 70.3 race intensity in training, with TSS numbers close to what you will find on race day, you will need to recover from these sessions much like you would need to recover from race day, especially if the runs off the bike are long.

If you wonder about the specific training for your race and goals, I would suggest reading chapter 12, Prerace Preparations, in order to better define what you want to specifically accomplish on race day.

Once you have your IF and TSS for the bike defined, you can now train specifically for those intensities and see how you handle it. You can track the training via metrics like peak power over durations specific to the race and your goals.

Table 10.4 lists the key metrics for tracking race-specific adaptations in your training. If these metrics are not improving, then it is important to address training and make the changes you need to keep the improvements happening.

TABLE 10.4 Specific Training Metrics to Track for Improvement

Event	Specific training metrics
70.3 bike	P120, P180
70.3 run	P30, P60, P90
Ironman bike	P180, P240
Ironman run	P90, P120

If these metrics aren't improving during this specific training phase, then you need to consider why and make changes. These might include the following:

- Resting more between key race-specific sessions
- Race-specific sessions shorter in duration and lower in TSS
- Lowering the TSS and IF goals of the bike and run
- Race and workout nutrition adjustments
- Recovery enhancements, such as massage, hydration, or sleep

You might also have a specific session that you repeat through the course of this period, so you can use it as a test set, tracking improvement specifically within that workout. If each week the power and pace numbers, as well as swim test sets, continue to improve, you can be confident you're doing things right.

It is also important to recognize that the numbers might not go up each and every week, because there are a number of factors influencing performance, but if the trend is improving over the course of weeks, you can be confident you are doing things right to prepare for the event.

SUMMARY

The most important aspect of this training period is that training sessions are designed to be specific to the demands of race day. Follow the metrics and specific numbers for the goal performance, along with the specific workout outputs, and you can be confident that you are truly preparing for the event's demands on race day.

11

TAPERING AND PEAKING

I think it's less about trying to achieve that big peak on those days than it is to have a performance that's predictable, that you know that if you line up your training in this planned way that you're going to have the best level of your season on those days.

Joel Filliol, Olympic triathlon coach

I once worked with an athlete for a number of seasons and had excellent success. When he came to me, he couldn't break 10 hours in Kona and had never won his age group in a 70.3. By the time we had our final season together, he had gone 9:16 and 9:35 in Kona and had finished eighth in his age group there, men 35 to 39. He had also won his age group at a number of 70.3s, was the top amateur overall at a few major 70.3 races, and finished ranked the number 1 triathlete in his age group by USA Triathlon. It was quite a successful stint.

The most interesting part of this was that when we first started together, he said, "I don't taper well. Please, let's not taper." I am always one to listen to my athletes, and I try to really learn from them. After all, they know themselves better than I do. But what I realized was that he just hadn't found the taper strategy that worked for him. Together, we would come up with the strategy that was right for him. And I do want to stress that this strategy was right *for him*. It wasn't something I would use with any other athlete regularly because he had a unique skill set. It became a great tool for us because we could run the same formula each season, and he was very consistent with it. In some cases, even if it wasn't the best possible taper, he believed it was, and he did very well with it. Confidence is everything, especially at the start line.

Finding the right taper for you is the point of this chapter. Sure, I will share this athlete's taper with you in this chapter, but I'm not going to tell you what approach, numbers, and ranges you must do. I will share the ones I find are most successful, and you can take this information to perfect your taper. We all approach races differently, based on travel (both the length of travel and timing to the race), our sleep patterns, time of year, amount of family traveling with us, weather, job demands, and more.

CTL AND TSB FOR TAPER PLANNING

One of the biggest challenges facing triathletes mentally is going to the start line feeling like you've done enough but have not overdone your preparation. Come the final weeks and days before the race, it is not uncommon to see athletes still killing themselves in training, thinking they might lose fitness or their sense of sharpness with their bodies. In Kona, you will see athletes excited and hammering their bikes down the Queen K or running intervals down Alii Drive, as late as the night before the World Championships. These athletes question if they've done enough to hold their fitness and fear they won't be sharp for the following morning. It's a rather silly thing to consider, since a workout the night before or even the week of isn't going to yield new fitness; it's more that these athletes have nothing to base their confidence on to make sure they are ready. This is where the performance management chart (PMC) with training stress balance (TSB), chronic training load (CTL), and peak values is your base for the confidence that you've done enough and you're ready to do well.

The basic way to taper is to raise TSB, your rest level, while still maximizing CTL, your fitness.

HOW MUCH CTL SHOULD I LOSE?

Many of you know CTL is representative of your fitness, and you might be wondering, *Why would I lose CTL? That's losing fitness!* Yes, you are correct. Remember that we discussed how you can't gain fitness without training stress and fatigue. So remove or reduce training stress and you face a loss of fitness. However, you can control how much fitness is lost by monitoring how much CTL is lost. How much CTL an athlete should lose depends on if it is a peak event. Obviously, if it isn't a peak event, then perhaps the athlete won't lose any CTL.

If it is a peak event, then generally 10 percent or less is the loss you're likely looking for. This isn't in individual sports, such as bike and run, but total CTL. So you might lose 6 percent of your run CTL and 3 percent of your bike CTL, for 9 percent total, or do it just the opposite. I'll determine the right amount for you shortly.

HOW HIGH SHOULD MY TSB GET?

Your TSB needs to be positive for a half Ironman, at the very least. If racing a peak event, you want it more than just positive. (See table 11.1 on guidelines for TSB.)

TABLE 11.1   Guidelines for Tapering with Combined PMC for Bike and Run

Race type	% loss of CTL	TSB value
70.3 training race	3% or less	<10
70.3 peak race	7% or less	<20
Ironman (peak-only event)	10% or less	<20

But believe it or not, you can still race well without a positive TSB. I was once told by a friend working with some Tour de France riders that a recent podium finisher at the Tour never had a positive TSB all year. I never got to see it because that information is protected, but it is believable, since in the Tour there is little chance to rest much, and professional riders are known for crazy amounts of training.

I believe an athlete can get a TSB as high as 20 and race well. I know some coaches have said even 25, but once your TSB gets beyond 20, you are sacrificing a lot of fitness and can easily begin to lose race sharpness.

TAPER TIMING AND LENGTH

There are a number of important factors to consider when determining the length and depth of a taper. They include the following.

• **How fit is the athlete?** If the athlete is very fit, a longer taper is fine, because there isn't much more fitness to be gained, and the bigger training sessions become more risky as the race day gets closer, leaving little time for recovery. If the athlete isn't very fit, then there is still some fitness that can be gained in the last few weeks, so a shorter taper is reasonable. Of course, you must have balance, so the athlete can be rested enough for race day. If you have more fitness, you can lose more CTL, but if you have a lower level of fitness, you can't afford to lose much.

• **How well does the athlete tend to taper?** If the athlete tends to not race well with a taper, then he or she may need to adjust the TSB gain and CTL loss to be on the lower end. The goal is to find the right TSB at which the athlete races really well and increase confidence in preparation. Realize, though, that as you age this number might change, so look for trends in your tapering as well as in your training.

• **Is it a peak race?** If the race is a key event, then a bit more taper is likely needed, because the stakes are higher.

• **How long is the race?** If the race is an Ironman, a little more taper is need-ed than for a half Ironman. I have seen athletes race very well on just two days of light training before a 70.3. I haven't found that to work well for an Ironman.

• **What does the athlete like to do?** How much you lose per sport should be an individual decision, based on the background and confidence of the athlete. I tend to have athletes back down a little more for the run, simply because it is so much more taxing on the body in training than cycling and swimming. However, if you're a runner by trade, then you might want to keep your run fitness up more, if you feel better and sharper that way.

The great thing about data, and collecting it over time, is that you can actually learn what works best for the athlete, through trial and error. And if you take an even more in-depth look at it, with some subjective notes as well, such as when you travel to an event, time zones changed, how many hours of travel it was, and the race conditions, you can begin to see what makes for the perfect taper.

TAPERING FOR INDIVIDUAL ATHLETES

The athlete I mentioned at the beginning of the chapter was a great experience for me as a coach because it forced me to test what I thought was a smart or standard taper. He forced me to be creative and come up with a tapering system that would work for him, rather than just having a taper I believed should work for all athletes and making him conform to it.

Back in 2009, we didn't know much about CTL and TSB yet, but there was a bit of information coming out, and what I saw from his past tapers in his PMCs showed me the traditional model of 10 percent CTL loss wasn't working. It appeared to be too much loss, with too high of a TSB value.

In figure 11.1, you can see how the season progressed for the first peak race of the year, a 70.3 race in Oceanside, California. This was where the athlete would qualify for Kona (back then the race had qualifying slots), and then we would shift the preparation plans to Kona. This image shows the CTL of both bike and run data, combined into one PMC.

You can see that in March, about one month out from the race, the athlete's CTL raised quite dramatically due to a training camp in Arizona. The athlete achieves a CTL plateau and is able to hold it quite well for the month leading into the race. CTL peaks at about 116 and drops to only 110 at its lowest, a loss of only about 5 percent. The interesting part of this is that the athlete actually drops to 110 twice, with a short three-day block of hard training sandwiched between the two three-day rest periods.

His TSB for the race was 16, which is moderate, right in the range of what most claim to be appropriate, 10 to 20 TSB. So even though he did fit in the TSB range, we had to adjust the approach of how we got to this range, to better meet his individual needs.

Again, it is important to consider the goals for the event, the athlete's history and individual fitness, and what the athlete will be confident in doing. Ideally, you will create a template you can simply follow for consistency purposes, allowing your best performance for the fitness and preparation you've been able to accomplish.

Table 11.1 shows some of the ranges likely needed to be prepared well enough to accomplish your goals for the event. If you're doing an Ironman, I don't believe you do that as a training race. That is very rare, for only the best in the world, who can qualify with not having their best performances.

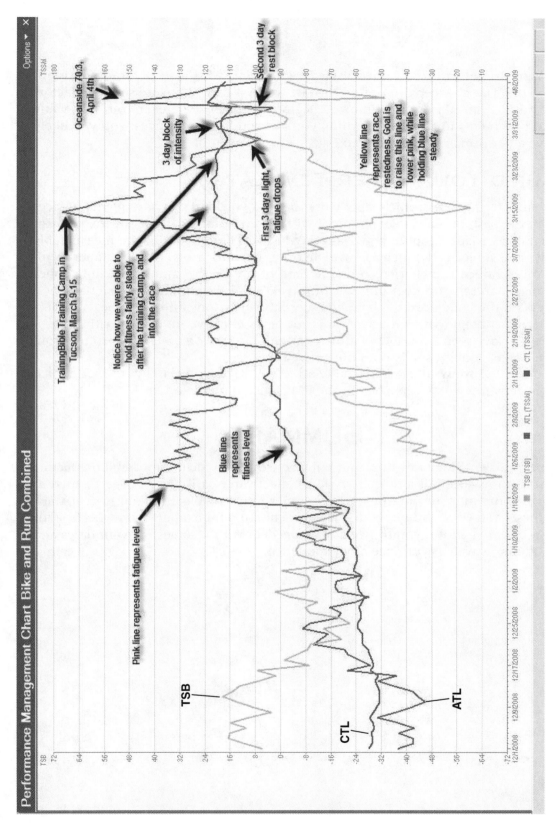

FIGURE 11.1 CTL of both bike and run data, combined into one PMC.

You can get to these values anyway you want, with a steady and consistent drop of CTL or a steep drop-off in the last week. Again, there are so many factors to consider, but if from the time you begin your taper (whatever your CTL value is at that point) to race day morning you are within these ranges, you will likely have a performance that will maximize your preparation.

BUILD YOUR TAPER TEMPLATE

If you're trying to see which taper works best for you, and you have plenty of races from the past, or want to experiment with different tapers in the future, you can use table 11.2 as a tool to better assess what was done, both in the measureable ways and subjectively, such as travel, in order to better assess how the taper went.

You'll notice the chart records the date of travel, the number of time zones changed, and the number of hours of travel. This is important because travel is a stress on the body during the taper, especially if it is long and tiresome. A perfect tapering strategy with no travel may not be as effective for a race with a lot of travel. I have seen a number of athletes attempt to race on quick turnaround from long travel, and it usually does not go well.

Table 11.3 shows the data from the athlete PMC described in figure 11.1, which helps illustrate what happened in the PMC, including the travel.

SUMMARY

Tapering is entirely individual and must be treated as such. Look at all the factors you can measure but also many whose effect can't easily be measured, such as travel hours and time out from race day, times zones traveled, and more. Keep track of these, and you can find the template or equation for a taper that works best for you, one that allows you to tweak it as needed, with changes in event dates and locations, as well as your age and experience.

TABLE 11.2 Sample Taper Template

Race event name	TSS	TSS/ day in taper	% of TSS/ wk	TSS/ wk	Athlete CTL	% of CTL on Mon. 1	TSB	% change of TSB	Workouts	Travel	Time zone change	Hours of travel	Race conditions
Mon. 1													
Tues. 1													
Wed. 1													
Thurs. 1													
Fri. 1													
Sat. 1													
Sun. 1													
Mon. 2													
Tues. 2													
Wed. 2													
Thurs. 2													
Fri. 2													
Sat. 2													
Race													

TABLE 11.3 Data From the Athlete PMC Described in Figure 11.1

Oceanside 70.3, Saturday, April 4, 2009	TSS	Avg. TSS/ day in taper	% of TSS/ wk	TSS/ wk	Athlete CTL	% of CTL on Mon. 1	TSB	% change of TSB	Workouts	Travel	Time zone change	Hours of travel	Race conditions
Mon. 1 (23rd)	98.8	98.8	14.89		115	100%	-8		run, swim				
Tues. 1 (24th)	138	118.6	20.86		116	101%	-10	125%	bike, run				
Wed. 1 (25th)	121	119.5	18.28		116	101%	-9	113%	run, swim				
Thurs. 1 (26th)	60	104.63	9.04		114	99%	-4	50%	bike, run, swim				
Fri. 1 (27th)	31.9	90.08	4.81		112	97%	6	-75%	run	X	-2	5	
Sat. 1 (28th)	60.6	85.17	9.13		110	96%	13	-163%	bike, run				
Sun. 1 (29th)	153	94.8	23	663.6	113	98%	8	-100%	Olympic tri				
Mon. 2 (30th)	165	103.58	36.9		113	98%	-1	13%	bike, run, swim				
Tues. 2 (31st)	122	105.6	27.24		113	98%	-2	25%	bike, run, swim				
Wed. 2 (1st)	87	103.74	19.46		112	97%	2	-25%	bike, run, swim				
Thurs. 2 (2nd)	20	96.13	4.47		111	97%	4	-50%	run				
Fri. 2 (3rd)	53.3	92.56	11.92	447.1	110	96%	10	-125%	bike, run				
Race day (4th)	334			781.1			16	-200%	race (70.3)				Perfect

PART IV

RACE ANALYSIS FOR WINNING RESULTS

12 PRERACE PREPARATIONS

Process + execution = results

Team slogan for Formula Endurance,
the nation's first USA Triathlon
High Performance Team
and USA Swimming team

The time has finally arrived, and you're ready to race! You've followed the plan of setting up the training year from general preparation to specific, and you're dialing in your taper to the proper training stress balance (TSB) to make your race day fitness shine through. Now you just need to make sure you have the proper plan and execute it on race day. You can't just go into the race hoping it goes well. You've worked too hard for that, and as New York City mayor Rudolph Giuliani once said, "Hope is not a strategy."

There are six keys to achieving high-performance goals. Whether you're an Olympian or a 60-plus age grouper trying to qualify for the World Championships or win them, high performance has six parts. The first three are preparation, preparation, and preparation. Get it wrong, and it doesn't matter how good a racer you are, you will likely not achieve the high goals you have set.

The next three are execution, execution, and execution. If your preparation has been perfect, it won't mean much if you're making poor pacing, nutrition, and equipment decisions on race day. All fitness does is give us a larger margin of error to work with, but the higher the goals, the more fit the competition is, so you either have to be exceptionally fitter than the rest or execute extremely well. I hope with this book you can and will do both.

When the event is extremely hot, pacing becomes a huge factor in the performance of athletes. Those who pace intelligently will likely do better than those who don't, if fitness levels are comparable or sometimes without even being comparable. We all know of incredible athletes who have had to walk the marathon of an Ironman. Fitness is not a license to be careless on race day.

This chapter is all about planning your execution, while the others have been more about preparation. But make no mistake, perfect preparation means practicing specific execution. When you toe the start line, your preparation should have you confident that the execution plan can and will happen because it has been rehearsed for many weeks.

If your specific preparation has been excellent, meaning you've been mimicking race day intensity, pacing, and course demands as close as possible, then the prerace preparations will be easy, since you've basically been doing them for about 10 to 16 weeks now. This includes training on a similar course, in similar conditions, and using the equipment and nutrition items you plan to use on race day. If the race is a local event for you, then you've likely been doing all this on the actual race course, which is a huge advantage.

When planning for a race, it's always good to get your plan in writing, so you can be specific and find the areas that could be miscalculated, underestimated or overestimated, or not considered and then review them over and over. Also, a postrace analysis is an incredibly useful tool to go back and review the plan, comparing it directly with what happened. This allows you to see where your planning was spot-on and where you missed in your projections. This will be especially helpful when you read chapter 14, Postrace Analysis.

Let's discuss the items to include in your race plan.

- **Travel to the event.** What day will you leave? When will you arrive? How many time zones will you be changing? How will you try to negate the effects of the travel if it is long and arduous?

- **Time you will get up on race morning.** Is this a usual time for you? Have you practiced it? If there is long travel, across many time zones, when and how will you begin preparing for this change of sleep patterns?

- **Breakfast.** What will you eat for breakfast? Have you tried this breakfast before? How many calories is the breakfast? What time will you eat breakfast, and how many hours is this before the race start? Any caffeine with breakfast?

- **Arrival to transition.** What time will you arrive at transition on race day? What will parking at the event be like? How long will it take you to warm up? Based on your wake-up time and travel to the event, will you have plenty of time to complete everything and be on the start line with time to spare and no stress? What can you do to make the time more efficient? What if there is an unexpected situation in the morning, such as a flat tire, loose bolt, ripped race suit, or broken goggles? Do you have the items, tools, and skills to take care of these quickly? If not, what do you need to do?

- **Temperature and precipitation.** What will the temperature be on race day? Will there be precipitation? How will these factors change as the day goes on, from the early morning, in the middle of the race, and even postrace? What will you do to prepare for these conditions? Will you bring extra clothes? Where will they be stored and how will you access them?

- **Warm-up.** What will your warm-up be? Can you get into the water for warm-up? Will you adjust your warm-up based on air or water temperatures? How so? If the race is a time trial start, how will you stay warm and loose when you have to stand in line?

- **Special needs bags.** If it's an Ironman or similarly longer race with special needs bags, what will you put in them? (Half Ironman events do not have special needs bags.) How will these items fair in the heat or cooler temperatures of the day, depending on the race? Have you practiced untying a special needs bag while riding? Or will you stop?

- **Swim.** Where will you line up for the start of the race? What is the typical direction of the current at the venue? How will you pace the swim? How many laps is the swim? What color are the turn buoys? Where will the sun be as you swim through the course? Is it a mass start or time trial start? What are the landmarks you will use to site off of?

- **Transition one (T1).** What is the route you must follow from the exit of the water to your transition spot? Any key landmarks to help guide you? How will you find your bike in the crowd of bikes? If there is a changing tent (full Ironman events), what will you do and change into there? Have you practiced this change, such as trying to put on a tri top or bike jersey with a wet body? Or will you not change at all?

  Is sunscreen something you apply in T1? Will you put your bike shoes on in T1 or once out on the road? Is it safe to run with them on your feet, given the surface and distance you will travel to your bike and to the mount line? Are there other choices or options?

- **Bike pacing.** What power range will you ride at during the race? For the entire course? Flats and hills? How will the temperatures and conditions affect this decision? This is a big and complex part of the plan, which will be addressed shortly in this chapter, and should be part of what you've done to prepare specifically in your training.

  If there are large packs of riders, you can draft in a race off a pack as long as you stay legal distance behind it. Will you use this to your advantage? To be clear, I don't condone drafting in a nondrafting event, but there are certain benefits even when riding legal or riding at a legal distance behind a pack of riders who are clearly drafting.

- **Bike nutrition.** What nutrition will you use on the bike? How soon into the bike until you start taking in nutrition? How many grams of carbohydrate and calories do you need per hour? Table 12.1 offers a simple guideline, based on the English or metric system.

TABLE 12.1   Nutritional Guideline Ranges for Long-Course Triathlon Bike Legs

	Grams of carbohydrate per hour, per pound of body weight (carbohydrate g/hr/lb)	Grams of carbohydrate per hour, per kg of body mass (carbohydrate g/hr/kg)	Calories per hour (Kcal/hr)
Bike nutrition	0.4–0.6	1.0–1.3	150–250

You can exceed or fall below these numbers, but you likely want to be sure you've proven it in training. Have you been training with this nutrition on your rides? Training with the same concentrations you will use on race day? Many athletes will suddenly change the concentrations of the drinks they have used in training, because they realize it will be a lot harder to carry the drinks with the amount of calories they need. Many times in training, they could stop and buy a new drink or mix another bottle. This isn't a good plan for race day, so make sure you've tested the concentrations.

Will you take on-course nutrition from the aid stations? How many aid stations are there? What items do they offer? You might think that you don't need to know this information, especially if your plan is to be almost entirely self-supported, except for water. However, it is fairly common for athletes to lose a bottle, drop some nutrition, or suddenly find that what they had planned for doesn't fit with their stomach on race day. If this is the case for you, even if just in case of emergency in the race, where you need nutrition, it is good to know what is available and what the calorie and carbohydrate numbers are. See table 12.1 for guidance on calories. Can you complete the race without having to use the special needs bags, perhaps using them as an insurance policy only? This might save you some time, being able to move past the crowded special needs area.

Realize that the goal of race nutrition is not to stuff as many calories into your body as possible but rather to optimize the calories needed, giving yourself the least amount necessary to achieve your goal. This amount should be practiced in your specific training phase, so you know what your needs are. The more calories you put into the stomach, and the higher the concentration levels of calories, along with the higher the intensity of the bike ride, the more likely the stomach will not be able to handle the calories you give it. You must know the concentrations and caloric counts (carbohydrate grams as well) that you need to accomplish your goal. Going above and beyond those numbers or a range you can handle is flirting with GI disaster.

Many athletes claim a need to eat solid food on the bike because their stomachs give them a hunger craving. This is understandable and can be fine for some athletes, but this should be practiced, especially at race intensity.

The slower the speed or intensity of the bike leg for the athlete, the more food he or she can process in the stomach, and the more solid the food can be, since the demands on the rest of the body are lower. See tables 12. 2 and 12.3 for more guidance on what type of nutrition strategy is best for you, based on your speed.

TABLE 12.2 Bike Nutrition Guidelines for Half Ironman (70.3)

Speed of the athlete (total race time)	Suggested nutrition strategy for calories
Sub 5 hours	Liquid-only sources
From 5 to 6.5 hours	Can have some solids, but mostly liquid calories are suggested
6.5+ hours	Athletes can eat whatever they want; all solids are fine

TABLE 12.3 Bike Nutrition Guidelines for Ironman

Speed of the athlete (total race time)	Suggested nutrition strategy for calories
Sub 11 hours	Liquid-only sources
From 11 to 13 hours	Can have some solids, but mostly liquid calories are suggested
13+ hours	Athletes can eat whatever they want; all solids are fine

With this information, you are likely ready and prepared to nail your nutrition plan. But remember, no nutrition plan in the world can make up for poor pacing on the bike or run. Execution is just as important as preparation. If you've prepared for a certain plan, execute it.

• **Transition two (T2).** What is the location of the dismount line? Will someone take your bike for you (typical in full Ironman races, not typical in 70.3), or will you need to rack your bike yourself? What landmarks will you use to find your spot? What is the exact path you will follow from dismount to run course start? If there is a changing tent, what will be done in the tent? Clothing change? Will you put on socks? Sunscreen? GPS watch? (I recommend recording the race.)

• **Run pacing.** How will you pace the run? How does this compare with your training paces? What will be your first mile or first 1 to 2K? How will the course profile likely affect pacing? Is it usually windy on the course? How will the temperatures and conditions affect this decision? More on run pacing shortly.

• **Run nutrition.** What will you use to get your calories and grams of carbohydrate on the run? How many will you consume per hour? What is that per aid station? How many aid stations are there? What will the aid stations be providing? How many calories do these items offer? See tables 12.4 and 12.5 for guidance on calories.

Again, you can go over or under these guidelines, but your chances of success are high if you're within these ranges. If you go outside these ranges, be sure to prove in your training that it will work well for you.

TABLE 12.4 Run Aid Stations

Drink	Calories	Carbs (g)	Sodium (mg)
Sports drink (4 oz)	25	-	-
Water	0	0	-
Cola (4 oz)	50	13	-
Pretzels (3 oz)	214	-	162
Soup broth	-	-	370
Banana	100	-	-
Gel	100–120	27	-
Bar (1/2)	120	00	-

TABLE 12.5 Nutritional Guideline Ranges for Long-Course Triathlon Run Legs

	Grams of CHO per hour, per pound of body weight (CHOg/hr/lb)	Grams of CHO per hour, per kg of body mass (CHOg/hr/kg)	Calories per hour (Kcal/hr)
Run nutrition	0.3–0.5	0.6–1.0	100–180

• **Finalize the plan.** If you can go through each of these segments of the race and write a plan, chances are you will execute much better. The amount of time and energy invested in training can be wasted if execution is poor, so this exercise can really pay off. In chapter 14, Postrace Analysis, this written plan becomes even more important because you will take each of these sections and compare them directly with what happened in the race. This will create an even better race learning experience, to help make you better at your preparation and execution.

DETERMINING BIKE PACING

One of the biggest challenges for any long-course triathlete is determining bike pacing. What further clouds it is the variance of courses, conditions, equipment, and fitness level. Luckily, if you have a power meter, this becomes much easier. It's almost like cheating, because we can dial in the perfect pacing strategy before and adjust it on the fly if necessary, given the conditions or other changes.

The adjustments on the fly to consider are the basis of chapter 13, In-Race Monitoring. However, the better your plan, the less likelihood you will need to adjust on the fly. But a good plan requires a lot of good research and experience with racing, or at least racing on the specific course. The quality of your research and your fitness will be directly correlated to the quality of your estimation of bike pacing and bike split.

New software programs can actually help you with this part of your race planning. Websites like BestBikeSplit.com can help you better estimate the coefficient of drag for your bike position, your speed at certain wattages, and how it specifically translates to the race course you want to do well at, accounting for likely wind and weather conditions, turns you'll slow for, hills, and even the equipment you'll use such as wheels and helmet. With this information, you'll be better able to accurately estimate your split, and how that might affect you in terms of TSS, on the course for a given power output. This can include planning by the following:

- TSS goal
- Time goal
- IF goal
- NP goal
- Directly comparing multiple plans to determine the best one
- Power outputs with headwinds
- Power outputs with tailwinds
- Power outputs on different inclines of hills and climbs
- Power outputs on different descents of hills and climbs

Once you start using this software, you can really gain a lot of confidence in your plan and even work backward from this plan to better identify what wattages or power zones are race specific. This is especially helpful software if you don't live near the course to train on it. If you have the advantage of living close enough to train on the race course during much of the build phase, you might not need this complex planning because you can dial in the perfect intensities for the course based on experience alone. Of course, as you've learned from this book, technology can likely still help you, no matter how successful you are.

This race planning guidance will continue on as if you don't use software for race planning, but you will likely want to use the software programs after seeing how much there is to plan and prep for. You might also wonder why there is so much emphasis on the bike plan but not the swim and run. We will get to the run, but the swim is limited in terms of time compared to the bike leg, and the execution of the bike for pacing and nutrition has the biggest effect on the race as a whole. There is usually not a lot of nutrition intake in the swim, and even poor swim pacing doesn't usually derail races.

If you don't live near the course, you will want to see what the weather conditions are usually like at this race. What are the normal temperatures, levels of humidity, and wind conditions? Once you know that, you have to make sure your pacing takes that into consideration. You also have to take altitude into account; an event at elevation will tend to be slower than an event at sea level. Again, software programs can help you dial in all these things pretty accurately and give you good guidance on how to handle them.

Once you have made your estimation, you are going to want to choose a TSS value to ride the race at. Remember, don't choose a TSS that is going to give you the fastest bike split; this is a triathlon, not a bike race. So many athletes want to push hard on the bike for that 5- to 10-minute faster split, without recognizing that if they walk just one mile of the run, they will lose close to 10 minutes. And usually athletes who walk one mile walk more than just one mile. Patience and pacing are the key to performance.

To help better illustrate what good bike pacing looks like, let's take a look at Frederik Van Lierde's 2013 Ironman World Championship power file (see figure 12.1).

You'll notice his TSS was 280. He knew that he had to pace himself really well to win. His NP for the ride was 303 watts with an IF of 0.80, which equals out to be approximately 80 percent of his FTP, which generated a bike split just under 4:30. Another interesting observation: he did not come off the bike in first place, and yet he ran away with the race. (Again, it's a swim-bike-run race.)

For Ironman-distance races, figure 12.2 shows the estimated TSS based on the interplay of IF and bike split.

So if you want to ride 5:30 for your Ironman-distance race and you want to keep your TSS from 260 to 300, you will need to ride at an IF from roughly 0.69 to 0.74, based on your NP. Of course, if 0.69 to 0.74 IF won't yield a speed on your bike to ride a 5:30 split, then you'll need to readdress your plan. More on that soon.

Remember, this is the range, but getting close to a TSS of 300 might not make a lot of practical sense on race day. If you look closely at the ranges, they indicate that you probably could have ridden harder, but the gray boxes are safe areas, showing there will be enough left in your tank for the run. Once you get into the yellow boxes it's a danger zone unless you are a really strong runner. Getting into the orange boxes will usually result in running a few miles and then walking. If you get up over 320, it will most likely be a 26.2-mile walk.

First-time Ironman-distance athletes should keep their TSS within the white or gray boxes to maximize running ability on race day.

Figure 12.3 is the same basic table but for a 70.3 distance race.

Now you have your estimated bike split, IF, and TSS. This is going to be refined as you continue to prepare for the race, which is good.

The next thing to take a look at is the speed your estimations are giving you back. This is why your estimations are so important. Keep in mind, though, that the flatter the course, the less variable that number will be on race day, where a hilly course will be further from the speed estimation. That said, we cannot account for possible wind in this process; that is where the flexibility will come in on race day. (Another reason for great software programs to help.)

Let's look at an example of an athlete who plans on riding a 5:00 bike split at an Ironman-distance race, with a goal TSS of 280, based around an FTP of 300 watts. I believe athletes should look at a time plus or minus 15 minutes from their goal or estimated time when figuring their plans. When we add in the ranges to increase our flexibility on race day to account for possible unknown conditions, we are looking at a bike split of 4:45 to 5:15.

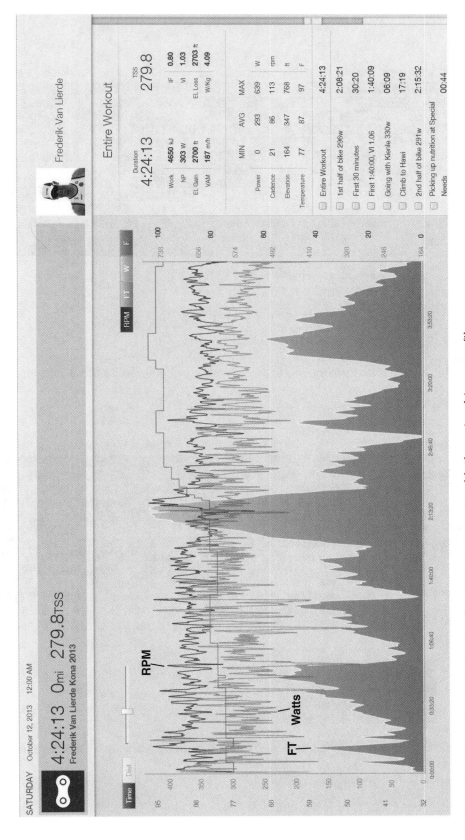

FIGURE 12.1 Frederik Van Lierde's 2013 Ironman World Championship power file.

Time\IF	67%	68%	69%	70%	71%	72%	73%	74%	75%	76%	77%	78%	79%	80%
6:30	292	301	309	319	328	337	346							
6:20	284	293	302	310	319	328	338	347						
6:10	277	285	294	302	311	320	329	338	347					
6:00	269	277	286	294	302	311	320	329	338	347				
5:50	262	270	278	286	294	302	311	319	328	337	346			
5:40	254	262	270	278	286	294	302	310	319	327	336	345		
5:30	247	254	262	270	277	285	293	301	309	318	326	335	343	352
5:20	239	247	254	261	269	276	284	292	300	308	316	324	333	341
5:19	232	239	246	253	260	268	275	283	291	298	306	314	322	331
5:00		231	238	245	252	259	266	274	281	289	296	304	312	320
4:50			230	237	244	251	258	265	272	279	287	294	302	309
4:40				229	235	242	249	256	263	270	277	284	291	299
4:30					227	233	240	246	253	260	267	274	281	288

Possibly too conservative.
Good conservative number.
Competitive athletes range.
Better be a top runner in your category.
You've likely overdone it.
Suicidal pace; you'll be suffering.

FIGURE 12.2 Relationship between bike intensity and bike time in an Ironman triathlon, expressed as TSS.

© Rick Ashburn. Descriptions adapted with permission.

Bike split	75%	76%	77%	78%	79%	80%	81%	82%	83%	84%	85%	86%	87%	88%
3:30	197	202	208	213	218	224	230							
3:20	188	193	198	203	208	213	219	224						
3:13	181	186	191	196	201	206	211	216	222					
3:06	174	179	184	189	193	198	203	208	214	219				
2:59	168	172	177	182	186	191	196	201	206	211	216			
2:52	161	166	170	174	179	183	188	193	197	202	207	212		
2:45	155	159	163	167	172	176	180	185	189	194	199	203	208	213
2:38	148	152	156	160	164	169	173	177	181	186	190	195	199	204
2:31	142	145	149	153	157	161	165	169	173	178	182	186	190	195
2:24		139	142	146	150	154	157	161	165	169	173	178	182	186
2:17			135	139	143	146	150	154	157	161	165	169	173	177
2:10				132	135	139	142	146	149	153	157	160	164	168
2:03					128	131	135	138	141	145	148	152	155	159

Possibly too conservative.
Good conservative number.
Competitive athletes range.
Better be a top runner in your category.
You've likely overdone it.
Suicidal pace; you'll be suffering.

FIGURE 12.3 Relationship between bike intensity and bike time in a 70.3 distance race, expressed as TSS.

© Rick Ashburn. Descriptions adapted with permission.

If this athlete refers to the chart in figure 12.2, he or she will see that a 5:00 bike split with a TSS of 280 tells the athlete his or her IF should be 0.75. The athlete also has to account for the range of 15 minutes, which in this case, we have to estimate when looking at the columns for 5:10 and 5:20 and 4:40 and 4:50, respectively. When we do this, the new IF range is 0.73 to 0.77. The NP that comes back is 285 watts (using IF = NP / FTP).

Based on these estimations, this athlete would have to ride at an average of 22.4 miles per hour in order to execute this plan perfectly. The athlete next needs to repeat the calculations to account for the range that was estimated. Those numbers tell the athlete that he or she needs to ride from 21.3 miles per hour to 23.6 miles per hour to account for the estimated range.

So far you know how to calculate a goal time (plus or minus 15 minutes) and can clearly estimate the demands required to execute it. Now you are at a key point: you have to ask yourself if you can realistically execute that plan based off the demands. This is where race split prediction software is a great tool.

On race day, you have to be flexible. You have to know and understand how close you are to your predicted time and what conditions have been playing into it. Ultimately, you will have to give yourself a time range for a goal time of plus or minus 15 minutes for an Ironman-distance race, plus or minus 10 minutes for a half Ironman–distance race, and 5 minutes for an Olympic-distance race. More on using this range to your advantage in chapter 13.

Remember, the better you plan, the easier your execution is and the more likely you are to succeed at reaching your goals.

DETERMINING RUN PACING

Many athletes speak about the pace they want to run off the bike in an Ironman. They say things like, "I want to start off at 7:00 minutes per mile and hold on. If I feel good after halfway, I will push the second-half pace." Or they will say, "I am going to push hard from the opening mile, trying to stay with my competitors or pull away from them."
There are a few problems with this approach.

This type of thinking is entirely *results* based, not *process* based. Athletes focused on a specific pace when they start the run put their confidence in jeopardy if they don't hit that pace. They will judge their race in that moment. Just because your legs don't give you a pace you hope for right away doesn't mean you can't get it or that you still can't run well. Athletes tend to begin pushing themselves more, early in the marathon or half marathon, looking for some confirmation that the pace they want to hit will happen if they can run it in the first few miles.

If you've ever done an Ironman or 70.3, you know there are peaks and valleys of performance and how you feel. Athletes must focus on being smooth and running easy early, seeing what the body gives them and not forcing it.

Remember, conditions can affect pacing as much as anything. In cool climates you can run faster. In hot climates you will likely run slower.

Pacing on the bike must be executed correctly in order to have a good run. So much of your run success begins before you ever take the first step on the run course.

Nutrition on the bike must be executed correctly in order to have a good run. Again, so much of your run success begins before you ever take the first step on the run course. (Yes, that is a repeat sentence.) But there is no nutritional plan that will make up for poor bike pacing for your run success. And of course, if you start the run too fast, no nutritional plan will solve that problem.

When athletes start their long runs in training, they rarely focus on or care about what the first mile or two of the run is paced at. They are just getting started and realize there is a lot of running to do. The same approach should happen for athletes when coming off the bike, especially in an Ironman. In 70.3 races, there might be a little more urgency, but it should still be relaxed and quick.

Many faster athletes might think this makes sense for mid- to back-of-the-packers but not for elites or top age groupers. But actually what tends to happen is those faster athletes are already running fairly quickly off the bike, even running relatively easy. Think about it: athletes who have a threshold pace of close to 5:00 per mile are easily running a 6:00 to 7:00 minute pace off the bike, with hardly any effort. The point? Don't rush the pace the first few miles; it will happen on its own.

How does this equate to writing a race plan if the plan is to base on feel, holding back early? Great question.

Recent studying I have done of paces for the first mile off the bike for pro men and women in Kona shows that if they run the first mile more than 20 seconds faster than the average pace they hope to realistically run, they're likely going to pay the price. This is for the faster people, where it is especially difficult to run faster, but extrapolate it out and that means about 5 percent for the age grouper. What is the takeaway for you? If your first mile is more than 5 percent faster than the average pace you can realistically run for the marathon, you're likely committing race suicide.

Almost always, the athletes with the smallest differential between the mile-1 split of the marathon and the total marathon time have one of the fastest marathons of the day. The same is true for 70.3 events. Pacing is a skill that must be honed.

When athletes run a half or full marathon fresh, they can handle a little aggressive pacing early but will still pay the price eventually if they do it too much. Now think about the difference when an athlete starts a marathon in an Ironman or a half marathon in a 70.3.

Most open marathons and half marathons are run with the athlete fresh and tapered. They also tend to be completed in the cooler morning hours. Ironman and 70.3 run legs are not started with fresh legs and tend to be run in the afternoon, in the hotter times of the day. Add in hot and humid conditions at a lot of races, and you begin to see the need to be one of the best pacers in the race, to maximize potential.

Stop focusing on the pace and focus more on executing good pacing. Plan accordingly for the pace your training shows you can realistically run and keep within 5 percent of that pace or less for the first mile (1 percent is better than a 5 percent differential) and be even closer in the following miles, and you should likely see yourself running close to the planned pace and split time.

CONFIDENCE

In all my experience, both as an elite triathlete and a coach, I have learned that the attitude you have on the start line is the biggest determinant of the race result. If I could peek into the thoughts of each athlete on the start line, I could likely tell you who is going to win, and even more likely, I could tell you who won't race well or to their potential.

Athletes focused on all the negative possibilities or worried about the competition, questioning their own preparation, or anything not in their control, are not going to perform well. Athletes on the start line who are focused on their race, not worried about the competition, eager to show the fitness they have, are the ones who are going to do well.

The mental aspect is not easy. Confidence can't really be faked; you either believe in yourself and your preparation or you don't. Confidence is built over many weeks, months, and even years. But the great thing about collecting data is that you can see your preparation objectively and know you are well prepared, building your confidence as you see the charts of your output show the improvement over the course of the season.

Go back and review your best performances and your worst performances, and I'm fairly certain the attitude you had on the start line is likely the key difference between them. Use data tracking to build your confidence, bring that confidence to the start line, and I'm sure you'll have the performances you're capable of.

SUMMARY

This is specificity you are training for. Whatever the plan for your race is, it should clearly be seen in the training you're doing, because if you're going to race a certain way on race day, it should be clear and defined so training can better represent it, preparing you for that performance.

A lot of athletes don't even consider many aspects of a race that need to be planned for. This includes travel time, venue specifics affecting warm-up, and more. If you write out your race plan and go through every step and part of the race, you will make sure to eliminate anything you might have overlooked and be better prepared for a great race. It will also help in the postrace analysis, helping to see where things were planned well and where they weren't, making for a smarter and better athlete for the future.

There are software programs out there to help you plan more effectively, down to the watts you should ride in a race, based on the equipment you will use and whether you are going uphill or downhill or with a tailwind or headwind. These programs can help you finalize the details and compare different race plans to maximize your performance potential.

13 In-Race Monitoring

Everyone has a plan 'til they get punched in the mouth.

Mike Tyson

Mike Tyson was one of the most feared fighters in the history of boxing. Yet there were plenty of experts in the sport who spoke of his weaknesses and how to beat him, as though it were not that hard. Many of his opponents trained and planned to beat him by using his weaknesses against him. And much like the quote from Tyson, those plans may have been very well devised, but once the match started and they took those first few punches, dealing with the adversity of the match, it became a challenge to stick to the plan.

That's triathlon and racing. No matter how well you plan, when you get into the big races, against the toughest competition, your resolve and steadfastness to that plan will be tested greatly. Your plan better not be good—it must be great. And it should have contingencies if the punch to the mouth was more than you expected.

This chapter shows you how to better execute your race plan, especially if things begin to unravel or you get that big punch to the mouth.

There are two types of athletes: scientists and artists. Scientists use the numbers and data to train and race to their potential, while artists use the feel of their fitness to train and race to success. A few athletes, and usually the most successful, would be categorized as both, using the best of both worlds to be successful.

Many of today's top professional triathletes get into the wind tunnel, measuring the drag of their bike position. This is a perfect example of the science side of racing helping athletes. When they use this information in a race while facing the strategic decisions of attacking at certain points, reading their opportunities and opponents to use it, it only enhances the art of racing to their advantage.

If you were to listen to an interview with two-time Ironman world champion Chris McCormack, he would tell you a lot about the art of racing. He does not like power meters and GPS watches.

He's an athlete who adjusted on the fly, reading his opponents and pushing the pace, taking risks in the race and putting pressure on his competitors. Sometimes it worked for him, and sometimes it didn't.

Unfortunately, Chris believed so much in the art of racing that he was very resistant to science. One wonders how many Ironman World Championships he might have won if he were as committed to the science of training and racing as he was to the art of racing.

Chris has spoken out about reading races and going with your gut, using your perceived exertion in the moment and having faith in your training and fitness.

I agree that athletes need to race and quit staring at the numbers. Athletes need to build trust in their perceptions, take risks, and learn what they're capable of. Chances are they are more capable than they realize of better performance. Many simply need to break the chains of the power meter zone or running at a set pace.

Our perceived exertion levels are only as reliable and good as their connection with the reality of our fitness and capabilities, though. Chris simply doesn't like to use the common power meter and GPS or stopwatch for running to determine this. The better he sees the skill of perceived exertion being correct for him, the better feedback he gets for himself.

But this is an acquired skill that takes months, if not years, of development and has to happen over the course of each season as well. Chris is a guy who doesn't balance a full-time job with training. He can conduct the sessions required to learn this skill in a much more rapid time frame than the average age grouper. He does this well, and the results are clear, but that's not reality for many athletes in the sport.

I get the sense it is better for him to say it is all art, and not science, because then it sounds like he is the only one capable of doing it correctly. It is certainly an art and science mix, but to say one artist's way is the only way is not something most would ever agree with.

I was coached for a period by Peter Reid during my professional Ironman racing days. Peter was a three-time Ironman world champion and probably one of the most consistent Ironman world championship racers ever. He was really big on athletes not getting stuck on the numbers and not letting the power meter control the athlete. I agreed, because if you really train properly, then on race day, you're going to ask more of your body than you ever have before, and the expectation is your body should perform better than it ever has before. If you're feeling good on race day, go with it, but be smart about it. If your race day goal is 225 watts and you're thinking the first hour at 280 watts is easy and you can hold it, that's probably a little too dramatic of a change.

The wind and conditions might change, so maybe you're going much faster or slower than you predicted. It's important to know your estimated and training tested range, from your build phase and race plan.

This is going to come down to how well you know your body as an athlete. What abilities are you confident in? If you're confident in your run ability, you may not need to take as much risk on your bike. If you're not confident in your run, maybe you do.

Let's say the race is a two-loop bike course and you're five minutes slower on the lap than what you expected on your goal watts. Now it's looking like you're going to be out there for 10 minutes more than you expected. You likely need to adjust your power numbers to the slower part of the range or closer to it.

THE EMOTIONAL COMPONENT OF LONG-COURSE RACING

If you've ever done long-course triathlon racing, an Ironman or half Ironman, you've likely seen that there are periods where you feel great and like the race is going exactly as planned, with a euphoria and happiness that makes all the sacrifice worth it. This tends to be followed by periods where things are not going well. This usually leads to feelings of doubt, anger, frustration, and crankiness. This lasts until either the race is over or you come out of it, beginning to feel better, and the cycle viciously repeats itself.

The challenge many athletes face is that when things are going well, they tend to feel invincible, not being patient and lacking respect for the distance and time they still have to travel. This is exactly why chapter 12, Prerace Preparations, was written, to get athletes to see a bigger picture, a written plan, and not let them stray from it.

When athletes feel great early on, it is easy to make poor pacing and nutritional decisions, as though they are invincible. But the opposite tends to happen after this. When athletes begin to struggle, battling fatigue, headwinds, cramps, and more, it's easy for the negative thoughts to creep into their head. This makes it very hard to rebound, because suddenly everything is a negative in their mind, and barring some sudden change in how they feel physically (usually only brought on by a dramatic slowing, which doesn't please them), they won't rebound quickly from this negative mind-set, and their performance will no doubt suffer from it.

If we can identify the things to monitor and make sure the race plan is executed precisely, or adjusted with intelligent decisions on the fly, then the athlete's success is highly probable.

You shouldn't have to stray from your plan, and these metrics during the race should help you avoid the emotional roller coaster, or at least the lows.

RACE DAY EXECUTION MONITORING

So how do you execute the plan on race day? You need to monitor your output. Since you're riding with a power meter, you can monitor and pace the bike according to certain metrics you want to accomplish, based on your race plan. Most modern bike computers can show multiple fields on a single screen. With a computer head unit mounted to your bike, you should consider having some of the following metrics displayed on the screen, tracking them throughout the race. This will tell you very quickly and directly if you are on or off your plan.

- **TSS (training stress score).** This will help you see how the race is going according to TSS, and if the course is consistent in terms of laps or elevation, you can likely foresee early in the race if you're on pace to get the TSS you planned for.
- **NP (normalized power).** This is related to TSS because you can't get TSS without NP, but this metric becomes extremely important in races that have a lot of up and down or extremely steep faces. If you know your goal NP value and your goal TSS value seems to be on point with your plan, you won't need IF on the screen.
- **IF (intensity factor).** Your IF is related to your NP, so if your screen is limited and you must eliminate something, this is the one I would suggest. However, it can really help an athlete see how he or she is doing, supporting the NP and TSS numbers.
- **Time.** Though this may seem unnecessary, it is actually crucial. The amount of time you are under intensity is the key factor in determining TSS. If you are doing a multilap course, the time for each lap can help you estimate how close you'll be at the current intensity to your goal time on the bike.
- **Current power.** This is a real-time power output. It helps you see in the moment if you're following the plan for power output. If you look at average, or some long-term time range for power output, you can miss much of the real-time outputs, especially if the course is hilly or with long climbs and descents.
  What about setting alarms if you're out of your desired zone? This would be helpful on a flat course but not very helpful on a hilly course where you will definitely exceed the power zone or power range quite a bit. Something to consider for your racing.
- **Average speed.** If your race course isn't multiple laps, or the laps aren't equal in length, you can track average speed in mph instead, while tracking real-time power and NP, so you can see how you're doing, projecting how the bike split might go in terms of time and TSS.
  If you will know when you are at the halfway point of a 112-mile ride, and your planned TSS is 280, your TSS at the 56-mile mark should be 140. Knowing that your speed ranges, average speed is going to let you know whether you are on track or not.
  Current speed, relative to average speed, is not that important if you're monitoring current power. Using and watching average speed can really help an athlete monitor and establish a bike split during the race. Know the mph average for your bike split estimated range, and you'll know how to adjust. Tables 13.1 and 13.2 show bike splits relative to bike speed for half Ironman (70.3) and Ironman, respectively.
- **RPM.** If you have a goal rpm, you'll probably want cadence up on the screen. This can help you if you're the type to become a masher, especially as you tire. The

TABLE 13.1 70.3 Bike Splits and Speed

Split	MPH	KPH
2:00	28.00	45.06
2:05	26.88	43.26
2:10	25.85	41.60
2:15	24.89	40.05
2:20	24.00	38.62
2:25	23.17	37.29
2:30	22.40	36.05
2:35	21.68	34.89
2:40	21.00	33.80
2:45	20.36	32.77
2:50	19.76	31.81
2:55	19.20	30.90
3:00	18.67	30.04
3:05	18.16	29.23
3:10	17.68	28.46
3:15	17.23	27.73
3:20	16.80	27.04
3:25	16.39	26.38
3:30	16.00	25.75

TABLE 13.2 Ironman Bike Splits and Speed

Split	MPH	KPH
4:10	26.88	43.26
4:20	25.85	41.60
4:30	24.89	40.05
4:40	24.00	38.62
4:50	23.17	37.29
5:00	22.40	36.05
5:10	21.68	34.89
5:20	21.00	33.80
5:30	20.36	32.77
5:40	19.76	31.81
5:50	18.67	30.90
6:00	18.16	30.04
6:10	18.67	29.23
6:20	17.68	28.46
6:30	17.23	27.73
6:40	16.80	27.04
6:50	16.39	26.38
7:00	16.00	25.75

great part of this metric on the screen is that it is process oriented and keeps you focused in the moment on pedaling your bike efficiently. Depending on your power meter, you might even be able to set the metric on the screen to be power balance (left leg vs right leg) or pedal engagement, which tells you the actual degree within the circle of the pedal stroke at which the foot produces a force on the pedal. This is another great process-oriented metric that helps your pacing execution.

If you are controlling your power correctly, within the limits of your plan, and you know your distance traveled or remaining, the TSS is going to line up. The IF is going to line up. It's simple math. As long as you're riding at the proper power output and your average speed is where it needs to be, the race will fall in line.

Put these metrics together and have them show that your planned race numbers for the bike are coming together, and your confidence for executing a great bike split in the race should be sky high. This will help you avoid the emotional roller coaster, because things are going exactly as you planned or even better than planned. It will help show you are mastering the art of racing.

What about heart rate? I will explain that shortly.

RACE NUTRITION

You also need to take into consideration your nutrition plan. Are you taking in solids and liquids as planned, and what are the possible stomach issues that could accompany the higher intensity that you would hold? Remember, at higher intensities, your stomach will process less. If you are going to push the pace a little more than planned, try to stick with mostly liquid nutrition; your system will be able to process that more efficiently at higher intensities.

Sometimes in a race your stomach just doesn't agree with what you planned and practiced. It could be that the drink you're using just doesn't taste very good on race day, so you might need a change on the fly. What if you drop your bottle or a hole in the road tosses it out of the cage? You'll need to know what else you need and what is available on the course to make up for it. Refer to the charts of nutritional items available at bike and run aid stations, should they be needed, from chapter 12.

OTHER VARIABLES IN RACING

What about a flat tire or mechanical issue? Should you pick up the pace and push it a little bit? My answer is no. When you try to make up time, you are changing your game plan, which inevitably leads to problems. Remember, you've been training for a specific pace. If you try to make up for whatever's lost and you haven't trained for that, your body is not going to handle that well. As much as that probably doesn't sound like a good plan to you, the rest and recovery you get from fixing the issue can sometimes lead to a much better run split. I have seen more than a few athletes run their best splits ever after a flat, or even after they had to serve a few minutes in the penalty tent. Use the poor circumstances to your advantage, and you might be amazed at what can happen.

Elites should consider the number of matches in their matchbook. Matches are big surges and attacks from the competition. The competition is certainly going to determine your race strategy and your race specificity, so if you're an athlete who's going to race off the front, it's now a much different type of strategy and specificity. Or if you're an elite who has to hold to a position within the line of athletes, and go with the moves and surges of the group, your specificity is much different, and you need to know how many big attacks or moves you can counter, and how big, until it affects your legs for the run.

HEART RATE

You'll notice I have not mentioned anything about heart rate. That is because I'm not a believer in monitoring heart rate on race day. Other people may disagree with me, and that's fine. I think heart rate tells you something you already know on race day, that you're going hard.

I think it's a great tool for training, giving you a lot of feedback in terms of how you're responding to the training stimulus. If you're seeing your heart rate stay the same with power increasing, or increasing with an output at a faster pace, it is an improvement in fitness.

On race day, you're going out to express that fitness. You don't need to worry about heart rate. The race is not won by, and there are no awards given to, those who had the highest or lowest heart rate in a race.

You have to cross the finish line first based on output. If your power outputs on the bike are where you want them and you know that you've trained to produce those values, your heart rate shouldn't really matter.

RUN PERFORMANCE

I've seen athletes use an aggressive run to their advantage (out of sight, out of mind), and I've seen plenty of aggressive run strategies fail. The better the runner, the more margin of error the athlete will have. However, if you ride the bike in a manner that is aggressive and overreaching, and try the same strategy on the run, you'll likely find yourself walking quite a bit.

If you can stay stoic through the early miles of the run, for the first 10 miles especially, sticking with the pacing plan you have, you're likely to do quite well.

Athletes need to have a GPS unit they can grab in transition two (T2) that has been fully charged and is ready with a connection to the satellites before the race starts. (I always preach to keep the bike and run computer units separate.) These watches should be able to hold the charge for the whole day, waiting for you in T2. If you have to turn it on in T2 and wait for it to connect, it likely won't connect until sometime after you leave T2, missing the crucial first mile split, which was discussed in chapter 12.

Once you grab the watch and leave T2, it's important to have the screen set to the following metrics to monitor as you run.

• **Current pace.** This one is obvious, because you need to know in the moment if you're going too fast.

• **Last lap.** This gives you the actual time for the last lap. It is very important for helping you see what your splits are and how effectively you're pacing the race.

• **Cadence.** This is based off your foot pod and may not seem that important early, but as you tire, seeing this metric can help keep you focused in the moment on moving quickly. This is another process-oriented metric, helping you see how well you are executing running fast. In long-course triathlon, the slower your cadence, the slower you are.

Those are the three critical items to monitor. There are a couple others to consider, if you really want them.

- **Total time.** This is optional, because some athletes late want to see their potential to get a great split and use it as motivation. Of course, sometimes it can have the opposite effect, especially if the race isn't going as well as planned.

- **Auto lap.** This isn't really a metric to display, but I think it's an important setting. I believe the GPS should be set to automatically take lap splits at the mile marker because it records your mile split without you having to remember (and it is likely you will forget a few times) and can help you track your pace as you go. Sometimes mile markers on the course are not as accurate as they should be, and this can help alleviate that.

Execution of the run is so much about pacing. Staying in the moment and focusing on the process of good pacing is vital for success. I think it's important to share some pacing charts to help you better plan and execute. Tables 13.3 and 13.4 show mile splits and how those translate to half and full marathon splits, respectively, to help better understand pacing.

TABLE 13.3   Half Marathon Splits

Finish time	Finish time (min)	Pace (mile^-1)	Pace (km^-1)
1:08	68	5:11	3:13
1:10	70	5:20	3:19
1:12	72	5:30	3:25
1:14	74	5:39	3:30
1:16	76	5:48	3:36
1:18	78	5:57	3:42
1:20	80	6:06	3:47
1:22	82	6:15	3:53
1:24	84	6:24	3:59
1:26	86	6:34	4:04.8
1:28	88	6:43	4:10
1:30	90	6:52	4:16
1:32	92	7:01	4:21.8
1:34	94	7:10	4:27.5
1:36	96	7:20	4:33
1:38	98	7:29	4:38.9
1:40	100	7:38	4:44.6
1:42	102	7:47	4:50.3

Finish time	Finish time (min)	Pace (mile^-1)	Pace (km^-1)
1:44	104	7:56	4:55.9
1:46	106	8:05	5:01.6
1:48	108	8:15	5:07.3
1:50	110	8:24	5:13
1:52	112	8:33	5:18.7
1:54	114	8:42	5:24.4
1:56	116	8:51	5:30
1:58	118	9:00	5:35.8
2:00	120	9:09.6	5:41.5
2:02	122	9:18.8	5:47.2
2:04	124	9:28	5:52.9
2:06	126	9:37	5:58.6
2:08	128	9:46	6:04.3
2:10	130	9:55	6:10
2:12	132	10:04	6:15.6
2:14	134	10:13	6:21.4
2:16	136	10:23	6:27.0
2:18	138	10:32	6:32.7
2:20	140	10:41	6:38.4

TABLE 13.4 Marathon Splits

Finish time	Finish time (min)	Pace (mile^-1)	Pace (km^-1)
2:30	150	5:43.5	3:33
2:34	154	5:52.7	3:39
2:38	158	6:01.8	3:44.8
2:42	162	6:11	3:50.5
2:46	166	6:20.1	3:56.2
2:50	170	6:29.3	4:01.9
2:54	174	6:38.5	4:07.5
2:58	178	6:47.6	4:13.3
3:02	182	6:56.8	4:18.9
3:06	186	7:05.9	4:24.7
3:10	190	7:15.1	4:30.4
3:14	194	7:24.2	4:36.1
3:18	198	7:33.4	4:41.7
3:22	202	7:42.6	4:47.4
3:26	206	7:51.7	4:53.1
3:30	210	8:00	4:58.8
3:34	218	8:10.1	5:04.5
3:38	218	8:19.2	5:10.2
3:42	222	8:28.3	5:15.9
3:46	226	8:37.5	5:21.6
3:50	230	8:46.7	5:27.3
3:54	234	8:55.8	5:33.0
3:58	238	9:04	5:38.7
4:02	242	9:14.2	5:44.4
4:06	246	9:23.4	5:50
4:10	250	9:32.5	5:55.7
4:14	254	9:41.7	6:01.4
4:18	258	9:50.8	6:07.1
4:22	262	10:00	6:16.8
4:26	266	10:09.1	6:18.5
4:30	270	10:18.3	6:24.2

SUMMARY

Race day execution begins long before race day. This ultimately means knowing your goal TSS, NP, and IF and the speed you will need to hold to reach your goal bike split. You can also use software programs to help plan this. Fine-tune your estimate in training. You need to understand and accept the flexibility that you can and cannot have on race day.

When it comes to the run, you've got to keep yourself under control early, so choose metrics that will help you monitor your performance to keep you focused on executing the pacing successfully, and use your best judgment if you feel great and want to push the watts and pace a little, but be smart.

Then, on race day, execute the plan and monitor the correct metrics. It is all about execution on race day.

14
POSTRACE ANALYSIS

There are too many factors you have to take into account that you have no control over. . . . The most important factor you can keep in your own hands is yourself. I always placed the greatest emphasis on that.

Eddy Merckx, Belgian, five-time Tour de France champion

This chapter teaches you how to assess your race performance and execution by looking more closely after the event at your pacing, the intensity at which you raced, and how your nutrition played a role. With that in hand, we will then tie it back to your preparation.

What role did your preparation play in the performance outcome? How can we then use that data in the future to perfect your training for the next race? The most important training you do may happen *after* the race, and it's not physical training.

Racing, at any level, is a combination of art and science. The art of racing is understanding how a race works and how to read a race, like the dynamics of what is happening around you, reading your competition's moves, and making moves to beat them. The art of racing is being flexible with your race plan as the race unfolds. This is going by feel on race day and is a psychological aspect of racing. The science of racing, the physiological demands of the race, is backed up with real numbers. These numbers come from a power meter and a GPS device. With this data, real feedback is now available to the artist.

POSTRACE REPORTS

If you visit any running, cycling, or triathlon forums on the Internet, you'll notice the popularity of race reports. We all seem to love the storytelling that goes with our adventures, especially in longer races, where so many things happen that the toughest part is remembering them all for the report.

Many athletes enjoy writing the report and talking about the funny instances, the pain and discomfort (at times), and the lows and highs of their performance. However, most are missing a quality opportunity to assess their race, performance, strategy, nutrition, pace, and even confidence or motivation in some cases.

If you're tempted to write a race report, it's fine to make it enjoyable for others to read, but be sure to use it as a tool to be honest and objective with yourself. In fact, a race report should be more for your use as an evaluation tool than as an entertainment tool for others.

With as much time as athletes put into training and preparation for an event, probably the most effective use of time comes after the race in truthfully assessing your performance and how closely it matched your expectations. If it didn't match, what were some of the causes? Were you underconfident in yourself and performed much better than you expected? Did you overestimate your fitness or underestimate the course, competition, or conditions?

What types of things can be learned from this reflection and evaluation? It may seem unimportant once the race is over, but if you ever plan to return to a similar endeavor, or this race, this opportunity is golden.

As mentioned in chapter 13, a postrace analysis is an incredibly useful tool that allows you to go back and review the written plan discussed in chapter 12 and compare it directly with what happened, step by step. This allows you to see where your planning was spot-on and where you missed in your projections. This exercise of writing the plan and then comparing it with what actually happened are opportunities to learn about both the science and art of racing. They are both learned skills and can come a lot faster if given the attention.

OVERALL LEAD-UP

Before we get to the written plan, you should record and assess how your peak and taper went as you came into the event, whether it was a peak event or just a training race. Here are a few key numbers to know and record.

TSB

What was your training stress balance (TSB) on race day? What was it for the bike performance management chart (PMC), run PMC, and the overall PMC? Did it fall within the parameters outlined for TSB in chapter 11?

Peak Power

Did race day present a top 10 peak power performance for the season, in the metrics you were training specifically for in this race? If not, how far off from a top 10 was it? Remember, if you did it right, you likely asked more of yourself for this race than you have all season. If it wasn't a top 10, it should be close, or you need to review and dissect your plan for both the race and the training year.

Peak Pace

This one may not have been a top 10 for the season for you, since you started this run in a fatigued state, whereas training runs were likely started much fresher. But this performance should still be one of your best race performances compared to others in the past or commensurate with the quality of training completed.

If it ends up that your race performance is a top 10 for the season in the peak pace metrics you tracked specific to either 70.3 or full Ironman, even better.

Race Plan

In the written plan, you wrote out the details that were beyond swim-bike-run, such as travel plans to the city, wake-up time on race morning, what you would eat for breakfast, what time you would leave for the event, when you would arrive, and more. These are all good opportunities to see if you underestimated the timing or importance of these items.

It's not uncommon at a race to see people rushing, or at least feeling rushed, before the race start. Sometimes a little better planning, with buffers put in for things like the time it takes to find parking, bathroom breaks, setting up transitions, and other needs can go a long way.

SWIM PERFORMANCE

No matter how you feel about how the swim leg went for you, you should assess if your preparation and plan were effective. Did you train properly to perform the swim split you wanted? There may not be a lot of numbers that are easy to assess and measure, but one simple measure is to see how your test sets and race-specific workouts equated to the performance. Were the swim test times similar to other races, and how did that compare with your time and place within your age group at the race?

Did the current, water temperature, or sighting challenges affect you? Were you able to handle the crowds if it was a mass start? What helped or hurt you with that?

If it was a time trial start, how effective do you feel your warm-up was? If you swam in a wetsuit, how did it feel?

BIKE PERFORMANCE

Now we can really begin to dive into the data and see how you did, not only in the race execution but also in how well your training actually prepared you for the demands of race day, so you can make adjustments in your future training decisions. Remember too that the bike is about 50 percent of the race time, so a lot can be gleaned from this data, in terms of analysis of your success.

Estimate Versus Actual Bike Split

In the race plan, you estimated your bike split, and now it's time to compare that estimation and the plan from it with what the actual split was. What effect did your estimation have on your race? If you were way off with your estimation, that can be very bad for your performance, no matter if you were much faster or much slower. What conditions on race day played into this? Was it hotter than expected? Was it windier than expected? Did you ride with better or worse equipment you didn't realize would affect your split? Did you end up carrying a lot more items than you do in training? All of these can have a major effect on your actual bike split versus your estimated bike split.

If you used a race planning software program, how did the plan compare with what actually happened? Again, if there were major differences, what might have caused them?

TSS on the Bike

You will need to look back at your bike split estimations and see what the goal training stress score (TSS) was. Was your TSS on race day within the acceptable ranges?

Remember, TSS is the representation of the load you put on your body during the bike leg (see figure 12.2). What effect did this have on your run and therefore your overall result? If you raced an Ironman-distance event and had a TSS of 315, how much of an effect did that have on your run? If you started out on the run in an overly fatigued state from riding too hard, what effect did that have? Or did you hold back too much on the bike?

It's important to note that you can hit your target normalized power (NP), intensity factor (IF), and TSS but do it in a very poor manner, such as riding the first half of the bike well over the planned values and the latter parts of the bike well under. Hopefully, you didn't abandon your specific training preparation and ride well above what you prepared yourself for.

If you had a great run, despite being over 300 TSS, perhaps your taper was excellent and you were able to race harder due to being fresher. Maybe the taper helped raise your functional threshold power (FTP) and therefore gave you the ability to push harder. This is critical information to know, because it can give you a lot of confidence in your taper for the future and even in your ability to race at a high level when it matters.

If your ride generated a TSS of 140 in a 70.3 event, what effect did that have on your run? Could you have ridden harder and still had a good run?

What external factors had an effect on your TSS that we can't necessarily see? Was it hotter or colder than expected? Was it windier than expected on race day? All of these conditions can play a role in increasing or decreasing your TSS on race day, in ways that are not exactly measureable. For instance, a super hot and humid day, even with a lower TSS ride, can still affect you. Riding a specific wattage in cooler temps may produce the same TSS as in hotter temps, but we would likely agree that the body's effort to have to cool itself in the hotter temps is an additional stress on the body that must be accounted for.

These are the numbers you have to take a look at to truly evaluate your race performance. You want to look at and learn from these numbers to guide your estimations and plans for future races.

ASSESSING YOUR RACE
AND MAKING IMPROVEMENT GOALS

Our sample athlete in this case study raced an Ironman-distance event with a goal TSS of 280 and an estimated bike split of 5:00, which generates a range of 4:45 to 5:15. His FTP was 300 watts and his goal IF was .75.

When you do the math based on these numbers, using the equation IF = NP / FTP, you get the following numbers for the full range (see table 14.1):

TABLE 14.1 Sample race assessment

Goal time	TSS	IF	NP	Average speed
4:45	280	.77	231w	23.6 mph
5:00	280	.75	225w	22.4 mph
5:15	280	.74	222w	21.3 mph

These numbers were the specificity for this athlete on race day and are the basis for his specific race plan.

After the event, this athlete would need to go back and see where his numbers fell in relation to the number range in the chart.

If this athlete's results fell within this range, that is solid execution of the race plan. Remember, great execution does not always equal great results. If this athlete was happy with his results, then it was most likely a good day. If he was not happy with his results, then he needs to dig deeper into what happened.

Was his estimation off? Was he more or less fit than expected? Was he stronger or weaker than he thought he would be on race day?

Based on that analysis, this athlete would need to examine his training leading into this event. Did the specific training reflect the specific demands of the race? Did the specific training reflect the demands of his race estimations, which generated the race plan? Did he execute his nutrition plan?

If this athlete rode a 300 TSS but never once completed a transition run off a 300 TSS ride at his goal running pace, he would be asking his body to do something that it has not trained for.

This is the type of analysis you will need to perform after each big race you take part in. This will allow you to scientifically assess your race and then make the necessary adjustments to your training going forward.

Pacing

This is where the metric variability index (VI) comes into play. Remember, VI is NP / AP for the bike and NGP / AP for the run. NP is what your power would have been if you rode perfectly smooth for the entire ride, where your AP is the mathematical average of every power reading throughout the ride.

In triathlon, your goal VI is 1.0, which is evidence that you rode smoothly the entire ride, without big spikes in power output. The upper limit you want to avoid going above for VI is 1.05 because anything greater than that usually indicates erratic pacing throughout the ride.

Keep in mind that terrain can play a big role in VI. If you are on a flat course, it will be a lot easier to control your power output versus riding on a really hilly course where you will have larger power surges going uphill and a large number of zeros when you are coming back down. I have seen athletes race quite well with high VIs, but those always tend to be on courses with long or many climbs and allow the athlete to also have long periods of coasting on long descents. The descents can greatly affect VI because the zero-watt output is included when calculating VI, AP, and even NP.

Race dynamics can also play a role in VI. If there are a lot of surges and attacks, like we see a lot in the professional race, the VI will be higher. Earlier in the race, where riders will jostle for position, there might be far more variance. As the race progresses, athletes tend to be able to settle in and ride more smoothly, barring any course demands that would force surges.

Let's take a look at some of the bike files from some of the best athletes in the sport, and even some age groupers, for Ironman and 70.3 distance.

Looking at Frederik Van Lierde's bike file (see figure 14.1) from his winning performance at the Ironman World Championships in 2013, he rode with a VI of 1.03, which is really low for riding in the elite race at Kona. There was a lot of jostling for position in the first two-thirds of the race before it settled down for the last third. He finished with an IF of 0.80 overall, which means he rode at the equivalent of 80 percent of his bFTP for the whole ride. Many people think because these pros are going so fast, they are going much harder than everyone else and carrying more fatigue. That's not really the case, in terms of TSS because his was 280, which is right in line with the guidelines here for most athletes. The difference is just that he can produce much more force per pedal stroke than the typical age grouper, allowing him to travel at a faster speed. Yes, because these pros are out there for a shorter period, they are racing at a higher intensity, but in terms of overall fatigue or TSS, it is very similar or sometimes even less than that of other athletes in the race, especially compared to those who overcook themselves on the bike.

All in all though, this was an impressive and nearly perfectly paced bike leg for Frederik Van Lierde. We would use this file to guide his training to be prepared for some jostling and surges in the first part of the race, all within a ride of 280 TSS.

Figure 14.2 shows that Luke McKenzie went off the front and had a VI of 1.05, which was more variable than Van Lierde's in the same race. He had quite a few surges early in the race, and rode a TSS of 293, but was out there for a shorter period of time than Van Lierde. Because he was out there for a shorter period, he was able to hold a higher IF of 0.82.

McKenzie was second off the bike and was passed by only Van Lierde in the run leg to finish second overall in 2013, so he raced a nearly perfect race. More on McKenzie and his 2013 race in chapter 15.

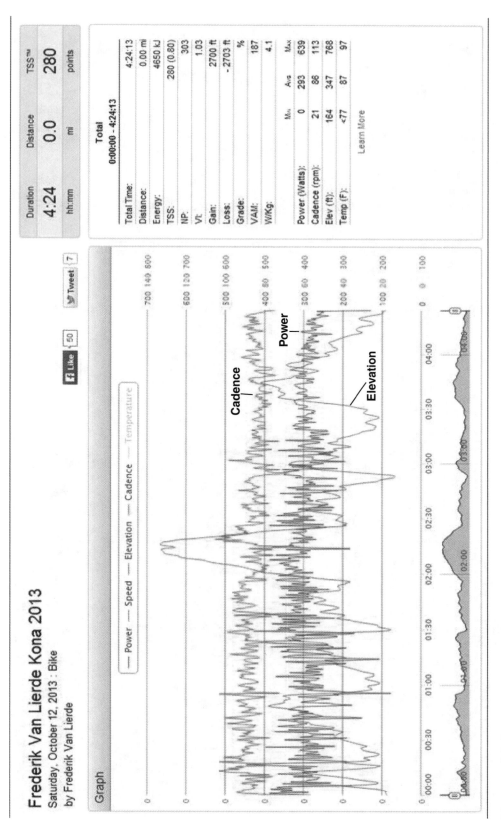

FIGURE 14.1 Frederik Van Lierde's bike file.

175

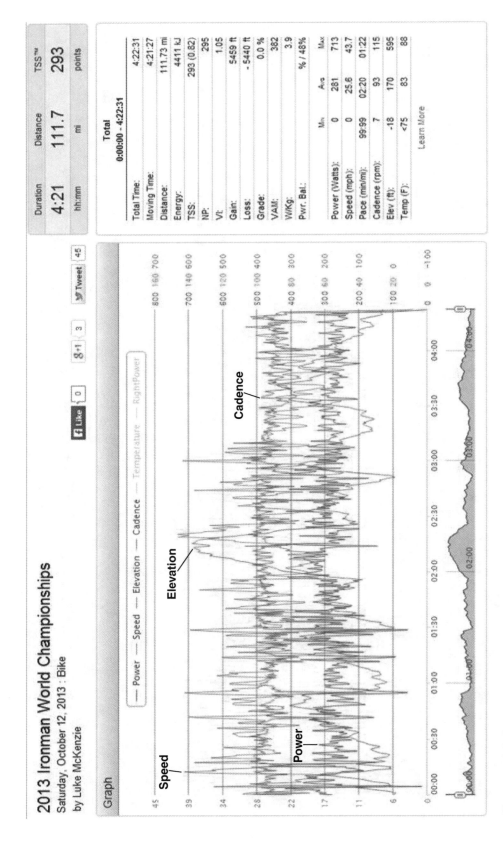

FIGURE 14.2 Luke McKenzie's Kona 2013 file.

Figure 14.3 is a great example of an athlete who rode too hard in the earlier part of the race. This power file from Ironman Arizona shows how the demands of the race were uphill to the turnaround and then back downhill. There was a declining power overall, with a pretty good TSS and IF, but the VI was too high, and the early watts were too much. With the overall declining power, that is a clear indicator that he went out too hard and wasn't able to use the strong winds to his advantage. This athlete flatted on the bike, as evidenced by the late gap in the data, but still couldn't recover well enough despite the time to rest.

Figure 14.4 is an interesting power file, because it comes from Ironman Wisconsin, which is a very challenging course, featuring a lot of climbing, with especially steep pitches and not many sustained climbs—just up and down a lot. This athlete rode a perfectly steady trend with his power output, despite the course being so up and down, as also evidenced by his high VI of 1.09. This athlete also had a flat tire (the gap in the file) and yet made the smart choice of not trying to push the pace to make up for the lost time.

A TSS of 298 and IF of 0.75 seem okay, but when compared with his VI of 1.09, it would seem likely he would have blown up. But looking at the file and all the metrics together, the VI is a single outlier from the typical numbers because it doesn't tell the entire story. He used the uphills to go hard and recovered well on the downhills, as evidenced by all the dips in his power output. Despite the 1.09 VI, he ran a three-hour marathon, the fastest age group run split overall and the fourth fastest overall counting the elites, and finished in the top 25 overall.

How was he able to do this? The biggest reason is that this athlete was able to train a lot on the course, living nearby. He did many of his key, race-specific workouts on the course, preparing to be able to handle the up and down of the roads, using it to his advantage, and knowing he could still run well off it. Few things can match pure, race-specific preparation that training on the course provides.

Now let's look at some 70.3 power files to learn more about how athletes raced and the specificity of the race demands they competed in.

Figure 14.5 is a file from Jesse Thomas, a professional triathlete, racing at the Oceanside 70.3 triathlon in 2013. I reviewed this file for his coach Matt Dixon, and my analysis of it included figure 14.5. Jesse lost this race in a running sprint finish to Andy Potts, who was first out of the water and well up the road by himself until late in the run. Andy's race was a steady ride at his watts, no surges needed. He just had to get up to race intensity and hold it. Jesse had to come from behind and catch the main chase pack. I've highlighted in the file how he had to put in an early, very hard time trial effort, until he caught the pack. Once he caught the pack, the movement and attacks started. You can see the dotted line in figure 14.5 is his actual bFTP, and he spends a good amount of the race above it.

On the right in figure 14.5, you can see I've found 19 surges in the race where he went over 500 watts for at least five seconds. He had nearly 40 surges in the race over 400 watts. He came off the bike and was able to catch Potts but didn't have the legs for the sprint finish. I believe he would have won if he was smarter earlier on the bike, limiting his surges.

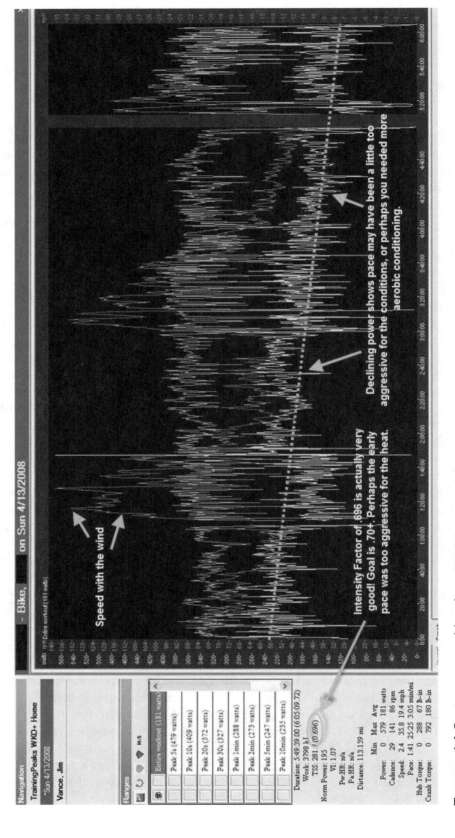

FIGURE 14.3 Age group athlete from 2008 Ironman Arizona.

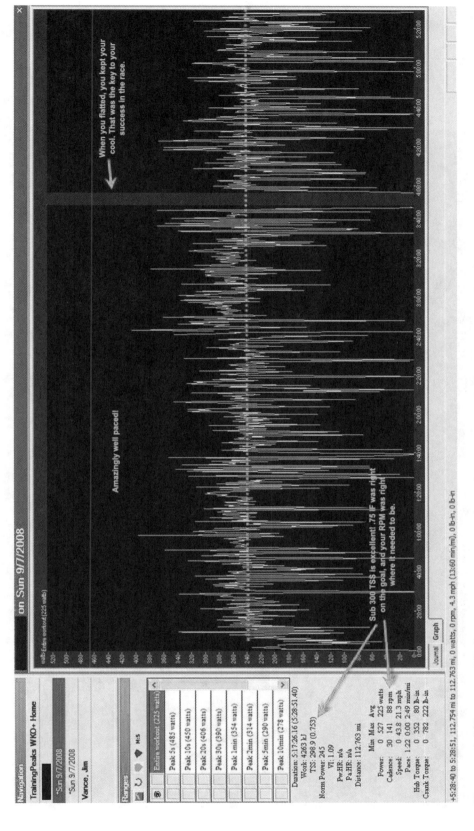

FIGURE 14.4 Power file from 2008 Ironman Wisconsin.

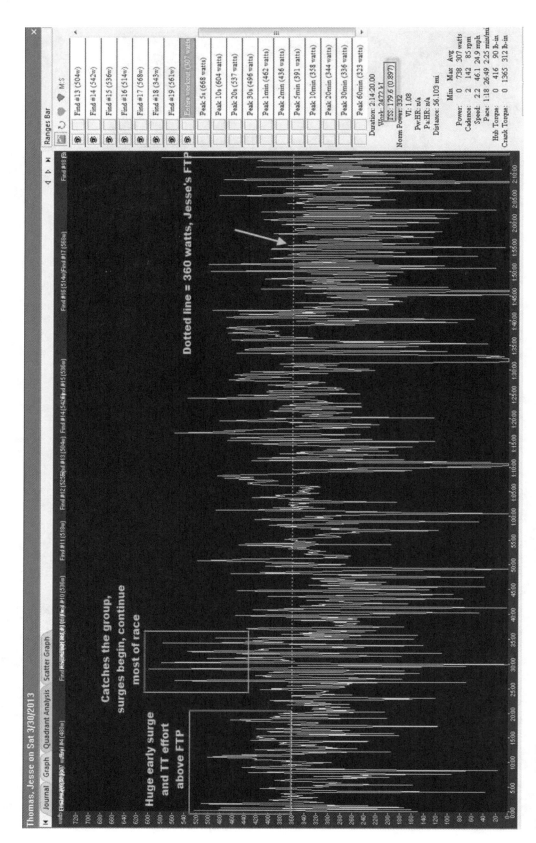

FIGURE 14.5 Jesse Thomas's Oceanside 70.3 file.

One might ask, why did he do so many surges? The reason is that there is a drafting benefit to being with a pack, even when riding legal, and there is still a mental benefit to keeping your competitors nearby. The problem is that he went with nearly every surge or attack, not knowing which ones to respect. Though his TSS and IF were right in line with what we identify as normal, the 1.08 VI of his ride is far from what we would expect someone to run as well as he did. Perhaps the only thing that saved him was the number of drops in his power to almost zero, coasting along to reassess or not enter draft zones.

Just how much was he jumping around with his power? Figure 14.6 shows the distribution of power in 20-watt ranges.

The longest total amount of time he spent in any 20-watt range was 11 minutes, in the 320 to 340 watt range, which was only 8.8 percent of his total time on the bike. This is not a steady-paced effort by any means. It's probably the worst way to ride a 70.3 bike leg, and he still nearly won the race. One month later he would win Wildflower again on a much hillier course and would have a lower VI, learning from the race file at Oceanside to keep under control and make smarter pacing decisions.

Now contrast his racing style with the winning power file for Emma-Kate Lidbury at Texas 70.3 in 2013 shown in figure 14.7.

Emma-Kate rode almost perfectly steady. In fact, it might be impossible to ride much steadier. No surges, she just stayed on her numbers and rode away from the field. Her TSS and IF numbers were actually higher than Jesse's, but the way she rode was entirely different, with hardly any surges above bFTP, much less well beyond that.

In figure 14.8, you can see how unlike Jesse's short time in many different watt ranges, Emma-Kate spends nearly two-thirds of the race in two 20-watt ranges. This is the clear difference in the two races and helps identify the difference between professional men and women, in terms of race specificity. The men's race is tighter, with many more surges, while the women's race is more spread out and less volatile. This may change in the future, and those women who prepare for the change will be the more successful ones.

Next, figure 14.9, is a 70.3 power file, also from Oceanside, from an older athlete in his 60s. This athlete did an exceptional job of holding back early, working into the effort and riding really well. He raises his power output through the ride, pushing hard. He actually came off the bike and ran a great split, despite being above 190 TSS. His VI was extremely high, but that might be as much about the drops in power as anything else. His late surges seemed to be unnecessary, and he would benefit from eliminating them in the future.

You have to take TSS and VI into account independently and together to get the full picture for a postrace analysis of the data. VI is not something we normally want to be high, but if the ride includes a lot of drops in power to help recover, athletes can handle a high VI, especially if they are prepared for that type of riding. They can also overcome high VI and TSS numbers if they pace themselves well.

One of the biggest takeaways from analyzing a race file should be answering the question of whether your training specifically prepared you for that race. If it did,

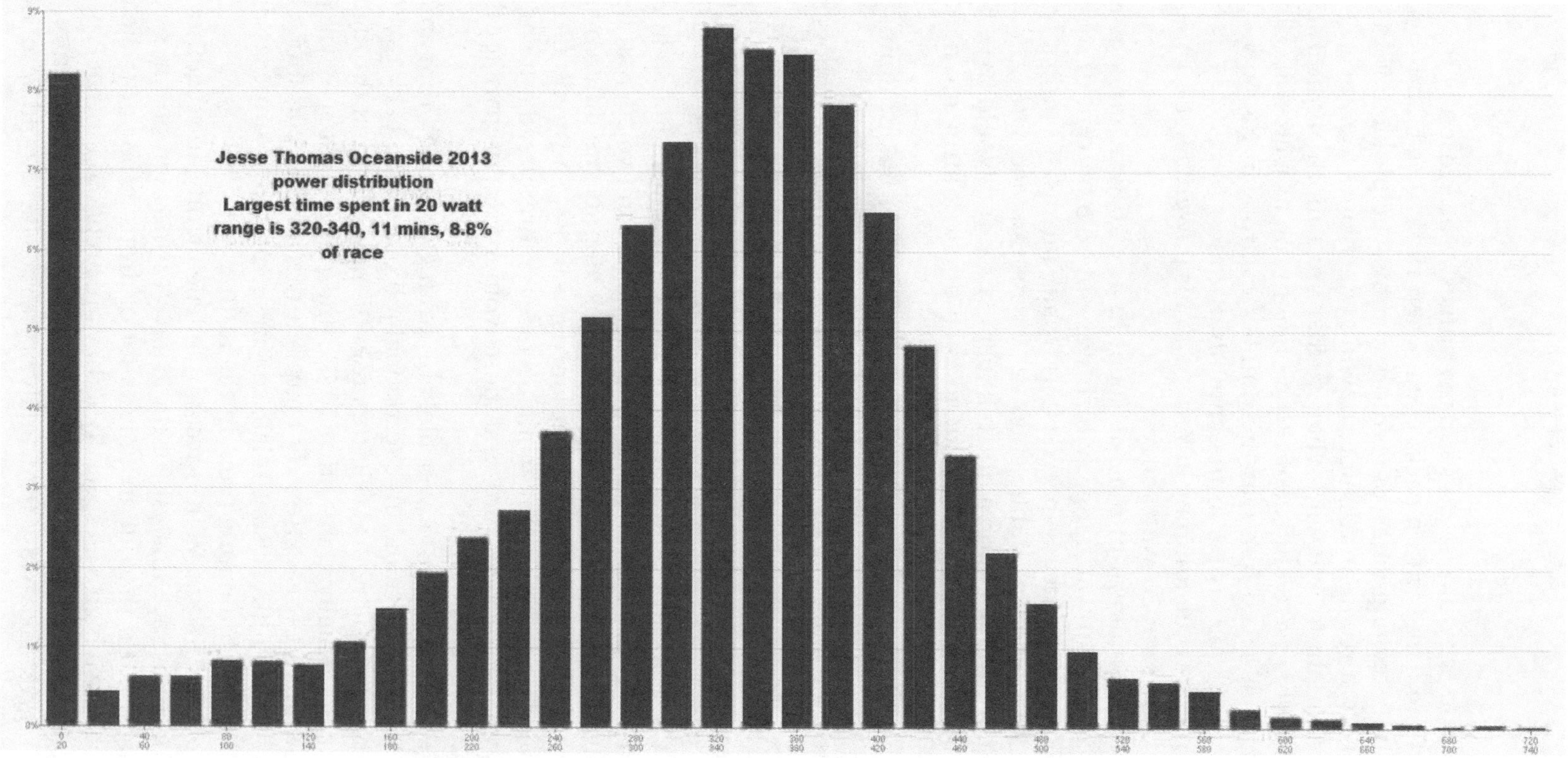
Jesse Thomas Oceanside 2013
power distribution
Largest time spent in 20 watt
range is 320-340, 11 mins, 8.8%
of race

FIGURE 14.6 Distribution of power in 20-watt ranges.

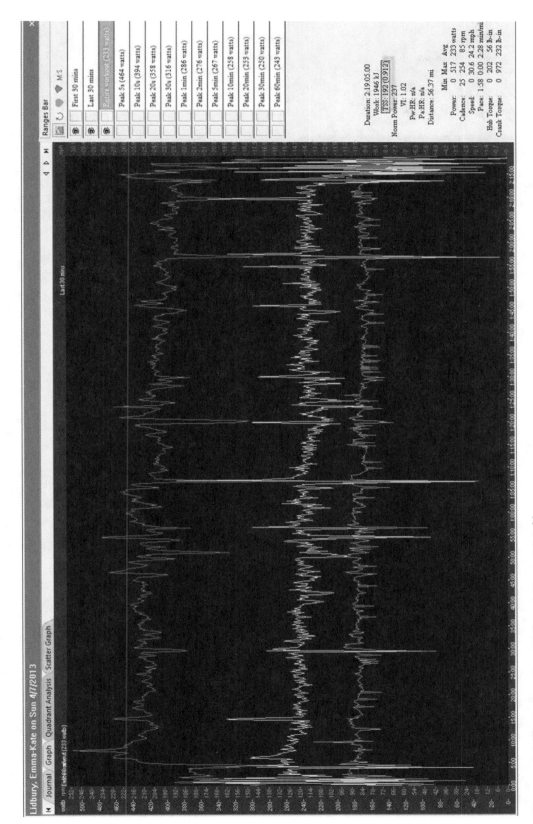

FIGURE 14.7 Emma-Kate Lidbury's Texas 70.3 file.

183

FIGURE 14.8 Unlike Jesse's short time in many different watt ranges, Emma-Kate spends nearly two-thirds of the race in two 20-watt ranges.

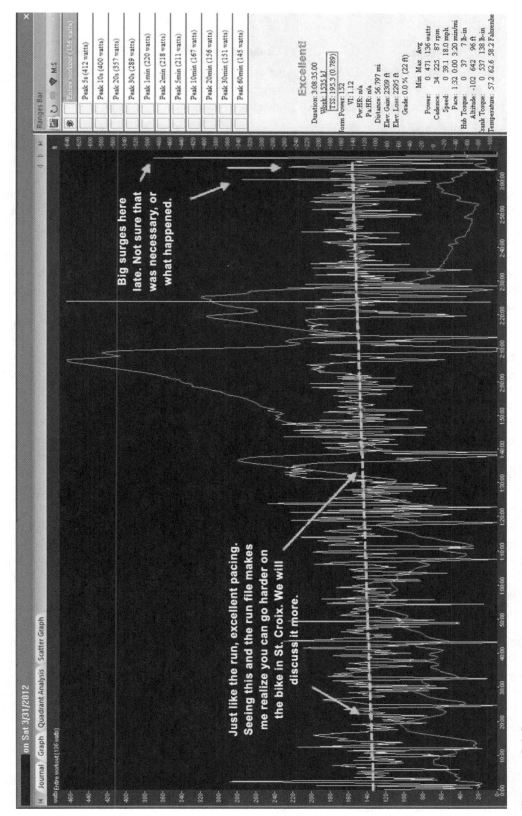

FIGURE 14.9 An older athlete's power file.

continue to tweak what you're doing, but you're on the right path. If it didn't, you need to review the previous plan and compare that with the specifics of the race dynamics you see in the power files to make the changes to get you to the next level.

Quadrant Analysis

One of the common questions triathletes have is if their cadence choice is the correct one when riding. The answer to that question is as varied as the different events in triathlon alone. However, using quadrant analysis can give athletes and coaches a better idea of the right cadence and force relationship for their specific event or goals as well as their tendencies, strengths, and weaknesses.

But the information and data need to be specific to the athlete, so that the inferences made from the data will lead to better training and racing. Figure 14.10, a quadrant analysis graph, shows how the single data points of watts recorded in the ride are dispersed throughout the screen, based on two factors, cadence and force. The quadrant analysis has cadence on the bottom (circumferential pedal velocity, or CPV), measured in meters per second (m/s), and force on the left (average effective pedal force, or AEPF), measured in newtons (N). Don't worry as much about the units; the concept is still the same that it is the speed of your rpm and how hard you press on the pedals. The threshold wattage of the athlete is the curved line going through the center, set in the user settings for the athlete. Four quadrants (I, II, III, and IV) each represent a relationship with cadence and force.

QI, the top-right quadrant on the graph, represents the highest force and highest cadence outputs. All of QI is above threshold, so it makes sense that these are hard, sprintlike efforts, or close to it. This is certainly *not* a quadrant an athlete could expect to ride in for very long in a long-course triathlon.

QII, the top-left quadrant, correlates to slower cadence but high force outputs. This is very much a slow, masher-of-the-pedals quadrant.

QIII, the bottom-left quadrant, correlates to slower cadence and lower force. Any light pedaling or coasting would appear in this quadrant.

QIV, the bottom-right quadrant, correlates to higher-cadence, lower-force pedaling. One would expect that an athlete who rides at a high cadence is likely to have a lot of samples in this quadrant, due to the high rpm.

You're probably wondering what quadrant you should be in. It depends on a number of factors, from goals to training and performance history, but one of the best things you can do is to simply look at the quadrant analysis graph and see how your power data samples distribute on it. Are you a masher in QII? A high spinner in QIV? Or are your data perfectly clustered at the middle? Once you recognize your tendencies, you can begin to understand more about your strengths and weaknesses.

Did your race-specific training sessions actually match up in the quadrant analysis distribution your files show? Meaning, do you train as a high-cadence spinner in QIV a lot but then on race day become a masher, with a lot of QII?

If you're training for an event that has a lot of steep inclines, are you really preparing specifically for the big-gear outputs you'll likely encounter on a course like that?

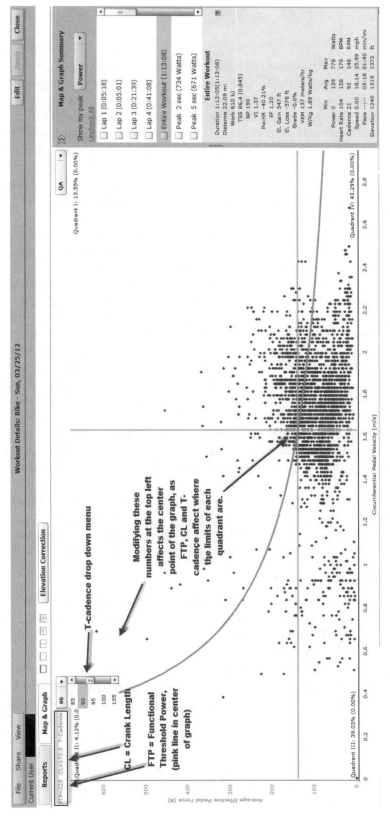

Figure 14.10 A quadrant analysis graph showing how the single data points of watts recorded in your ride are dispersed throughout the screen, based on cadence and force.

It's important that athletes set this graph up properly, in order to keep the information accurate for analysis. One of the ways to do this is to make sure your bike equipment is set correctly, because the bike you ride makes a difference. You should be sure to include the measurement of the crank arms (likely from 165 to 175mm). The crank length (CL) is important, because this is the lever you use to apply force. Longer levers may allow athletes to push with more force, but they tend to move slower than shorter levers. Longer levers also require a greater arch speed at the pedal than shorter levers, for a given cadence. Arch speed is the time it takes for the end of the crank to travel the same distance around the center, compared to the end of a shorter crank lever.

The other main setting that needs to be addressed for this chart is the athlete's threshold cadence (T-cadence). This is simply the cadence that the athlete rides at when riding at threshold. This is an important setting because it helps set the basis of the neurological cost of cadence for the athlete. For example, if during a 40K TT you tend to ride at 100 rpm, and another athlete does it at 90 rpm, a cadence of 95 rpm is a below-threshold effort for you but above threshold for the other athlete.

If you are unsure what your cadence tends to be when you ride or race at threshold, you can review a 40K TT you did either in an Olympic-distance triathlon or stand-alone TT. If you don't have one of those, just review some workouts where you did threshold intervals and see what the average cadence was for *all* the intervals you did at that intensity. Finally, be sure that your functional threshold power (FTP) is up to date.

When you manipulate these values (FTP, CL, and T-cadence), it moves the center point of the graph. Since most of the samples in the graph tend to be centralized, a small shift in a certain direction can dramatically change the distribution of the samples in the quadrants.

In the next chapter, we do a postseason analysis and use the quadrant analysis more to show how you can use it to become better at racing, training specifically and determining the best cadence for you. In the meantime, assessing how you rode the race compared to your preparation for the race is vital information to consider.

Cadence Fade Versus Power Fade

I have studied several elite Ironman triathletes and tried to answer the same question you likely have about finding the proper cadence. Using race files, I have tried to see if there is any clear indication when an athlete rode in too low or high a gear.

Table 14.2 is a measurement tool I created to determine whether an athlete pushed too hard in terms of too low a gear versus too high, or if they did it just right. I isolate the first hour and last hour of an Ironman bike to see how the effort fatigued the athlete. I compare the average cadence and the normalized power for those two hours and calculate the percentage lost or gained. This also highlights good or poor pacing, but when compared with bFTP, it should be easy to determine if the early pacing was too fast.

In table 14.2, you can see how Luke McKenzie rode at three cadences and what it meant for his performances at the Ironman World Championships in each of the three years. Though this is a small sample size, you can see that as he raised his cadence

TABLE 14.2 Luke McKenzie Cadence Fade Versus Power Fade

Athlete	Race	Place	Year	Cadence hour 1	NP	Cadence last hour	NP	Cadence fade %	Power fade %
Luke McKenzie	Kona	24	2012	77	306	68	239	13.24%	28.03%
Luke McKenzie	Kona	9	2011	87	278	80	247	8.75%	12.55%
Luke McKenzie	Kona	2	2013	94	290	89	279	5.62%	3.94%

and trained to be able to ride at a higher cadence, his finish in the race improved, and his fade percentages improved as well, showing less of a drop in cadence and power.

So if you're looking at your race files and wondering if your cadence is where it should be, then this fade measurement can help you to better determine if your chosen cadence is the right one for you or if you simply need to better train it.

A general rule for judging the performance of an Ironman ride is that the total fade percentage for both cadence and power should not exceed 20 percent . If an athlete has 3 percent cadence fade but 16 percent power fade, I would still classify that as a good to excellent ride (see table 14.3).

Pacing will have a lot to do with this, but it is good for athletes to consider and see what their tendencies are and how their cadence and power fades rank on this chart.

What about 70.3 distance? Great question. When we look at 70.3 distance, we compare the first and last 30 minutes of the bike split, for average cadence and normalized power. The numbers are a little leaner, because the event is half as long, so the fades shouldn't be as great (see table 14.4).

It should be noted that no change or even a negative percentage change in cadence fade (meaning the cadence actually got higher in the last 30 minutes than in the first) is not that uncommon in a 70.3, since the race is shorter and courses can sometimes be a big factor in the cadence, with a long, moderate descent or tailwind possibly affecting performance.

A general rule for judging the performance of a 70.3 ride is that the total fade percentage for both cadence and power should not exceed 13 percent. The reason the fade percentages aren't exactly half for this race is because the 70.3 is a much more intense race than a full Ironman.

TABLE 14.3 Recommended Cadence Fade and Power Fade Ranges for Ironman Performance Analysis

Ironman	Cadence fade %	Power fade %
Excellent	0–5%	0–7%
Good	5–8%	7–15%
Needs improvement	8–12%	15–20%
Poor	12+%	20+%

TABLE 14.4 Recommended Cadence Fade and Power Fade Ranges for 70.3 Performance Analysis

70.3	Cadence fade %	Power fade %
Excellent	0–3%	0–4%
Good	4–5%	5–8%
Needs improvement	6–7%	9–14%
Poor	8+%	14+%

When athletes ride at a very low cadence, 70 rpm and below, it requires a lot of force on the pedal. High force outputs require a lot more recruitment of fast-twitch muscle fibers, which won't last very long. The lower the gear, the more force required and the more fast-twitch fiber recruitment.

Even though long-course triathlon is considered an aerobic sport, these athletes are still going quite hard, so four to five hours of high force is something that is extremely taxing, and likely an athlete can't hold it. The amount of drop-off in force production can signal a cadence that is possibly too low.

The opposite can also be true because too high a cadence recruits a lot of fast-twitch muscle fibers as well because the speed of the movement is so high it's difficult to do with slow-twitch fibers.

Look at your cadence fade versus power fade, comparing what you see on race day to your race-specific training sessions. If you're racing at a cadence you don't train at, that's not specific enough training, and you're likely seeing a big cadence fade versus power fade value. Also, if you begin to track this from your past race files, and future files, you'll likely assess where your best cadence range is. More of this is discussed in chapter 15, Postseason Analysis, especially looking at Luke McKenzie and what he did in his postseason analysis and race analysis to make changes to become a podium finisher at the Ironman World Championships.

RUN PERFORMANCE

Remember, we have a goal TSS for a very specific reason: to leave enough gas in your tank to run as well as you can. Use the bike to set up the run.

If the run did not go either how you wanted or expected, how did your bike TSS factor into this? If your TSS is fine, how did you get to that number? Was the pace too hard early and you slowed considerably late? If you had a great run, what do the numbers tell you?

If your run did not go how you wanted or expected, and TSS doesn't appear to have been the main factor, then the next step is to look at VI from the bike. Were there too many early surges? Were there too many surges overall, throughout the bike? Remember, surges can be in response to another athlete, such as passing, or to overcome terrain.

Did you run the first mile 5 percent faster than your goal pace for the event? Was your goal pace realistic, given the course and your training? What metrics did you see in your training that made you feel you could run that pace?

What external factors on race day had an effect on your run split? The hottest part of the day is usually in the afternoon, when athletes are on the run course. Was it hotter than expected when you were on the run course? Was it windier than expected on the run course?

You have to look at the metrics from the power meter and your run training independently and combined and factor in external conditions.

Finally, did you execute your nutrition plan to support the run performance you wanted? More on that shortly.

FLEXIBILITY

We've spent a lot of time talking about the importance of flexibility with your estimated bike time. This is the main reason for creating ranges with your goal time. So were you flexible on race day? Flexibility is the art of racing, being able to adjust on the fly as you're reading the race.

If your training was specific to your needs and your estimated bike split, you ultimately asked more from your body than you have ever asked before; you were asking it to perform better than it ever has before.

Did you adjust your race plan as the race progressed throughout the day? Did you adjust your strategy on the fly due to unexpected conditions such as a hotter or windier day? Did you adjust your strategy if you simply were not able to generate the power output that you wanted? Did you adjust your strategy if you were stronger than you thought you would be on race day?

How did your nutrition play a role in your flexibility? Did your nutrition plan work? Was there a good mixture of solid foods and liquid calories? Did you have gastrointestinal issues during the race? If you did, what affect did that have on your ability to stick to your plan? What were some of the potential causes? Concentration of the nutrition? Too much solid food? Not enough?

SUMMARY

This chapter has shown you that racing is an art and a science. You have to consider the variables you can control such as pacing, nutrition, NP, TSS, and VI, and the external variables you cannot control, such as weather.

First look at them independently. How did these affect your race? Then bring them all together and look at the whole picture. Did the numbers match up to your strengths as an athlete? Was your training specific to the race plan? What could have been different with your training that would have supported the race plan? What are your weaknesses that you need to work on?

What can all this tell you about future races that will match your strengths? If your run struggles at a high VI value at a race, that is great information to have for choosing future races. Perhaps you'll find that the opposite is actually true. This will guide you in laying out your training for a high VI race and develop a goal race time and strategy for it.

How well did you handle the TSS? Did you train for a specific TSS, and did you execute that TSS on race day? How did it affect your run? Did it give you the run and the overall result you wanted? Use this information to adjust your training for future races.

You also need to look at how flexible you were on race day. Were you able to make adjustments on the fly, or did you refuse to make adjustments because you stuck to the plan no matter what? Learn from each race and see where you made good adjustments and where you could have made better adjustments. Go back and adjust your plans for the future, based on what you learned from this race, so you can be confident in races that if you make a choice to change the plan, you're making a smart decision.

When you use science to make yourself a better artist, you are doing everything you can to put yourself in the best position possible to have a great race every time.

15 POSTSEASON ANALYSIS

Without reflection, we go blindly on our way, creating more unintended consequences, and failing to achieve anything useful.

Margaret J. Wheatley, American writer
and management consultant

Once the season is over, it's time to pause and review how the year went from a training and racing perspective. If you've been collecting data from the season, the things you can learn about your training approach and decisions can be the most important lessons of all. After all, if you're going to make the next breakthrough in your training and racing, you will at some point have to change what you do in your approach. It is highly unlikely that the approach and training decisions you are making now will always work and take you to the peak of your potential. If they do, you've become the first person with the perfect plan.

IMPORTANT QUESTIONS FOR NEXT SEASON'S TRAINING

You need to ask yourself some questions at the end of every season so you can better plan and adjust your training accordingly for the next season. Here are those questions.

What was your peak bike CTL?

Once you find the value, divide your bFTP by this value and then compare it with past seasons to see if you really saw the improvement you wanted to see.

If you were at a much higher ratio but saw little improvement, then the type of training you're doing is probably in need of change. If your cycling was better this year, whether higher or lower in ratio, you know you've likely made some great training decisions.

What was your peak run CTL?

Much like you did with your bike CTL, now take this peak value and divide your rFTP in kph by this number and compare with past seasons. Do you feel this value could be higher? Is it necessary for it to be higher? Were you faster than in other seasons?

How much did CTL raise in the base phase?

From the end of the preparation phase to the completion of the base phase, how much did your CTL rise for bike, for the run, and combined, by actual number and percentage per week? This will really help you identify times when maybe you pushed too hard with a big jump in training stress. It also helps with planning for the following season.

How much did CTL raise in the build phase?

Follow the same process as just mentioned, but begin from the end of the base phase. Determine the percentage of CTL gained per week, or per training cycle, and review how you responded to that.

What were the specific metrics you identified as important to your training and preparation, and did they improve with your training?

Go back and look at the trend of the specific metrics you identified in the different parts of the year as important to your goals and determine if the training decisions you made actually had them improve continuously and steadily. Did you see the race-specific metrics show a cluster of top 10 performances for the season in the days and weeks leading up to the goal event?

Look at your mean max power curve and pace curve and see how those metrics performed relative to other seasons or all seasons past. Look at the weekly average watts or average pace through the season and see if you saw the improvement you wanted to see.

Review your P30 by week for the season. I've never seen an athlete who showed steady, continuous improvement in this chart not have a fantastic season. For many samples, even if there is a dip, as the training gets specific to long-course triathlon, the positive trend should still be there.

What was the peak CTL value for your combined PMC?

Take this value and compare with seasons past and how far out you were from your goal event when you achieved it. Could it have been closer to the peak event? Should it have been achieved further out, allowing for more rest and taper?

How much CTL did you lose from your peak CTL values by race day?

This shows how well you held the fitness from your peak, through your taper period. Go back and use table 11.1 from chapter 11, Tapering and Peaking, to see if the taper approach you had worked.

What were the training stress balance (TSB) values on race day for you at the goal events?

What was it for bike, run, and bike and run combined? How did you feel you performed with these values? Should they have been higher? Should they have been lower? This is really where you begin to see where you may need more bike training in your taper, or less running, or wherever you felt could have performed better, in order to stay sharper for race day. You may find your swim needs more attention too.

What were the lowest TSB values achieved for the season?

We are looking for a TSB floor where we can find a training stress load that is just too much, relative to your fitness. This floor usually represents sickness, injury, or very poor training following, due to the load being too much.

Look at the quality of the training prior to and following this TSB value. It might be that you handled it fine. It might be that you got sick or injured in the days following, or suddenly there was a decline or clear plateau in the specific metrics you were focused on improving. Once you know this number, it can be really helpful for avoiding injury and illness from breakdown in the seasons ahead.

You might ask yourself the following questions:

- Based on what I am seeing, did I have a tendency to push myself too hard?
- Did I not push hard enough?
- Did I lack the consistency needed to make the jump in performance I am looking for?

Answer those questions truthfully, and you'll likely find yourself improving quite a bit.

ANALYZING A PERFORMANCE MANAGEMENT CHART (PMC) FOR THE SEASON

I think one of the best ways you can learn to analyze your season as a whole is to look at some examples of what you have done in the past to see how you can use the charts and data to learn from that and guide future training decisions. Here are some PMC analyses I have put together.

PMC ANALYSIS 1—PREDICTING INJURY

Figure 15.1 is a PMC for an athlete who got hurt a few years ago and unfortunately was not able to start his Ironman event. Any time you work with an athlete, you're dealing with a unique experiment of one. You can bring experience from other athletes and training philosophies, but in the end, no two athletes are the same.

Figure 15.1 helps illustrate why review of a season, the training approach and decisions made, is more powerful and effective when used with data. This athlete got injured, and I wondered what the trigger might have been. Was there a mistake I made in planning, or he made in possibly not following the plan, that we can learn from for doing better training next time?

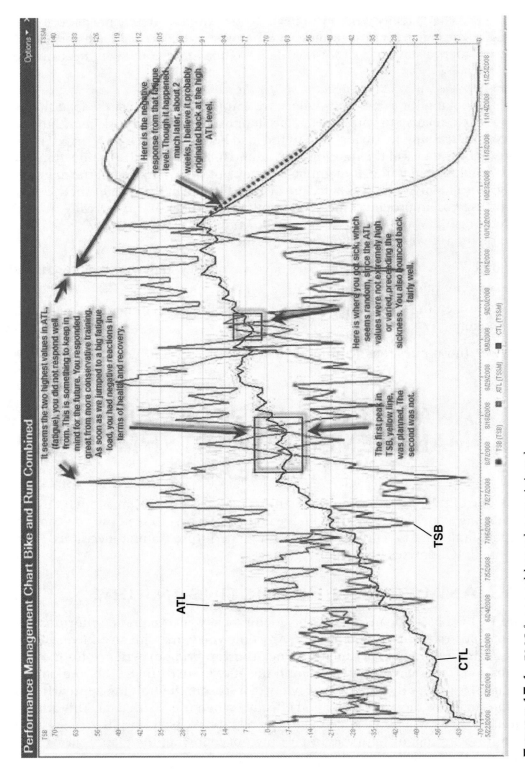

FIGURE 15.1 PMC for an athlete who was injured.

In figure 15.1, you can see that I identified two instances where acute training load (ATL) shows a very large jump, and in the first instance, TSB reaches a -65 value, followed not much later by an injury. It would appear from this that the TSB floor value should be higher than -65 in the future.

Also, the two large jumps in ATL were about 21 percent to 25 percent higher than the peak before them, one week before. This leads me to believe that this jump was too great for the athlete to handle, and TSS should not increase that much next time.

There's another moment identified in figure 15.1 where the athlete is sick, but I point out that it seems random, since it is not preceded by any large changes in TSB or ATL. Not everything is cause and effect just because it correlates, but it is just as powerful to know things are not related as it is to know they are.

PMC ANALYSIS 2—ANALYZING TRAINING LEVEL ACHIEVED

I coached a very talented collegiate triathlete who was an impressive swimmer and rider. He committed to the training data, and we prepared for the USA Triathlon Collegiate National Championships, which is an Olympic-distance competition.

Figure 15.2 shows his PMC for bike and run training coming into the event.

In this figure, you can see he reached a peak CTL of 45.7 and did his race at +1.7 TSB, losing only 8 percent of his CTL. These are pretty good numbers, and he went on to set the bike course record at the event, coming off the bike in first place and holding on for a great finish.

Some might think this CTL isn't very high for bike and run, and that is correct. But this athlete didn't start training until a few months before the event, which was only an Olympic-distance race, not long course, and he was injury prone. This meant we had to be conservative, and the plan worked to maximize the training he put in.

PMC ANALYSIS 3—ANALYZING TRAINING SUCCESS

The PMC in figure 15.3 shows this athlete's run training. As she reaches the peak before the 70.3, in a four-week span she has seen a number of top 10 peak pace performances in training for a number of time ranges. Even though the training has been more specific to the 70.3, she is still seeing some best peak paces of the year for time intervals as low as 30 seconds to 1 minute. This happened at the same time the athlete saw top 10 peak performances for 6 minutes five times, 30 minutes six times, 60 minutes five times, and 90 minutes three times, with almost all of these ranges showing her best performance overall in that time frame.

This athlete's confidence was soaring after seeing this success, and the race performance showed it for her.

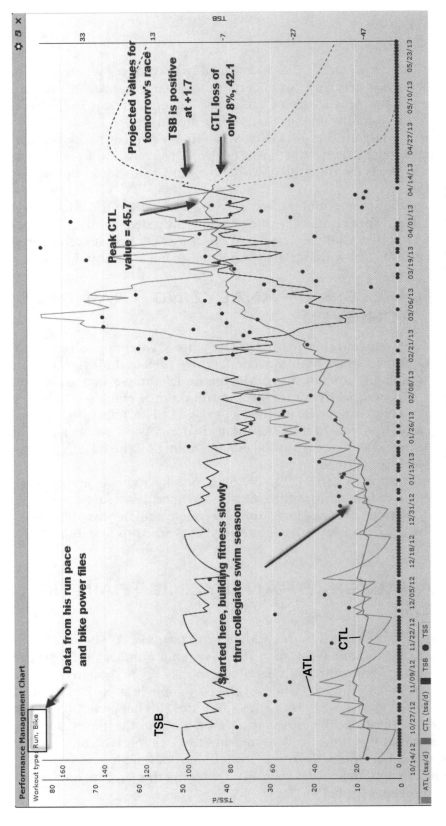

FIGURE 15.2 PMC for bike and run training coming into USA Triathlon Collegiate National Championships.

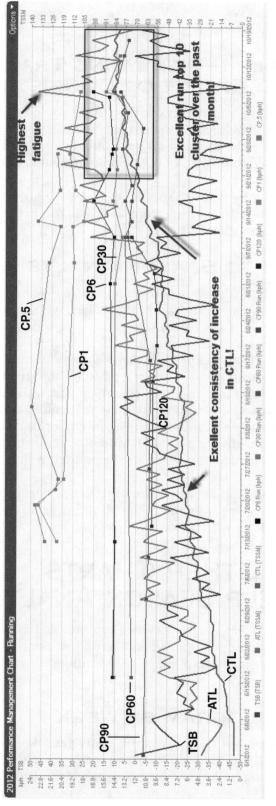

FIGURE 15.3 PMC for running, showing the successful training response of key peak run metric values seen in the days leading up to competition.

PMC Analysis 4—Analyzing Training Success and Effect of Consistency

If you've really done things right with your training, you'll see a PMC like figure 15.4, where the athlete has a huge cluster of peak paces in the last six weeks before tapering and heading into the race, for all peak intervals tracked. This shows how fit the athlete is compared to the rest of the year and how the consistency of training paid off for the athlete.

So when looking at a long period like that, one can see how fitness really came into form and compare it with training from the past. You can even use a PMC to compare seasons to one another.

PMC Season-to-Season Analysis

Here are a few examples of season-to-season or multiple-season comparisons and how you can directly compare one season to another, within the PMC.

Figure 15.5 is from a short-course athlete, looking at shorter intervals, but you can see the athlete is night-and-day better in 2012. This type of clarity in the results and comparison to the season before help the athlete stay motivated, build confidence in the training plan, and provide clear feedback about the training decisions.

The PMC in figure 15.6 compares three seasons for the athlete and helps show the ups and downs of fitness and how the athlete responded, including the recent period on the right showing a trend of top peak power outputs for the three-year period. This helps give the athlete a ton of confidence about how things are going and helps the athlete recognize how he or she responded well to the training decisions in that period.

Figure 15.7 is a run PMC that shows the athlete's performances over a period of more than four years to see how the athlete is doing relative to the entire time he or she has been working with a coach.

Other Charts to Help Season Analysis

There are a number of other charts besides the PMC that can help with season analysis and season-to-season comparisons. The following are a few I have found to be successful in analyzing athlete response to training throughout the year and from years past.

Watts per Kilogram by Week

Figure 15.8 is a periodic chart that shows the watts per kilogram by week for an athlete who was coaching himself and came to me to review his season. You can see the athlete had a good buildup of fitness through the first part of the season, then took two weeks off for downtime and transition period, and after that trained

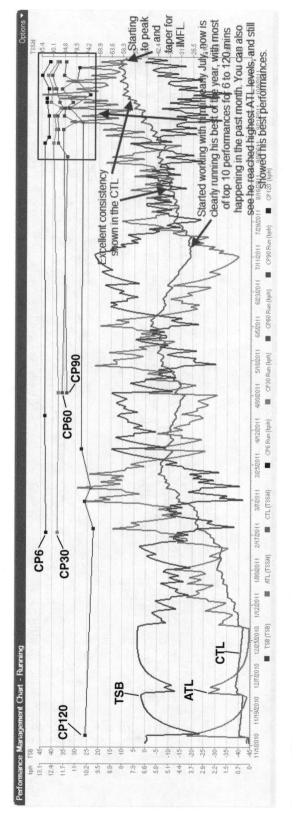

FIGURE 15.4 PMC for running, with the athlete's consistency in training showing many top 10 performances before the taper for Iron-man Florida.

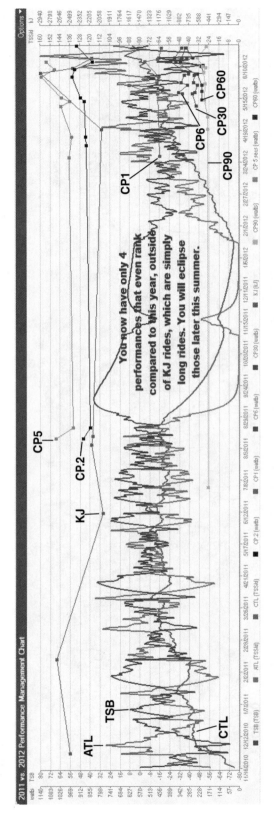

FIGURE 15.5 PMC for cycling, comparing two seasons and how the training response was from season to season.

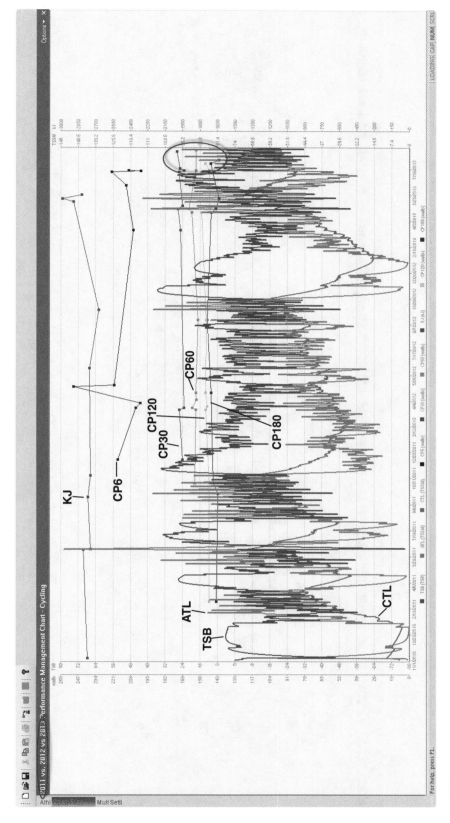

FIGURE 15.6 PMC for cycling comparing three seasons, 2011, 2012, and 2013, and highlighting how the training response was much better in 2013 than in the prior two seasons.

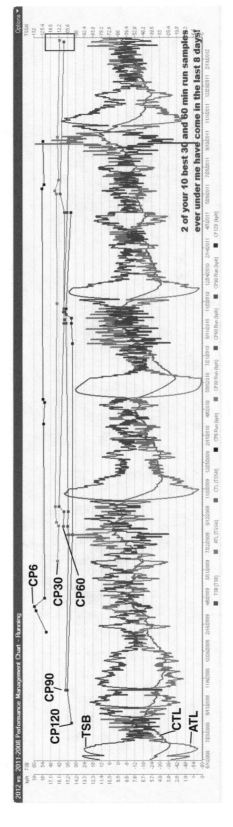

FIGURE 15.7 PMC for running comparing the past four seasons, and how recent performances compare to those in the past.

randomly with no direction or clear event to peak for. He was frustrated he couldn't continue the improvement, but he learned and saw the importance of training with purpose just by looking at this summary of his season.

TSS PER WEEK FOR SEASON

The athlete in figure 15.9 was training for an Ironman on his own, and completed the race in April, before starting with me immediately following for another Ironman in November. The athlete pushed himself very hard, and it took some time for me to convince him we were training plenty because he felt we should have done more.

Training on his own, two weeks before his April Ironman race, his TSS total for the week was over 1,300. Under me, he never went above 1,100 in a week and only five times went over 1,000 TSS total in a week. The athlete finished more than an hour faster in November than in the race on the same course in April. This helped to prove that the athlete didn't need as much volume to do well.

PEAK POWER BY TRAINING PHASE

Monitoring the peak power outputs for the different phases of training can really help an athlete and coach see if the training response went as planned. Figure 15.10a shows how this athlete prepared for the Ironman in November and the different peak outputs through each phase of training. This progression of the metrics most specific to Ironman racing, P180 in the build phase, should improve through each phase and show an overall peak during the race. This athlete saw his best 60-, 90-, and 180-minute power outputs for the year happen during the race.

You can see it's very similar for this athlete in Figure 15.10b. He didn't do any three-hour rides in the peak phase, instead waiting for race day. He hit his best outputs for the entire spectrum, from one minute to three hours, on race day.

In figure 15.10c, we take this same type of chart for a different athlete and compare the athlete's current season to his past season, as he progresses toward his June Ironman event, after coming from a short-course racing season the year before.

AP PER WEEK FOR SEASON

I started working with the athlete in figure 15.11a in July, and you can see the progress from when we started through the base phase. I highlight how he responded in figure 15.11, but what I wanted to know was whether we could keep that trend going. Is it realistic to expect continuous improvement?

Figure 15.11b shows that the athlete kept this trend up for 17 weeks, 3 weeks out from the goal event. This is what you want to see! Though not every single week was better than the week before it, the trend of improvement is very clear.

P30 PER WEEK FOR SEASON

In figure 15.12, we've tracked the peak 30-minute power output each week of the season and plotted it on the graph, following the trend. You'll notice a big drop

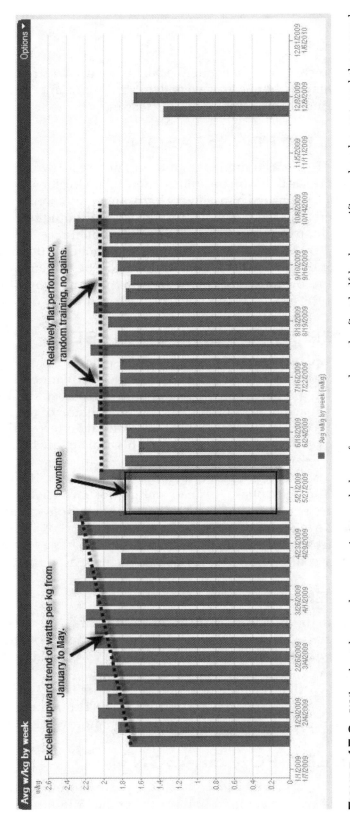

FIGURE 15.8 W/kg chart by week, comparing two halves of a season, where the first half had a specific goal and event, and the second half was random training, with no goal event.

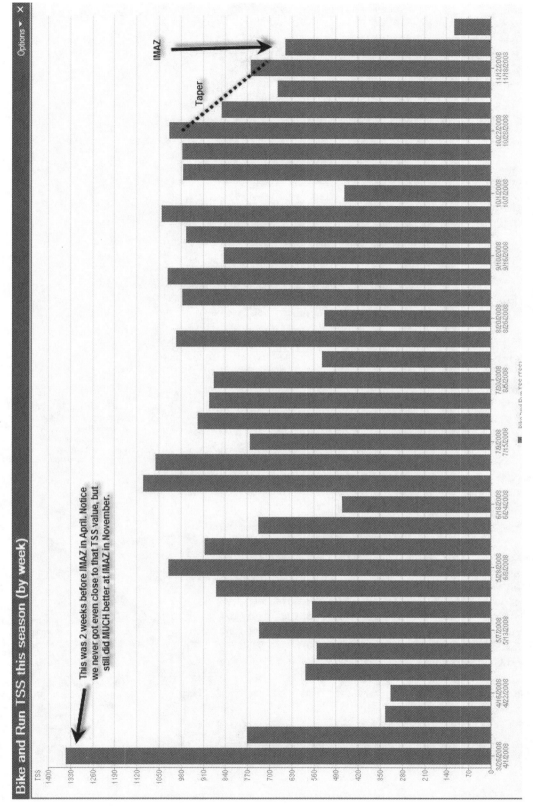

FIGURE 15.9 TSS per week for a season, for an athlete preparing coming off a spring Ironman, preparing for a fall Ironman.

Table a

Period or Ride Date	CP .2	CP 1	CP 6	CP 12	CP 30	CP 60	CP 90	CP 180	Graph It
Base 1 (max CP) Last Ride: 8/20/2008	436	300	266	254	246	205	162	0	☐
Base 2 (max CP) Last Ride: 9/8/2008	477	311	289	258	245	196	183	173	☐
Base 3 (max CP) Last Ride: 9/29/2008	475	353	318	252	247	208	193	175	☐
Build 1 (max CP) Last Ride: 10/20/2008	508	316	296	254	245	205	200	190	☐
Build 2 (max CP) Last Ride: 11/12/2008	456	282	230	227	203	198	194	183	☐
Peak (max CP) Last Ride: 11/23/2008	403	284	238	229	222	214	204	197	☐
Personal Best CP Values (all time)	508	353	318	258	247	214	204	197	☐
	10/11/08	9//08	9//08	9/5/08	9/26/08	11/23/08	11/23/08	11/23/08	

a

Table b

Period or Ride Date	CP .2	CP 1	CP 6	CP 12	CP 30	CP 60	CP 90	CP 180	Graph It
Preparation (max CP)	535	426	325	294	291	250	232	0	☐
Base 1 (max CP)	482	329	297	295	282	245	237	216	☐
Base 2 (max CP)	512	364	321	311	299	244	232	218	☐
Base 3 (max CP)	508	373	318	317	309	256	249	219	☐
Build 1 (max CP)	490	402	332	319	314	260	254	236	☐
Build 2 (max CP)	418	342	323	309	307	255	254	235	☐
Peak (max CP)	503	374	300	297	289	254	244	0	☐
Race (max CP)	411	290	257	255	253	248	245	238	☐
Personal Best CP Values (all time)	535	426	332	319	314	284	275	238	☐
	5/15/08	4/26/08	10/2/08	9/19/08	9/19/08	3/26/08	3/26/08	11/23/08	

b

Table c

Period or Ride Date	CP .2	CP 1	CP 6	CP 12	CP 30	CP 60	CP 90	CP 180	Graph It
Base 1 (max CP) Last Ride: 1/29/2008	466	310	235	215	198	169	0	0	☐
Base 2 (max CP) Last Ride: 3/1/2008	782	431	262	245	204	186	178	0	☐
Base 3 (max CP) Last Ride: 3/24/2008	232	229	223	222	214	171	161	0	☐
Build 1 (max CP) Last Ride: 4/24/2008	630	330	255	250	229	207	166	159	☐
Build 2 (max CP) Last Ride: 4/30/2008	620	350	253	237	209	181	173	0	☐
Peak (max CP) Last Ride: 5/12/2008	433	364	255	242	196	163	157	0	☐
Race (max CP) Last Ride: 5/20/2008	160	155	147	146	136	0	0	0	☐
Transition (max CP) Last Ride: 6/15/2008	520	290	242	228	217	0	0	0	☐
Race (max CP) Last Ride: 6/22/2008	523	327	245	222	176	160	158	0	☐
Build 1 (max CP) Last Ride: 7/7/2008	493	345	248	242	192	172	155	0	☐
Peak (max CP) Last Ride: 7/20/2008	532	352	265	233	213	188	165	142	☐
Race (max CP) Last Ride: 7/26/2008	448	371	242	229	215	0	0	0	☐
Build 2 (max CP) Last Ride: 7/29/2008	795	373	253	223	198	191	185	0	☐
Peak (max CP) Last Ride: 8/10/2008	522	334	244	232	219	217	214	0	☐
Race (max CP) Last Ride: 9/7/2008	480	402	245	216	201	176	170	0	☐
Base 2 (max CP) Last Ride: 9/15/2008	513	358	247	204	174	166	0	0	☐
Base 3 (max CP) Last Ride: 10/25/2008	540	390	264	239	209	192	176	0	☐
Race (max CP) Last Ride: 10/27/2008	515	353	238	213	187	176	170	0	☐
Transition (max CP) Last Ride: 1/5/2009	629	357	254	247	223	190	177	0	☐
Preparation (max CP) Last Ride: 1/13/2009	147	142	137	134	113	106	0	0	☐
Base 1 (max CP) Last Ride: 2/11/2009	398	325	224	193	183	160	148	127	☐
Base 2 (max CP) Last Ride: 3/11/2009	557	327	272	260	212	189	169	143	☐
Base 3 (max CP) Last Ride: 4/6/2009	595	346	285	264	253	236	227	199	☐
Build 1 (max CP) Last Ride: 5/7/2009	520	372	252	239	206	177	166	149	☐
Personal Best CP Values (all time)	795	431	285	264	253	236	227	199	☐
	7/27/08	3/1/08	3/14/09	3/14/09	3/14/09	3/14/09	3/14/09	3/14/09	

Ramon, these are the power values for you for last season and this season, for all the data collected and uploaded. Might not include other rides, (Alcatraz last year). It has them broken into the phases, and shows what the best for each time interval in each phase was.

Last year

This year

CP180 value is most important for us, but 30, 60, and 90 help tell us as well about how you're doing. Your best ride ever was the one on March 14th, at the camp. Since then, you haven't been riding at that intensity, but we've backed off on purpose to focus on IMCDA specific intensities. And yet, you're still better in watts than before Arizona. Good signs!

c

FIGURE 15.10a–c Breakdown of the power outputs for different phases of the season, based on the periodization model and the different time intervals, for three different athletes.

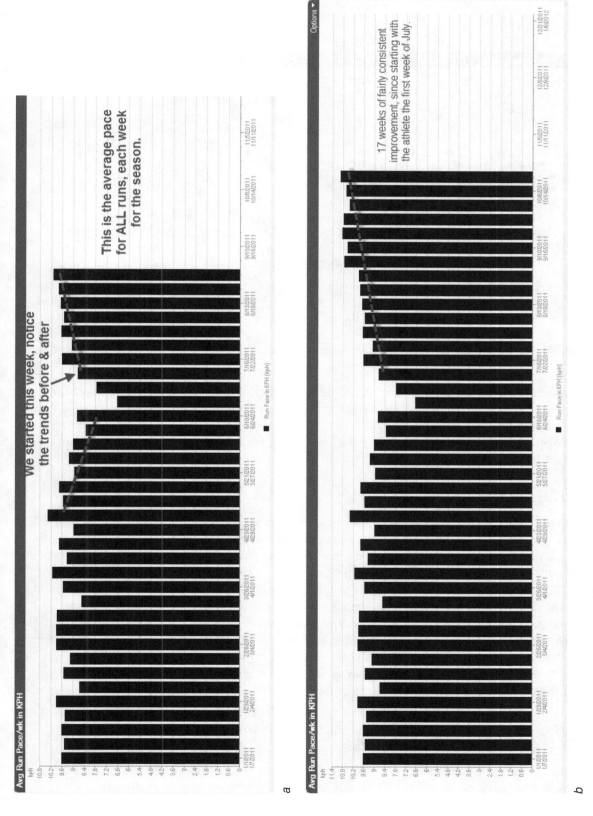

FIGURE 15.11 (*a*) The average pace for all runs in a week in the early part of the season; (*b*) further into the season.

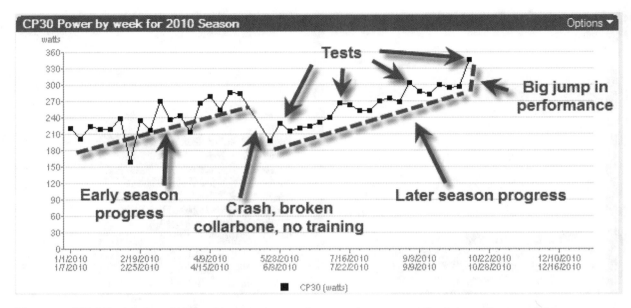

FIGURE 15.12   The peak 30-min watts by week, over the course of a season for an athlete.

and gap in the middle, where the athlete suffered a broken collar bone in a bike crash and yet was able to come back incredibly steady and test at 346 watts for a bFTP test before a key event.

You can also do the same thing with running, tracking the P30 pace, since there are a lot of 30-minute samples through a season.

SUMMARY CHARTS

Perhaps the best way to really see the improvement, or the need for it, is in a summary chart, where you can see the best performances for numerous time intervals, highlighting the best outputs for each week, and each month, one after the other. Figure 15.13a–b provides two examples.

Figure 15.13a shows the athlete improving in every area of fitness, for all time frames, which helps provide the coach and athlete with feedback that the training is clearly working. You will want to look back and see if you saw the improvement you wanted to see within the summary chart.

In figure 15.13b, the athlete is really focused on improving his run, as he preps for a 70.3 and Ironman season, so we are focused on improving his P60 (rFTP) outputs through the cold winter months and are tracking his progress and response to the training.

MEAN MAX CURVES

One of the great things about collecting data from training is the data always tell the same story, with the same details. Ask a friend about her best time or a great

Summary

Recent Weeks

Ending	Duration	Distance	Weight	HR	TSS	kJ	Peak 1w	Peak 5w	Peak 20w	Peak 60w	Peak 1' min/mi	Peak 5' min/mi	Peak 20' min/mi	Peak 60' min/mi
12/11/2011	8:42:30	71.79	175.0	140	438	2035	280	235	198	176	6:38	8:16	9:20	9:39
12/4/2011	8:02:12	53.39	175.0	125	338	1623	269	197	178	170	6:57	8:52	9:28	9:52
11/27/2011	8:56:45	72.11	175.0	144	312	1843	233	191	177	172	7:56	8:46	9:01	10:10
11/20/2011	7:18:11	57.22	175.0	145	230	863	171	142	137	131	8:07	9:02	9:25	0:00
11/13/2011	8:39:33	65.83	175.0		331	2147	200	195	192	137	9:45	9:45	9:45	0:00
11/6/2011	0:00:00	0.00	0.0		0		0	0	0		0:00	0:00	0:00	0:00

Recent Months

Month	Duration	Distance	Weight	HR	TSS	kJ	Peak 1w	Peak 5w	Peak 20w	Peak 60w	Peak 1' min/mi	Peak 5' min/mi	Peak 20' min/mi	Peak 60' min/mi
Dec-2011	13:44:41	119.26	175.0	134	685	3006	280	235	198	176	6:38	8:16	9:20	9:39
Nov-2011	27:54:30	201.09	175.0	145	966	5505	233	195	192	172	7:56	8:46	9:01	10:10
Oct-2011	0:00:00	0.00	0.0		0	0	0	0	0	0	0:00	0:00	0:00	0:00
Sep-2011	0:00:00	0.00	0.0		0	0	0	0	0	0	0:00	0:00	0:00	0:00
Aug-2011	0:00:00	0.00	0.0		0	0	0	0	0	0				

With the lone exception of 20 min pace, everything is improving quite well. Great signs!

a

Summary

Recent Weeks

Ending	Duration	Distance	Weight	HR	TSS	kJ	Peak 1w	Peak 5w	Peak 20w	Peak 60w	Peak 1' min/mi	Peak 5' min/mi	Peak 20' min/mi	Peak 60' min/mi
2/8/2009	2:52:59	43.76	165.0	153	324	1305	250	225	210	203	6:31	6:40	6:44	0:00
2/1/2009	11:35:10	141.18	165.0	155	879	3724	428	279	241	220	5:58	6:21	6:30	6:38
1/25/2009	16:33:16	218.16	165.0	154	1065	6643	411	331	275	252	4:43	5:24	6:37	7:09
1/18/2009	11:45:11	157.53	165.0	88	799	4758	469	372	292	223	6:05	6:18	6:29	6:52
1/11/2009	9:55:35	98.40	165.0	141	544	2426	315	306	291	218	5:18	5:50	6:52	7:21
1/4/2009	7:41:44	100.48	165.0	114	489	2302	247	230	203	189	5:34	6:22	6:32	7:01

Recent Months

Month	Duration	Distance	Weight	HR	TSS	kJ	Peak 1w	Peak 5w	Peak 20w	Peak 60w	Peak 1' min/mi	Peak 5' min/mi	Peak 20' min/mi	Peak 60' min/mi
Feb-2009	5:02:16	65.62	165.0	156	527	1667	250	225	210	203	5:58	6:22	6:31	6:38
Jan-2009	52:24:13	647.73	165.0	128	3412	18199	469	372	292	252	4:43	5:21	6:29	6:52
Dec-2008	24:59:30	288.93	165.0	154	1793	9186	342	297	264	242	5:05	5:24	6:23	7:16
Nov-2008	19:31:01	209.76	165.0	88	1215	8394	597	334	288	278	5:36	6:01	6:23	10:59
Oct-2008	31:50:43	439.48	168.0	48	1816	15913	469	365	305	276	5:10	5:32	6:07	7:00
Sep-2008	48:46:57	725.98	165.0	1	2960	21276	363	320	305	257	5:33	6:08	6:39	6:55
Aug-2008	60:13:51	933.80	168.0	94	3318	28565	501	399	361	319	5:36	6:21	6:32	6:51
Jul-2008	29:44:12	530.64	165.0	99	1581	16619	543	406	299	275	5:34	5:51	6:00	7:01
Jun-2008	27:28:57	486.82	168.0	32	1529	16574	544	357	322	293	6:04	6:15	6:23	7:36
May-2008	28:20:50	498.65	165.0	127	1422	18185	440	377	338	290	6:04	6:23	6:31	7:21
Apr-2008	28:53:13	564.00	165.0	123	1402	21031	474	387	340	312	0:00	0:00	0:00	0:00
Mar-2008	34:59:52	691.55	168.0	137	1845	26055	498	352	320	289	0:00	0:00	0:00	0:00

b

FIGURE 15.13*a–b* Summary charts, showing the month to month improvement, and recent week-to-week improvements for the season.

season she had and the chances of her remembering and telling the story as accurately as she used to are slim. It's natural for athletes to embellish a bit. So a ride where an athlete averaged 290 watts might actually become 300 a few seasons or months after it, if left to the athlete telling the story. But if we refer back to past data, especially power and pace data, it will tell us the real story.

Athletes often get hung up on where their fitness is in a single moment. This is especially true after a few months of work back at training. Athletes can get impatient, wanting the fitness to get back to top form ASAP! They might even think they were much fitter last season than they are now, but is that really the case?

I hear many athletes ask questions like these:

- Where was I in my training and fitness last year at this time?
- How did my fitness look in the early months of that great season I had a few years ago?
- How am I doing right now with my fitness, compared to earlier this season?

With mean max curves, we can actually get a direct comparison of where fitness is right now compared to where it was at any other point in time, such as the exact moment last season. We can even compare this season to all seasons in the past from which we have data. We can do this with the mean max curve, for power or pace.

What is a mean max curve? It's a graph that plots out the best average performance for watts or pace over time. Time is represented on the x-axis (bottom horizontal line) and output of pace or watts on the y-axis (left vertical line).

The trend for the mean max curve for power will show it start high, then drop and flatten out. This is because we can hold higher output values for short periods, like 1 to 30 seconds, than we can for hours at a time.

The trend for the mean max curve for pace is usually the opposite, with a lower starting point that rises and plateaus (although some software programs will reverse this). This is because the faster paces are at the bottom, and again, we can only hold faster paces for shorter periods of time.

Figure 15.14 shows an athlete's mean max pace curve for the season. The dotted line represents the date range from the first half of the season, while the solid represents the second half. You can see certain time ranges where the performances were better or worse, comparatively.

Athletes can compare the off-season they're in now with the off-season from last year. The choices of what to compare are endless and can teach athletes and coaches a lot. Using these graphs to get a better sense of where athletes are at a point in time, compared with another point in time, is valuable for gaining confidence, recognizing weaknesses, and planning training.

Figure 15.14 shows how the athlete is performing in the build phase, training specifically for the 70.3 distance. This athlete is seeing much better peak values than in the first half of the season for anything from seven minutes to two hours.

The ability to compare time periods gives an idea of how the athlete is progressing compared to other seasons or even different parts of the current season. The fact you can do this for both power data and pace data is a valuable tool.

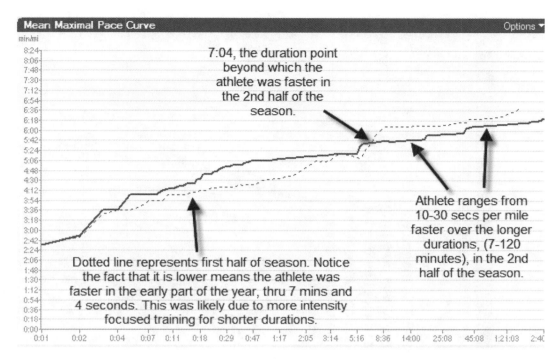

Mean Maximal Pace Curve   Options ▼

7:04, the duration point beyond which the athlete was faster in the 2nd half of the season.

Athlete ranges from 10-30 secs per mile faster over the longer durations, (7-120 minutes), in the 2nd half of the season.

Dotted line represents first half of season. Notice the fact that it is lower means the athlete was faster in the early part of the year, thru 7 mins and 4 seconds. This was likely due to more intensity focused training for shorter durations.

FIGURE 15.14 Mean max pace curve graph comparing the first and second half of a single season, for run paces over certain time intervals.

Figure 15.15 shows an athlete training through the winter who is already seeing power numbers as good as the entire year before from 25 seconds to 30 minutes. These data show that the attention to the speed skill and higher-intensity efforts during the winter are paying off quite well.

Figure 15.16 shows an older athlete who despite focusing solely on short durations of one minute or less for intensity, and easy longer rides, is seeing big improvements in both areas compared to his collection of all-time power data. Again, this is excellent feedback for the coach and him that the training is going well.

Those are some simple charts comparing general outputs, but what about season-to-season analysis of training? What about trying to figure out how much is enough?

RUN TRAINING ANALYSIS

How much should you run in training for Ironman? Maybe that's something you're wondering when you look at your past season and see the run training you did. It's a very common question, with the very common answer of, "it depends." It depends on goals and run ability, and it depends on what you've done in the past, but it is a great question to ask yourself. Experience is a great teacher, and the body tends to respond well to new stresses and fresh stimulus. So perhaps it doesn't matter how much you run but how you've done the run training in the past.

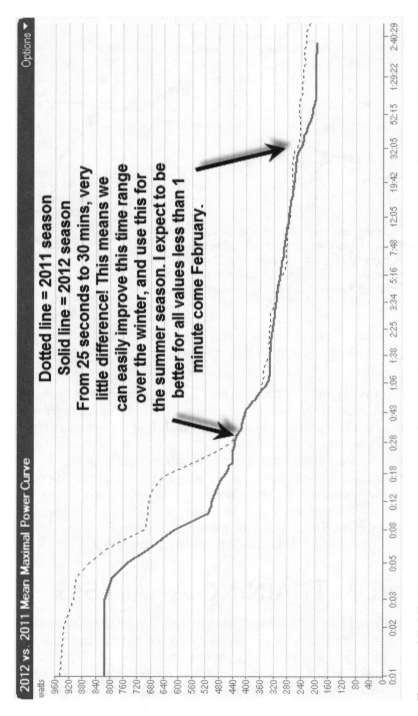

FIGURE 15.15 Mean max power curve graph comparing two winter seasons and the performance differences over certain time intervals.

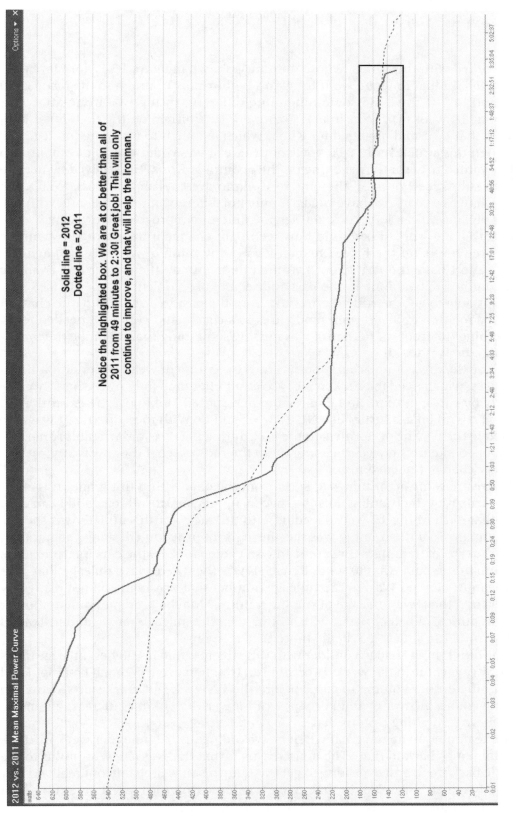

FIGURE 15.16 Mean max power curve graph comparing two seasons and an older athlete's performance differences.

I worked with the athlete whose training is shown in figure 15.17 for more than five years. In that time, he went from an 11-hour-plus Ironman to the results you see, and in 2012, we did something quite different, racing two Ironman events in about 14 weeks (Wisconsin and Cozumel). He finished on the podium at both events that year and qualified for Kona, which led me into planning for 2013.

When this athlete and I talked, we both agreed we would need a new approach if we wanted to accomplish getting on the podium in Kona. He believed he needed to run sub three hours off the bike in Kona to accomplish that goal. Well, after more than five years, we have tried a number of different approaches, and with five years of data we can look back and see the different approaches we've tried, what seems to have worked best, and how we might change it to accomplish running sub three hours off the bike. I had an idea in my mind of what we had actually done, and I have the PMCs, but I wanted to dive in a little deeper and examine the volume we had done in the past and see the bigger picture.

I was able to get the run volume data from the past five years into one chart. It showed me that I have certain tendencies as a coach, and perhaps I needed to try something different, or perhaps I was missing something that might be the breakthrough he was looking for.

Of course, this volume chart doesn't show execution or weather conditions from the races, which need to be taken into account rather than judging the performance strictly by run split time. So I dug further and started looking at the execution on race day, with bike statistics like NP, TSS, VI, and IF. With these metrics, I was able to isolate the way he performed on the bike during the race and what his run training looked like in the weeks leading up to the race to see if there was any pattern or clear change I needed to try.

There are some great things to learn from the data within this graph. It is absolutely true that the training must be specific to prepare the athlete, and I can confirm that each of the 12 weeks leading into the races for this athlete was specific to Ironman. So if the training was specific in its intensity and designed adaptation, then the type of training is consistent and isn't going to skew the data interpretation.

From this, what I want to see as a coach is whether there was a mileage that gave us the most benefit. Was there a mileage number that was high and not really any better than the lower mileage of specific training? Maybe I can pinpoint a number for this athlete, a bell curve in which I can keep the mileage range, and instead of doing more run miles, maybe do more bike or swim.

One other thing I had to consider with this athlete is that his highest mileage times have always come in the weeks preceding an Ironman event. What if I manipulated the timing of that volume to come before the 12-week-out mark starts? Now the athlete comes in strong, and perhaps I can lower the volume, increase intensity. Definitely something to consider.

Some might say he ran great when he was doing just 32 miles per week in 2008, so why not go back to that? The main reason is that this was a new stimulus to the athlete back then, and expecting to get the same result is probably not realistic. But certainly it is strong evidence that mileage volume isn't the biggest determinant of run performance in an Ironman, at least for this athlete.

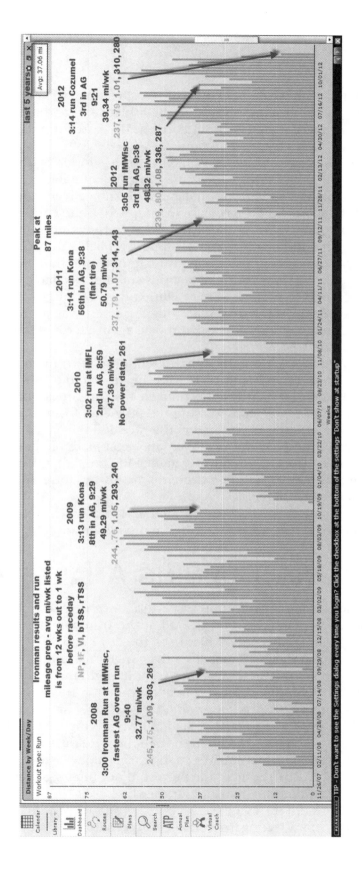

FIGURE 15.17 Run volume and race performance comparison over five seasons for an Ironman triathlete.

You can see that in 2011 we decided to do the most volume we had tried, thinking that would be the new training stimulus on the athlete and perhaps give him the breakthrough he needed. But that didn't happen. He flatted in the race at Kona, and still the run was not what we had hoped.

As some might suggest, running at Wisconsin or in Florida is not the same as running in Kona, and the performances may not be equitable, considering the conditions. This is always something that must be subjectively considered with analysis of the data, along with place in age group (AG), the course being favorable to an athlete's strengths or weaknesses, and even the mind-set of the athlete.

If you asked me, this athlete's best race all-time is probably Kona 2009, when he was eighth in his AG, against stellar competition in hot conditions. This takes into account all the subjective things and the fact this was a peak championship event. His next best performance was his 8:59 at Florida the year after (simply because of the significance of the 9:00 barrier), and his third best was probably Ironman Wisconsin in 2012, where he raced hard and well against a tough field, just missing a top 20 overall finish.

One colleague told me he thought VI mattered more in Ironman than even IF or TSS, but this athlete's two highest VIs were his fastest and third-fastest runs. Also TSS seems to have very little reflection on his run times because he runs either 3:13 to 3:14 or 3:00 to 3:05. Missing the bike data from Florida 2010 is a bummer because the unit malfunctioned in the race and the data are incomplete, and I didn't want to draw conclusions from an incomplete picture. So is it that this athlete handles courses that require a higher VI better than steady state, flat courses? That could be correct. Athlete strengths are always something to consider when choosing races and courses.

All of this is a lot of information to consider, and as a coach, reflection on the past is very important if you want to set the right path ahead.

CYCLING TRAINING ANALYSIS

In 2013, Luke McKenzie made a jump in performance that took him from just cracking the top 10 to placing second overall at the Ironman World Championship. I had studied some of his power files from the 2011 and 2012 races, and as I watched him compete at the 2013 race, I saw a change in his riding style that suddenly struck me and had me thinking about what it might mean for performance in other athletes. What was the change? It was his cadence. He went from an average cadence of 74 rpm in 2012 to 93 rpm in 2013. The fact he went from 24th in 2012 to 2nd in 2013 with such a change had me wondering if he had done some type of seasonal analysis that showed him the benefit of riding at a higher cadence.

It's fair to ask, was Luke McKenzie's change to a higher cadence (nearly 20 rpm more from 2012 to 2013) one of the biggest, if not the biggest, reason for his breakthrough race, both on the bike and for the run?

Before I go on to present the evidence, let me say I am not certain of this because there are so many factors affecting performance, especially preparation, conditions, race circumstances, decisions of competitors, and more. However, this change in riding style and performance was so great that it is unprecedented, and we must examine it closer, not just shrug it off as coincidence.

So let's look at the basic info for Luke's bike ride in 2011, compared with 2012 and 2013.

Table 15.1 provides the breakdown by quadrant for each year. His actual power file is shown in figure 15.18. Many would say 2011 was a higher-cadence year than 2012, and they would be right. However, looking at figure 15.18, you can see that even though his higher cadence gave him more time in Q4 (90 rpm or higher), he still had an average that was weighted heavily in Q3, and his average cadence for the whole ride was less than 90, at 86. His reduction of about 40 percent of his total ride time for 2013 in Q3 compared with 2011 and 2012 is incredible.

TABLE 15.1   Breakdown of the time spent in each quadrant during each of Luke McKenzie's cycling performances from 2011, 2012, and 2013 at the Ironman World Championships.

	Q1	Q2	Q3	Q4
Luke 2011	3.9%	18.9%	55.0%	22.2%
Luke 2012	0.1%	36.4%	58.5%	5.0%
Luke 2013	6.5%	7.4%	16.9%	69.2%

Perhaps in 2011 he rode too low still, and 86 rpm just wasn't high enough to see the advantages of the higher cadence. But let's look deeper and compare cadence fade to power fade, where we isolate the first hour and last hour of an Ironman bike to see how the effort fatigued the athlete. I compare the average cadence and the normalized power for those two hours and calculate the percentage lost or gained.

In table 15.2, I have sorted the years by place, with his worst finish, 2012, at the top; 2011 in the middle; and his best performance, 2013, at the bottom.

A few interesting correlations as finish place improves (albeit from a small sample size):

- Cadence was higher both in the first hour and last hour as place improves.
- The percentage loss of cadence fade is lower as cadence goes up, and place improves.
- The percentage loss of power is lower as cadence goes up.
- Run splits get faster as cadence goes up, and cadence fade goes down.
- IF goes up, but given the influence conditions can play on this, the data seem to lack any credibility.

Perhaps just as interesting is that TSS for each ride, NP for each ride, and VI for each ride show no statistical relevance.

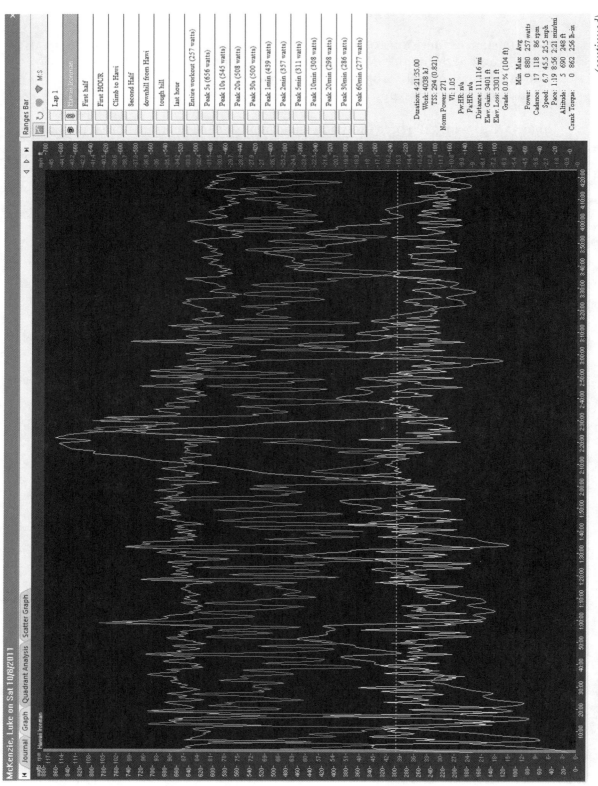

FIGURE 15.18a-c Luke McKenzie's power file from Ironman World Championship: (a) 2011.

(continued)

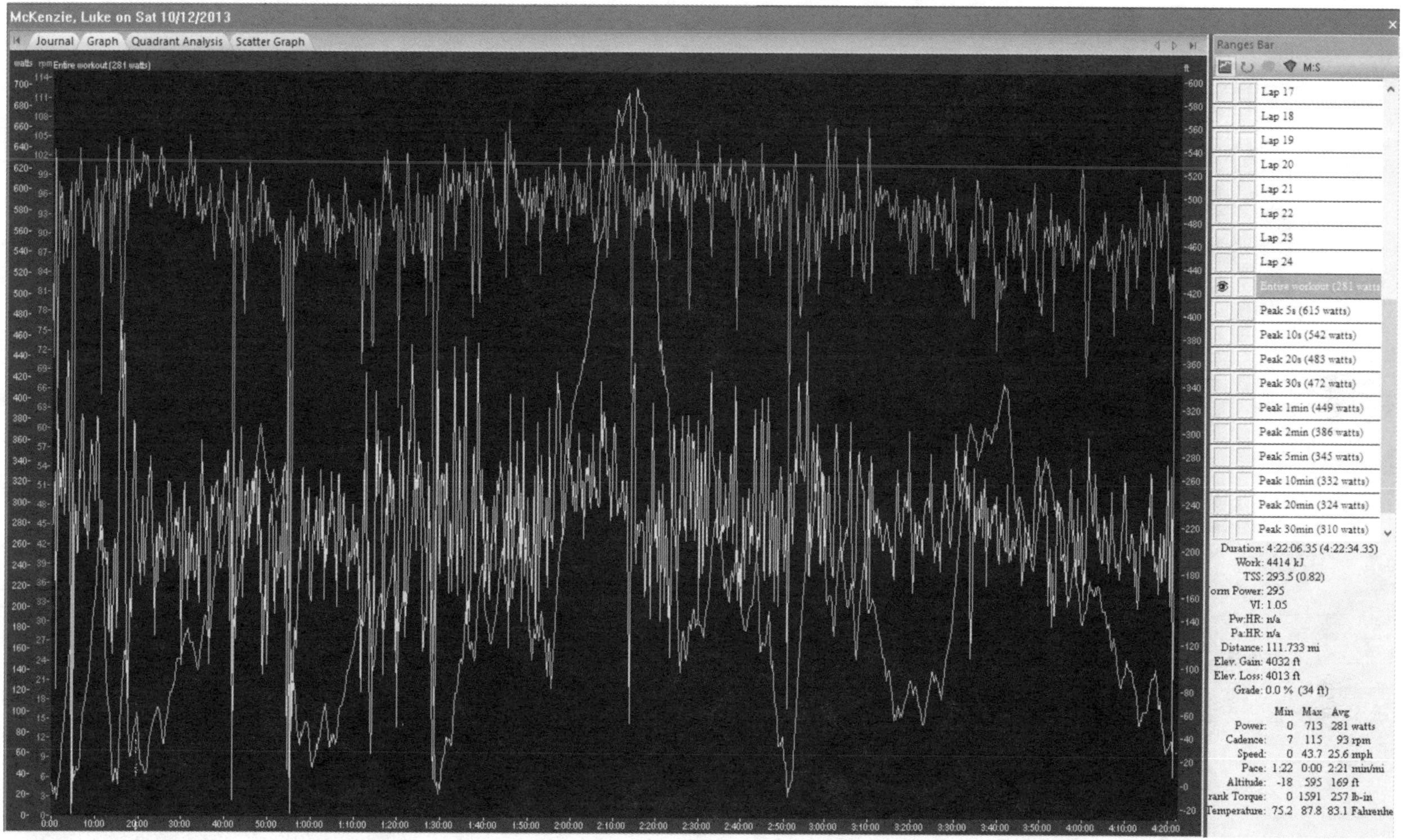

McKenzie, Luke on Sat 10/12/2013

Journal | Graph | Quadrant Analysis | Scatter Graph

watts — norm Entire workout (281 watts)

Ranges Bar

M:S

| Lap 17 |
| Lap 18 |
| Lap 19 |
| Lap 20 |
| Lap 21 |
| Lap 22 |
| Lap 23 |
| Lap 24 |

Entire workout (281 watts)

Peak 5s (615 watts)
Peak 10s (542 watts)
Peak 20s (483 watts)
Peak 30s (472 watts)
Peak 1min (449 watts)
Peak 2min (386 watts)
Peak 5min (345 watts)
Peak 10min (332 watts)
Peak 20min (324 watts)
Peak 30min (310 watts)

Duration: 4:22:06.35 (4:22:34.35)
Work: 4414 kJ
TSS: 293.5 (0.82)
Norm Power: 295
VI: 1.05
PwHR: n/a
PaHR: n/a
Distance: 111.733 mi
Elev. Gain: 4032 ft
Elev. Loss: 4013 ft
Grade: 0.0 % (34 ft)

	Min	Max	Avg
Power:	0	713	281 watts
Cadence:	7	115	93 rpm
Speed:	0	43.7	25.6 mph
Pace:	1:22	0:00	2:21 min/mi
Distance:			111.733 mi
Altitude:	-18	595	169 ft
Crank Torque:	0	1591	257 lb-in
Temperature:	75.2	87.8	83.1 Fahrenheit

FIGURE 15.18a–c   (b) 2012.

221

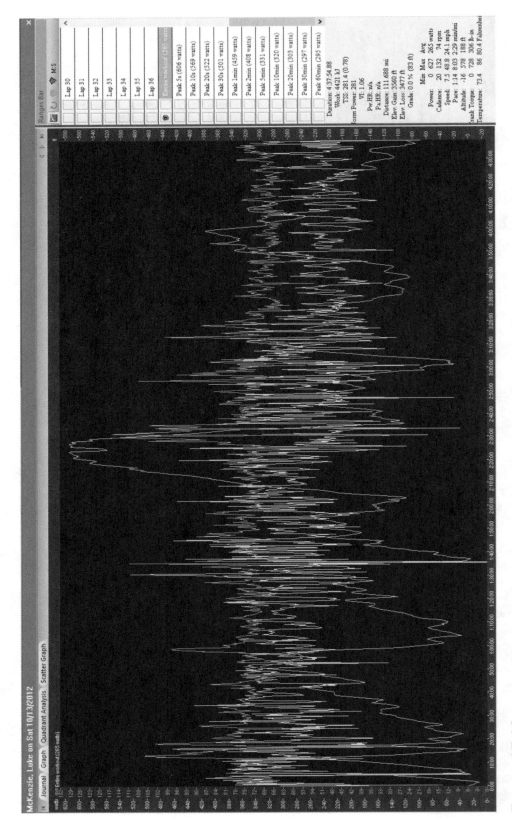

FIGURE 15.18*a–c*   (*c*) 2013.

TABLE 15.2 Luke McKenzie's performances at the 2011, 2012, and 2013 Ironman World Championships sorted by place.

Athlete	Race	Place	Year	Cadence hour 1	NP	Cadence last hour	NP	Percent cadence fade	Percent power fade	TSS for ride	IF for ride	VI ride	NP entire ride	Bike split	Run split
Luke McKenzie	Kona	24	2012	77	306	68	239	13.24%	28.3%	282	0.78	1.06	281	4.65	3:20:32
Luke McKenzie	Kona	9	2011	87	278	80	247	8.75%	12.55%	294	0.821	1.05	271	4.35	3:05:54
Luke McKenzie	Kona	2	2013	84	290	89	279	5.62%	3.94%	293	0.82	1.05	295	4.3	2:57:20

Of course, as place improves in the race, you would expect fitness and preparation to be better. One item of interest is that in 2011, Luke's reported FTP was 330 watts, when he got ninth. In 2012 and 2013, his worst and best performances, respectively, it is reported at 360 watts. Does this negate the preparation argument, since he had a higher FTP or better bike preparation in 2012 and 2013? Of course not. After all, FTP is only one measurement of fitness. But one could also argue that if Luke made the decision to ride over 90 rpm (which he clearly did), he made a decision to better prepare himself to do so and executed that in his daily training. This would give credence to the fact that his preparation was more effective when he focused on going over 90 rpm.

Was it because he did the race over 90 rpm or that his training to ride at 90+ had a more positive effect on his fitness and preparing his body? Was 90 the magic number where the changes in fitness happened for him?

There are no simple, clear answers because there are so many variables. But the question is was Luke McKenzie's change to 90+ rpm on the bike a big reason for his dramatic improvement in Kona? This type of postseason analysis you can do for yourself and is where you can find the breakthroughs you need, whether or not it is your cadence.

Of course, many factors contribute to a race, and proper pacing is probably one of the biggest. So let's look at how the pacing went in these races and if that played a role in the differences in the placings for Luke in Kona.

How can we assess pacing? In Kona, perhaps more than in any other Ironman, the first hour matters a lot. The first hour on the bike matters in all pro Ironman races, but in Kona it includes the town loop, with climbs on Kuakini and Palani, packed with screaming fans, and the desire to make the lead pack onto the Queen K, given the legal drafting benefit and the mental push of having the athletes around you to keep the pace high.

Considering Luke has always been a top swimmer, he comes out with the lead group and tends to stay with them early on the bike and throughout much of the race. The first hour of his bike will bring him well past the 25-mile mark, meaning he is traveling over 25 mph. In fact, the range of distance covered from 2011 to 2013 through the first hour is 26.1 to 27.8 miles. That's fast, and with the early surges and climbs in the town, you can bet there isn't much room for error. So I was curious. Did Luke just pace himself better in 2013 than in 2012 and 2011?

VI is a measurement that helps us see how much variance there was in the power output of the athlete. So let's isolate the first hour of the bike and see how volatile the pace was, with surges up the hills and staying with the pack.

In table 15.3, you can see that usually the pace is quite varied early and is much more settled down in the last hour. What is really interesting here is that I was expecting to see that in Luke's best performances, he likely paced himself better, limiting the surges. But what we actually see is the exact opposite. Luke's two biggest VIs were in his two best performances in Kona. His worst performance of the three, 2012, featured a significantly lower VI and a steadier, much better paced first hour.

So what was different about these three samples that set 2012 apart in terms of best pacing but worst performance? Let's review the basic data from the three rides again.

In table 15.3, you can see that his overall VI was higher in 2012. But don't forget that it also was his largest power fade of the three years.

When your power output drops nearly 30 percent from the start and you've paced yourself without surges extremely well at the beginning, the effort to produce the watts is too much to maintain. So was it fitness or the execution of the ride, in terms of cadence versus force on the pedals?

Remember, his FTP in 2012 was 360, the same as in 2013, and he actually produces a lower IF and lower TSS in 2012 than in 2013. Usually that means less stress on the body, which would signal a better opportunity to run well off the bike. But that didn't happen in 2012.

Part of pacing is also knowing that the intensity at which you're riding is correct. So let's compare Luke's hour 1 VI in Kona with the IF from that first hour to see if he just rode too hard, even if not varied (see table 15.5).

TABLE 15.3 The VI (Variability Index) of each of Luke McKenzie's rides for the first and last hour of his bike performances at the Ironman World Championships in 2011, 2012, and 2013.

	VI hr 1	VI last hr
2011	1.09	1.03
2012	1.04	1.02
2013	1.08	1.02

TABLE 15.4 The VI (Variability Index) of each of Luke McKenzie's rides for the first and last hour of his bike performances at the Ironman World Championships in 2011, 2012, and 2013.

	2011	2012	2013
AP	257	265	281
NP	271	281	295
IF	0.821	0.78	0.82
VI	1.05	1.06	1.05
Avg RPM	86	74	93
Bike split	4:24:15	4:39:09	4:22:25
Place	9	24	2

TABLE 15.5 Luke McKenzie's VI and IF in the first hour of the bike, from the Ironman World Championships, in 2011, 2012, and 2013.

	VI hr 1	First hr IF
2011	1.09	0.843
2012	1.04	0.847
2013	1.08	0.806

In table 15.5 you can see he actually had his highest IF in 2012, in that first hour, but it was only four-tenths of a percent more than in 2011. And 2011 was much more volatile in that first hour. In 2013, he was rather volatile, but the actual intensity of the watts relative to his FTP was lower than the previous two years by about 4 percent.

Finally, let's look at how he rode those watts, relative to force and cadence, with a quadrant analysis, isolating just the first hour of the bike each year (see table 15.6), and then compare that with the quadrant breakdown for the entire race (see table 15.7).

In table 15.6 we can see that Luke actually increased his Q2 percent in that first hour in 2011 and 2012, compared with how he rode the rest of the race, table 15.7. Remember, Q2 is high force, low cadence, below 90 rpm for him. But in 2012, he spent significantly more time in Q2 than in 2011. In 2013, he actually spent a smaller percentage of time in Q2 during the volatile first hour than he spent in the rest of the race, table 15.7. He even spent more Q4 time spinning over 90 rpm

TABLE 15.6 The quadrant analysis breakdown of time spent pedaling in each quadrant, during the first hour of the bike for Luke McKenzie, at the Ironman World Championships in 2011, 2012, and 2013.

Hour 1	Q1%	Q2%	Q3%	Q4%
Luke 2011	6.2%	24.5%	41.9%	27.4%
Luke 2012	0.2%	50.3%	41.8%	7.7%
Luke 2013	6.5%	5.8%	11.6%	76.2%

TABLE 15.7 Luke McKenzie's full race breakdown by pedaling quadrant, for 2011, 2012, and 2013 at the Ironman World Championships.

	Q1%	Q2%	Q3%	Q4%
Luke 2011	3.9%	18.9%	55.0%	22.2%
Luke 2012	0.1%	36.4%	58.5%	5.0%
Luke 2013	6.5%	7.4%	16.9%	69.2%

in that first hour than in the rest of the race, percentage wise. He spent the same percentage of time in Q1 in 2013, in the first hour, as he did during the entire race.

To summarize:

- In the most volatile hour of the 2013 race, Luke spent more than 76 percent of the time over 90 rpm, which was more than he actually did for the whole race.
- Luke's 2012 first hour of racing, his worst performance and lowest cadence year, was actually less volatile the first hour than in 2011 and 2013.
- Luke's 2012 first hour was about the same IF as in 2011 but about 4 percent higher than in 2013.
- Luke's Q2 time in the first hour of 2012 was significantly higher than in the other years, more than twice the 2011 figure and nearly 10 times more than in 2013, his best year.
- Luke's biggest power and cadence fade came in 2012, despite the lower volatility in the first hour and similar IF to his excellent 2011 performance.

From these data I think we can say pacing made very little difference because his small VI and similar IF early in the ride don't prove poor pacing on his part. (Although his IF in hour 1 was the lowest in 2013, and 4 percent might have made the difference.)

So what was the big difference in the performance? Was it that he was better able to tolerate the volatility based on the higher cadence he rode in 2011 and 2013 in that hour, compared with 2012? Did his mashing, high Q2 time catch up with him and sap the run out of his legs?

Yes, the sample size here is very small, but these are questions that coaches and Ironman athletes need to ask themselves.

SUMMARY

There are a number of ways to analyze training and performance from season to season, or race to race, in order to review and assess training approach, decisions, injury and sickness causes, and more. Use the totality of the data and information to understand what the athlete responds best to and you will find yourself making intelligent, well-informed training decisions. You'll also likely see a continuous improvement curve for performance.

GLOSSARY

aerobic endurance—Ability to perform at low intensities for a long time at a level at which oxygen and fuel needs can be met by the body's intake.

AeT—Aerobic threshold. Represents the pace an athlete can hold at the point they begin having labored breathing.

anaerobic endurance—Ability to perform at high intensities for a long period, beyond the demands the heart and lungs can supply.

AP—Average power. Average watts for a session.

ATL—Acute training load, from the PMC, which is a 7-day rolling average of TSS accomplished by the athlete, usually representing fatigue level.

ATP—Annual training plan. How the year is structured and how the foci of training various energy systems is determined, based on the athlete's race schedule and limiters for performance.

bFTP—Functional threshold power. The best watts an athlete can hold for approximately 60 minutes, or 40 km.

bTSS—Training stress score specifically from cycling workouts or races.

CP—Critical power or critical pace. The best power or pace an athlete can hold for a given time in minutes. CP6 is best power or pace an athlete can hold in 6 minutes; CP120 is best power or pace for 120 minutes.

CTL—Chronic training load. From the PMC, which is a 42-day rolling average of TSS accomplished by the athlete, usually representing fitness level.

EF—Efficiency factor. An aerobic fitness measurement, using either NP for bike workouts or NGP for run workouts and diving it by average HR. The higher the number, the better.

force—Ability of the muscle or group of muscles to exerting against a resistance.

HR—Heart rate, usually expressed as average or in real time.

hrTSS—Training stress score estimated based on heart rate. Can be used to estimate the TSS of both running and cycling workouts.

IF—Intensity factor. The quotient of FTP and NP or NGP of a workout, representing how intensive the session was relative to functional threshold.

IM—Ironman.

LTHR—Lactate threshold heart rate, which is determined in field tests.

muscular endurance—Ability of muscles to perform multiple contractions for a long time under load.

NGP—Normalized graded pace.

NP—Normalized power. A wattage value that estimates the physiological effort of a ride to account for spikes and surges in the effort.

P—Peak power. Same as critical power, just the new way of saying it. Still listed at P6, or P180, and so on.

Pa:HR—Aerobic decoupling. Represents the relationship of pace and HR for aerobic-intensity run workouts. The lower the decoupling, the better.

peaking—The peak amount of fitness or stress on the body before tapering.

PMC—Performance management chart, which helps illustrate training stress and performance potential of the athlete.

power—Ability to apply a tremendous amount of force in a very short time.

power meter—Tool on bike or trainer that measures the output of the rider in terms of work rate (watts).

Pw:HR—Aerobic decoupling. Represents the relationship of power and HR for aerobic-intensity cycling workouts. The lower the decoupling, the better.

rFTP—Functional threshold pace for running. The best pace an athlete can hold for approximately 60 minutes.

RI—Rest interval. Amount of recovery time between intervals or sets.

RPE—Rating of perceived exertion. A scale of 1 to 20, where 1 is easy and 20 is maximum effort.

rpm—Revolutions per minute. A measurement of complete pedal strokes, steps, or swim strokes in 1 minute.

rTSS—Training stress score specifically from running workouts or races.

speed skill—Ability to move with speed and efficiency; technically proficient.

taper—Reduction in training volume before major race event.

tempo—Subthreshold effort, normally very steady and long but intense.

test—Very hard effort designed to set a performance or training benchmark.

threshold—General term for the point at which energy systems and demands change in the body.

TSB—Training stress balance. Simply the CTL value minus the ATL value, usually representing the restedness and performance potential of the athlete.

TSS—Training stress score (TSS). A way to measure the stress put on the body from a workout or race. TSS is calculated using normalized power (NP) or normalized graded pace (NGP), intensity factor (IF), and duration of the session.

TT—Time trial. Best effort for the given distance or time.

VI—Variability index. Shows the difference between the NP and the AP of a ride.

$\dot{V}O_2$max—Capacity for oxygen consumption by the body to produce high outputs at maximal intensities.

volume—Combination of frequency of workouts and their duration.

w/kg—Watts produced per kilogram of body mass. A cycling performance metric.

Z—Power zone or HR zone (Z1-2 is zones 1 to 2).

REFERENCES

Coggan, A. 2008. "Power Training Zones for Cycling." TrainingPeaks. http://home.train-ingpeaks.com/articles/cycling/power-training-levels,-by-andrew-coggan.aspx.

Dallam, G. 2013. Running biomechanics for triathlon. In *Triathlon science*, ed. J. Friel & J. Vance, 90–98. Champaign, IL: Human Kinetics.

Friel, J. 2009. *The triathlete's training bible*. Boulder, CO: Velopress.

INDEX

PLEASE NOTE: A page number followed by an italicized *f* or *t* indicate that there is a figure or table to be found on that page, respectively. Italicized *ff* or *tt* indicate multiple figures or tables will be found on that page, respectively.

ABOUT THE AUTHOR

Jim Vance is a former elite triathlete and currently an international triathlon, running, and cycling elite coach with TrainingBible Coaching. After a college career as a cross country and track athlete at the University of Nebraska, where he earned his degree in physical and health education, Vance turned to triathlon and trained at the Olympic Training Center. Later he moved to Ironman racing where he had many top finishes, including a third-place finish at Ironman Florida with a personal best time of 8:37:09.

Vance is the founder and head coach of the nonprofit organization Formula Endurance, the nation's first USA Swimming and USA Triathlon high-performance team that develops elite youth and junior triathletes for Olympic-style racing, based in San Diego, California. Formula Endurance is annually named one of the top development programs in the United States.

With Joe Friel, Vance coedited and contributed to *Triathlon Science* (Human Kinetics, 2013), a book that focuses on science and research in the sport.